Women in American Operas of the 1950s

Eastman Studies in Music

Ralph P. Locke, Senior Editor
Eastman School of Music

Additional Titles of Interest

Aaron Copland and the American Legacy of Gustav Mahler
Matthew Mugmon

Aaron Copland's Hollywood Film Scores
Paula Musegades

Anneliese Landau's Life in Music: Nazi Germany to Émigré California
Lily E. Hirsch

Building the Operatic Museum: Eighteenth-Century Opera in Fin-de-Siècle Paris
William Gibbons

Dance in Handel's London Operas
Sarah McCleave

Elliott Carter's "What Next?": Communication, Cooperation, and Separation
Guy Capuzzo

Laughter between Two Revolutions: Opera Buffa *in Italy, 1831–48*
Francesco Izzo

Not Russian Enough?: Nationalism and Cosmopolitanism in Nineteenth-Century Russian Opera
Rutger Helmers

Opera and Ideology in Prague: Polemics and Practice at the National Theater, 1900–1938
Brian S. Locke

Wagner's Visions: Poetry, Politics, and the Psyche in the Operas through "Die Walküre"
Katherine R. Syer

A complete list of titles in the Eastman Studies in Music Series
may be found on our website, www.urpress.com.

Women in American Operas of the 1950s

Undoing Gendered Archetypes

Monica A. Hershberger

UNIVERSITY OF ROCHESTER PRESS

The University of Rochester Press gratefully acknowledges generous support from the Howard Hanson Institute for American Music and the AMS 75 PAYS Fund of the American Musicological Society, supported in part by the National Endowment for the Humanities and the Andrew W. Mellon Foundation.

Copyright © 2023 Monica A. Hershberger

All rights reserved. Except as permitted under current legislation, no part of this work may be photocopied, stored in a retrieval system, published, performed in public, adapted, broadcast, transmitted, recorded, or reproduced in any form or by any means, without the prior permission of the copyright owner.

First published 2023
Reprinted in paperback 2024

University of Rochester Press
668 Mt. Hope Avenue, Rochester, NY 14620, USA
www.urpress.com
and Boydell & Brewer Limited
PO Box 9, Woodbridge, Suffolk IP12 3DF, UK
www.boydellandbrewer.com

ISBN-13: 978-1-64825-061-3 (hardcover); ISBN-13: 978-1-64825-066-8 (paperback)
ISSN: 1071-9989 ; v. 187

Library of Congress Cataloging-in-Publication Data

Names: Hershberger, Monica A., author.
Title: Women in American operas of the 1950s : undoing gendered archetypes / Monica A Hershberger.
Other titles: Eastman studies in music ; 187.
Description: Rochester : University of Rochester Press, 2023. | Series: Eastman studies in music, 1071-09989 ; 187 | Includes bibliographical references and index.
Identifiers: LCCN 2022046285 (print) | LCCN 2022046286 (ebook) | ISBN 9781648250613 (hardback) | ISBN 9781648250668 (paperback) | ISBN 9781800109100 (pdf) | ISBN 9781800109117 (epub)
Subjects: LCSH: Women in opera. | Opera—United States—20th century.
Classification: LCC ML1711.9 .H47 2023 (print) | LCC ML1711.9 (ebook) | DDC 782.1/40973—dc23/eng/20220930
LC record available at https://lccn.loc.gov/2022046285
LC ebook record available at https://lccn.loc.gov/2022046286

A catalogue record for this title is available from the British Library.

To my mother, with love and gratitude.

Contents

	Acknowledgments	ix
	Introduction: *Peyton Place*, USA	1
1	American Opera at Mid-Century	17
2	A Conniving Gold Digger: Elizabeth "Baby Doe" Tabor	37
3	A "Really Vicious Monster": Lizzie Andrew Borden	77
4	A Chaste White Woman: Laurie Moss	113
5	A Dangerous Jezebel: Susannah Polk	151
	Epilogue: "The World So Wide"—Beyond the Virgin or the Whore in the Twenty-First Century	186
	Bibliography	195
	Index	219

Acknowledgments

When I began studying American opera, I would not have predicted that I would go on to write a book about women, gender, and American operas of the 1950s. I am grateful that throughout all the stages of the research and writing process, I have been supported by a vast and overlapping network of colleagues, friends, and family. I am especially grateful to Carol J. Oja, Anne C. Shreffler, and Sindhumathi Revuluri for their thoughtfulness and guidance as I worked to develop this project, first as a dissertation and then a book. I am also grateful to Carol A. Hess and Kevin Bartig for helping me find my scholarly voice. More broadly, I am indebted to an enormous number of feminist music scholars whose work has informed my own.

I feel very fortunate that over the course of my research, I was able to speak with key figures in American operas of the 1950s. I am grateful to composer Carlisle Floyd (1926–2021), who allowed me to interview him in his home in Tallahassee, Florida. Floyd's niece, Jane Matheny, graciously helped with many of the logistics of this interview. I am also grateful to Phyllis Curtin (1921–2016), the soprano who created the title role in *Susannah*, and Brenda Lewis (1921–2017), the soprano who created the title role in *Lizzie Borden*. Both singers were remarkably patient with me when I interviewed them. Similarly, Alice Hotopp (b. 1932), who sang the role of Laurie Moss in *The Tender Land* at Oberlin College in 1955, was generous with her time and patience in telephone and email correspondence. Sopranos Sharon Daniels and Phyllis Treigle, both of whom sang the role of Susannah after the 1950s, provided keen insights that helped shape my understanding of how perspectives on *Susannah* changed over the latter half of the twentieth century.

The archival research for this book would not have been possible without the help of dedicated librarians and archivists across the country. I am particularly grateful to Graham Duncan (South Caroliniana Library at the University of South Carolina), Jennifer B. Lee (Rare Book & Manuscript Library at Columbia University), and Jane Parr (Howard Gotlieb Archival Research Center at Boston University).

The State University of New York at Geneseo (SUNY Geneseo) supported this book in many ways, including course releases, a Summer Faculty Fellowship, a Faculty Incentive Award, and several Pre-Tenure Faculty Research Support Grants. I am also grateful to the Society for American

Music, which awarded me the Virgil Thomson Fellowship in 2018, allowing me to complete outstanding archival research for Chapter 3.

Sonia Kane of the University of Rochester Press and Eastman Studies in Music series editor Ralph P. Locke supported this book from start to finish. I am grateful to them for their guidance and enthusiasm for my work.

I am grateful to many colleagues. In the Department of Music & Musical Theatre at SUNY Geneseo, Andrew Bergevin, Tammy Farrell, Gerard Floriano, Joan Floriano, Jonathan Gonder, Don Kot, Michael Masci, Leah McGray, James Kimball, and Pamela Kurau have proven unfailingly kind and supportive. So too have my SUNY Geneseo colleagues outside music, particularly Catherine Adams, Melanie Blood, and Katelynn Kochalski. Beyond SUNY Geneseo, I am grateful to Lucy Caplan, Grace Edgar, John Gabriel, Isidora Miranda, Samuel Parler, Caitlin Schmid, Anne Searcy, Sarah Suhadolnik, and Michael Uy for investing so much of their time and expertise reading and re-reading my work. William Cheng and Kristen M. Turner also supplied incisive feedback at crucial stages in my research and writing process. Since our years in graduate school, Krystal Klingenberg and Caitlin Schmid have shared their friendship and intelligence with me. I could not have written this book without their support.

My family has accompanied me on this journey in a variety of ways. My husband Dan listened to conference papers, read chapter drafts, and engraved my musical examples. In May 2020, Dan and I welcomed our son Anton James into the world. Learning to be a parent has been a challenge and a joy, and I am grateful to share the work with Dan. I am also grateful for support from Dan's parents, Ken and Helen, and Dan's sister, Corrie. My sister Margaret, brother-in-law Stefan, and niece Lena have been sources of inspiration and support as well.

While working on this book I have thought often of my grandmothers, Alice Hershberger and Eunice Smith. Both were born around the same time as many of the sopranos discussed in the following pages, and both began having their children in the 1950s. I am indebted to my grandmothers and to my parents whom they raised. My father died in 2011, long before I began this project, but my memories of his love and sense of humor have continued to sustain me. My mother has spent hours talking to me about this book. She has accompanied me to the opera and on research trips. More broadly, she has been a role model, helping me learn to navigate the different aspects of my identity (scholar, teacher, mother, daughter, spouse, etc.). Thank you, Susan Smith Hershberger, for all that you taught me.

Introduction: *Peyton Place*, USA

In 1988, the University of Minnesota Press published an English translation of philosopher Catherine Clément's 1979 *L'opéra, ou, la défaite des femmes* (*Opera, or the Undoing of Women*). In this tract that is now famous among feminist music scholars, Clément argued that in opera after opera, women were the inevitable victims. Likening women in opera to jewels, she explained that "the role of jewel, a decorative object, is not the deciding role; and on the opera stage women perpetually sing their eternal undoing."[1] Musicologist Joseph Kerman sought to clarify Clément's perspective in 2006. He argued that when Clément wrote of "opera," she was referring not to "the genre [of] opera over its entire history" but to "the repertory of the Paris Opéra when she grew up in and around the 1950s."[2] He pointed out that this was the same repertory—which included such staples as *Lucia di Lammermoor*, *La Traviata*, *Carmen*, *Tosca*, *Salome*—that many Americans understood as "opera" during Rudolf Bing's tenure as general manager of the Metropolitan Opera Company (Met) from 1950 to 1972. Kerman ultimately admitted that Clément's perspective had a ring of truth to it, concluding that it was impossible to deny "that our basic, traditional operatic repertory drips with female blood."[3]

Kerman's assessment notwithstanding, many opera scholars continue to dismiss Clément. Yet in the 1950s, at the very moment that Clément was beginning to see a pattern of gendered violence, ostensibly at the Paris Opéra, opera in the US was conforming to a similar pattern. In fact, composers and librettists in the US were influenced by many of the same operas that eventually inspired Clément's blistering critique. As they absorbed the European opera canon through the live performances and weekly radio broadcasts of the Met, they created new operas.[4] Aaron Copland and Erik Johns wrote *The Tender Land* (1954, rev. 1955); Carlisle Floyd wrote *Susannah* (1955); Douglas Moore and John Latouche wrote *The Ballad*

---

1 Clément, *Opera, or the Undoing of Women*, 5.
2 Kerman, "Verdi and the Undoing of Women," 21.
3 Ibid., 21.
4 See Jackson, *Sign-Off for the Old Met*. Also, for a New York music critic's perspective on the Met in the 1950s, see Briggs, *Requiem for a Yellow Brick Brewery*, 278–318.

of Baby Doe (1956); and Jack Beeson, Kenward Elmslie, and Richard Plant wrote *Lizzie Borden* (1965). In all four of these operas, women appeared, yet again, as the genre's inevitable victims. Remarkably, the singers who embodied these American victims did not always accept their victimhood. Sometimes they resisted, rewriting the roles they had been assigned through their performances. Sometimes they used their lived experience to invest in their roles a certain kind of authenticity. In this book, I examine some of the most performed yet understudied operas written in the US in the 1950s, asserting the significance of the pattern that Clément identified, as well as the significance of the women who resisted, years before the official resurgence of the US feminist movement.

Women in American Operas of the 1950s: Undoing Gendered Archetypes is the first feminist analysis of *The Tender Land, Susannah, The Ballad of Baby Doe,* and *Lizzie Borden*.[5] I have chosen these four operas both because of their privileged positions in the American-opera canon and because of how they demonstrate the gendered constraints of the decade. Indeed, each relies heavily on the paradigm of the virgin or the whore, that dichotomy that as film critic Molly Haskell argues "took hold with a vengeance in the uptight fifties, in the dialectical caricatures of the 'sexpot' and the 'nice girl.'"[6] Copland and Johns presented Laurie Moss (of *The Tender Land*) as a virgin. Floyd painted Susannah Polk (of *Susannah*) as a woman who is regarded as a whore. Moore and Latouche initially constructed Baby Doe (of *The Ballad of Baby Doe*) as a whore, yet over the course of the opera, they had her miraculously transform herself into a good woman by becoming a devoted and self-sacrificing wife. Beeson, Plant, and Elmslie depicted Lizzie Borden (of *Lizzie Borden*) as an angry and repressed spinster, an expired virgin.

The women who were tasked with portraying these "virgins" and "whores" did not necessarily take them as their male creators made them. For example, Beverly Sills (1929–2007) began singing the title role in *The Ballad of Baby Doe* in 1958, and as her memoirs reveal, she actively sought to challenge the gold digger and homewrecker stereotypes embedded in Moore and Latouche's text. She also downplayed Baby Doe's transformation into a good wife and widow at the end of the opera, thereby rejecting the notion that Baby Doe could only be a virgin *or* a whore, a good woman *or* a bad one. Importantly, Sills felt she had lived something of Baby Doe's plight. In 1956, she married Peter Greenough, wealthy and recently divorced from

---

5   Throughout this book, I generally use the term "American opera," rather than "US opera." Whereas the term "US opera" is in some ways more precise, "American opera" was the term in use during the 1950s. It is also the term most widely employed by its practitioners today.

6   Haskell, *From Reverence to Rape*, xiii.

a member of Cleveland's social elite. Like the real Elizabeth "Baby Doe" Tabor (1854–1935), an Irish-Catholic woman who married a much wealthier Protestant man, the Brooklyn-born Jewish Sills was regarded as something of an unwelcome outsider in Cleveland; like Baby Doe in Denver, Sills was never accepted into her husband's predominantly White Anglo-Saxon Protestant social circle. I maintain that Sills's work on *The Ballad of Baby Doe* allowed her to examine the constraints of her personal life, and to shape an American opera on her own terms. Sills did not simply accept Moore and Latouche's version of Baby Doe; through her performance, she sought to rewrite the role in a way that fit with her identity and lived experience.

As my discussion of Sills demonstrates, throughout this book, I alternate between the "real" and the "imaginary," contemplating and sometimes even smudging the line between the two. When I write of women in American operas, I write of historical women, women characters, and women performers. This three-dimensional approach underlines the continual overlapping of history and fiction on the opera stage and on the opera stage in the US, in particular.[7] *The Ballad of Baby Doe* and *Lizzie Borden* are based, loosely of course, on the lives of actual people. *The Tender Land* and *Susannah* are less clearly drawn from history, yet they are believable, featuring ordinary, relatable characters. To a certain extent, these four operas can be understood as an extension of the *verismo* tradition.[8] Although most often located in the late nineteenth century and associated with Italian composers Ruggiero Leoncavallo (1857–1919) and Pietro Mascagni (1863–1945), *verismo*, according to Elise K. Kirk, flourished in the US throughout the latter half of the twentieth century.[9] Kirk explains that "American verismo composers centered action around plausible, everyday characters and brought them into focus through richly expressive melodic and orchestral means."[10] "Plausible, everyday characters" have continued to populate American operas. Richard Taruskin situates two of John Adams's operas—*Nixon in China* (1987) and *The Death of Klinghoffer* (1991)—by explaining that at the end of the

---

7   Susan Rutherford has examined this overlap as well, focusing on the "mediated relationship between Verdi's operas and the life-world of the female audience." See *Verdi, Opera, Women*, 22.
8   *Verismo* began as a movement in Italian literature in the 1870s; by 1890, it had spread to opera. The operas of Giacomo Puccini, particularly *La bohème* (1896), *Tosca* (1900), and *Madama Butterfly* (1904–1907), are often understood as a synthesis of the older Verdian tradition and the newer *verismo* tradition.
9   Kirk, *American Opera*, 253. Kirk cites Kurt Weill, Elmer Rice, and Langston Hughes's *Street Scene* (1947), Marc Blitzstein's *Regina* (1949), and Gian-Carlo Menotti's *The Consul* (1950) as examples of *verismo*.
10 Ibid., 253.

twentieth century, composers and their patrons reached "a new consensus … that contemporary classical music can and should have the sort of topical relevance more usually found in popular culture."[11] Yet in contrast to Taruskin, I am not convinced such consensus was entirely "new." In this book, I emphasize the topical relevance of *The Tender Land*, *Susannah*, *The Ballad of Baby Doe*, and *Lizzie Borden*. I analyze the national and gendered anxieties that often colluded in the initial making of the heroines featured in these four American operas, and I argue that Clément's notion of the opera stage as a place where "women perpetually sing their eternal undoing" remains relevant.[12] Yet I also show how the stories of these operatic heroines, voiced and re-voiced by American women, offer a window into a burgeoning feminist resistance in the 1950s.

This is not the popular image of the 1950s, and to be sure, I do not seek to deny the conservatism of the decade, sparked during the waning days of World War II as many employers and public officials in the US sought to put women back in their "proper" place.[13] In January 1944, for example, FBI director J. Edgar Hoover reminded women that ultimately, their purview was the home. Writing in the popular magazine *Woman's Home Companion*, Hoover argued that "the mother of small children does not need to put on overalls to prove her patriotism," for "she already has her war job."[14] Hoover was concerned about juvenile delinquency, and he believed that by throwing their energies into cultivating a "happy home," mothers would help to protect "the nation and its youth."[15] James Madison Wood, the president of a private women's college in Missouri, agreed with Hoover. Writing in the same issue of the *Woman's Home Companion*, Wood tackled the question "Should We Draft Mothers?" Wood argued that he was "opposed to drafting American women for war work."[16] Yet he supported the idea of drafting women to work in their homes, explaining that if mothers failed "to recognize their responsibilities and act accordingly … mothers should be drafted—and ordered to accept their responsibilities for the protection

---

11   Taruskin, *The Oxford History of Western Music: Music in the Late Twentieth Century*, 517.
12   Clément, *Opera, or the Undoing of Women*, 5.
13   Historian Susan M. Hartmann points out that throughout World War II, "as women moved into the public sphere, they were reminded that their new positions were temporary." See *The Home Front and Beyond*, 23.
14   Hoover, "Mothers … Our Only Hope" in Walker, *Women's Magazines 1940–1960*, 46.
15   Ibid., 46–47.
16   Wood, "Should We Draft Mothers?" in Walker, *Women's Magazines 1940–1960*, 49.

of society."[17] Like Hoover, Wood maintained that he was thinking about the rising "tide of juvenile delinquency."[18] He urged his readers to remember "the basic responsibility of the American mother," concluding that "her patriotic duty is not on the factory front. It is on the *home* front!"[19]

Hoover's and Wood's words foreshadowed the decided shift that was to follow World War II.[20] As historian Elaine Tyler May argued in foundational scholarship about the status of women during the 1950s, the "independence of wartime women gave rise to fears of female sexuality as a dangerous force on the loose."[21] Single women—women whose sexuality could not be contained by marriage—were regarded with increasing suspicion. They were often construed as dangerous predators, or as May put it, "temptresses who seduced men into evil."[22] Concerns about female sexuality were compounded throughout the 1950s by growing anxieties about the Soviet Union and the spread of communism, and as May asserts, Americans increasingly turned inward—to the family—to assuage their anxieties. Nurtured by the mother who stayed at home and supported financially by the father who went to work, the nuclear family was widely regarded as the institution to foster the moral strength needed to resist communism. Thus, the nuclear family became a powerful metaphor in the US in the 1950s.

But not everyone bought into the metaphor. Not everyone could.[23] Moreover, as historian Joanne Meyerowitz argues, "an unrelenting focus on women's subordination erases much of the history of the postwar years."[24] Influenced by the writings of Meyerowitz and others, I work to recover some of the radical histories embedded in and around *The Tender Land*, *Susannah*, *The Ballad of Baby Doe*, and *Lizzie Borden*, while at the same time recognizing the conservative narratives that are often more readily on display. I argue

---

17   Ibid., 49.
18   Ibid., 50.
19   Ibid.
20   Hartmann explains that by 1946, the female labor force had declined dramatically. By 1947, however, "they had begun to climb again" and "at the end of the decade the number, but not the proportion [of all women in the job market], of employed women was slightly higher than that of the wartime peak." See *The Home Front and Beyond*, 24.
21   May, *Homeward Bound*, 68.
22   Ibid., 93.
23   Alice Childress's 1956 novel *Like One of the Family: Conversations from a Domestic's Life* clearly demonstrated that Black women often had no choice but to work outside the home. The chapters of Childress's book were first published in installments in the monthly newspaper *Freedom*, founded by Paul Robeson in 1950.
24   Meyerowitz, "Introduction" in *Not June Cleaver*, 4.

that by listening critically to the women's stories and voices that informed American operas during the 1950s, we can hear the rustlings of the feminist resurgence that would emerge in full force the following decade. In this way, *Women in American Operas of the 1950s* responds to Naomi André's call for an "engaged musicology," a framework that allows for reading opera as "an art form that has potential for being a site for critical inquiry, political activism, and social change."[25]

Throughout this book, my approach to American operas—and to the paradigm of the virgin or the whore—is heavily informed by some of the most popular literature from the 1950s. Drawing on historian Eugenia Kaledin, who argued that "during the 1950s the pen and the typewriter became the most powerful means women had to assert their individuality and their social imagination," I pay special attention to literature written by women.[26] One particularly powerful example occurred in 1956, when Grace Metalious's novel *Peyton Place* rocked the nation, selling sixty thousand copies within the first ten days of its release.[27] Set in a fictional town in New Hampshire, *Peyton Place* challenged the mythology of New England, turning the region's picturesque small towns, fall foliage, church steeples, and rocky coastlines inside out. The book centers on the lives of three women. Constance MacKenzie lives in considerable fear that someone might discover that she gave birth to her daughter Allison out of wedlock. Allison is restless and insecure, eager to escape the constraints of life in Peyton Place and become a famous writer. Most sobering is the story of Allison's friend Selena Cross, who comes from a poor family but is eager to better herself. After her stepfather rapes her, Selena gets an illegal abortion from a sympathetic town doctor. When her stepfather tries to rape her yet again, she kills him, protecting her autonomy but sacrificing her dream of climbing the social ladder in Peyton Place.

The story behind *Peyton Place*—like the stories behind so many of the operas featured in this book—was not entirely fictional. Metalious was inspired by the so-called "sheep pen murder," which she learned about after moving to the small town of Gilmanton, New Hampshire.[28] In September 1947, a woman named Barbara Roberts confessed to killing her father a few

---

25 André, *Black Opera*, 193.
26 Kaledin, *Mothers and More*, 125.
27 *Peyton Place* was Metalious's first novel, and as Ardis Cameron explains, during the 1950s, the average first novel sold just two thousand copies. See *Unbuttoning America*, 3.
28 Ibid., 38–53. Cameron discusses the story of the "sheep pen murder" at length. She notes that long before Metalious caught wind of the story, it had "circulated as family legend, local gossip, newspaper articles, court depositions, rural folklore, personal testimony, eyewitness accounts, memory, and small talk." See pp. 38–39.

days before Christmas 1946, burying his body beneath the family's sheep pen. According to Barbara, her father was a violent man. Approximately one year before her father's death, Barbara told the town's chief of police that her father abused her physically and sexually; on the night of his death, she asserted that he had tried to choke her.[29] As historian Ardis Cameron points out, "in postwar America, incest was a hushed and guarded secret," and with *Peyton Place*, Metalious sought to expose that secret, basing the character of Selena Cross on Barbara Roberts.[30] In fact, in Metalious's original manuscript, Selena is raped by her father, rather than her stepfather. The author's biographer Emily Toth explains that Metalious's publisher argued that "incest/rape could not be published, not in 1956."[31] According to Toth, Metalious was "heartbroken" about having to make Lucas Cross Selena's stepfather, and she believed her book to be "destroyed."[32] Yet Toth argues that "the story's impact was not lessened, since its power came from the point of view."[33] Toth asserts that Metalious "showed rape as it appeared to a woman: ugly, violent, a destruction of innocence."[34] Metalious refused to lay the blame for Lucas's crimes at Selena's feet, and she refused to saddle Selena with the label of "whore." During the 1950s and 1960s, *Peyton Place* loomed large. The "indecent" book was banned in Canada, as well as in several towns across the US, yet readers continued to seek out the story—in bookstores, in movie theaters, and on television.[35]

---

29 On December 3, 1947, the *Lewiston Evening Journal* (Lewiston, Maine) reported that Barbara Roberts, "a pretty 21-year-old woolen mill worker" had begun serving "a three- to five-year reformatory sentence for manslaughter." See "Laconia Girl Worries about Brother as She Starts Sentence."
30 Cameron, *Unbuttoning America*, 44.
31 Toth, *Inside Peyton Place*, 105. When Toth published her biography in 1981, her publisher requested that she not use Barbara Roberts's real name. Thus Toth referred to Roberts as Jane Glenn, her use of this pseudonym demonstrating, among other things, the stigma still attached to incest and rape at the end of the twentieth century. See p. 382.
32 Ibid., 105.
33 Ibid., 106.
34 Ibid.
35 20th Century Fox made *Peyton Place* into a film in 1957. Metalious published *Return to Peyton Place* in 1959, a sequel that was also made into a film (in 1961). From 1964 to 1969, *Peyton Place* ran as a prime-time soap opera on ABC, and from 1972 to 1974, *Return to Peyton Place* ran as a daytime serial on NBC, a spinoff of the prime-time series. As Toth documents, Metalious (who died in 1964) had very little to do with any of the film and television adaptations of *Peyton Place*.

In 1957, one year after *Peyton Place* appeared, Betty Friedan began surveying 200 of her classmates from Smith College. Fifteen years had passed since their college graduation, and Friedan wanted to know if her classmates had found "true feminine fulfillment" in the home.[36] In 1963, she published her findings in *The Feminine Mystique*, a now-famous book underpinned by the assertion that American women had been fooled by the propaganda of the early Cold War. "A baked potato is not as big as the world," Friedan insisted as she explicitly took up the feminist cause, countering contemporary portrayals of American suffragists as "man-hating, embittered, sex-starved spinsters" and arguing that "the feminist revolution had to be fought because women quite simply were stopped at a stage of evolution far short of their human capacity."[37] She maintained that women were still being deprived of their full capacities, and she encouraged women to build their lives outside the confines of the home.

The Feminine Mystique is generally regarded as a major catalyst for the second-wave feminist movement—particularly for the white women who considered themselves part of that movement.[38] Cameron, however, warns against interpreting feminism "as a movement always conscious of itself, certain of its aims, aware of life's roadblocks, singular in its efforts, and available only to those who labored under its flag."[39] Somewhat similarly, Toth identifies the arguments embedded in *Peyton Place*—"that wife-beating is not inevitable; that rape is an act of violence, not sexual pleasure; that abortion can mean saving a life—the mother's"—as the "'women's issues' of the 1970s and '80s."[40] She points out that many of "the women who created Women's Liberation in the late 1960s" were "the generation most influenced by *Peyton Place*."[41] If these women initially read *Peyton Place* because of its reputation as a "forbidden, 'sexy' book," she asserts, they "also absorbed its

---

36   Friedan, *The Feminine Mystique*, 18.
37   Ibid., 67, 82–85.
38   As anthropologist Johnnetta B. Cole points out, many second-wave feminists centered on the experiences and priorities of white women. She explains that "the battle cry, 'Out of the house and into the marketplace,' struck African American women as quite absurd because we have always worked—and often, in the homes of the grandmothers, mothers, sisters and aunts of these very women who seemed to have just discovered the workplace we have always known." Cole's words speak directly to the reality that Alice Childress sought to illuminate in her 1956 novel, *Like One of the Family*, cited previously. See Cole, *Conversations*, 93.
39   Cameron, *Unbuttoning America*, 13.
40   Toth, *Inside Peyton Place*, 143. Friedan did not regard *Peyton Place* in this way. See *The Feminine Mystique*, 264.
41   Toth, *Inside Peyton Place*, 367.

messages about women's movement issues."[42] Toth concludes that "without knowing it, they'd read—and loved—a feminist book."[43]

Another fundamental text of the era was Helen Gurley Brown's 1962 nonfiction manual *Sex and the Single Girl*.[44] Like *Peyton Place*, this book is scarcely taken seriously when it comes to discussions of feminism, yet historian Jennifer Scanlon asserts that *Sex and the Single Girl* played an important role in introducing "feminist thinking to millions of readers."[45] Scanlon also argues that in contrast to Friedan, "Brown sought to liberate not the married woman but the single woman, not the suburban but the urban dweller, not the college-educated victim but the working-class survivor."[46] As Scanlon's analysis illustrates, there was no single pathway to the feminist resurgence of the 1960s.

In this book, I look to the opera stage to uncover still more feminist pathways. I do not attempt to read American opera of the 1950s as an explicitly feminist venture; instead, I maintain that like *Peyton Place*, the arguments embedded in *The Tender Land*, *Susannah*, *The Ballad of Baby Doe*, and *Lizzie Borden* speak to women's issues. I show that as operas revolving around American women garnered more listeners than ever before, the line between the supposedly glittering and fictional world of opera and the real everyday began to fade, and sopranos such as Phyllis Curtin and Beverly Sills suggested that it might be possible to transform not only the world of opera, but also the world beyond. Like Toth, who argued that the power of *Peyton Place* came from its point of view, I argue that much of the power of American opera in the 1950s might be read similarly—from the perspectives of women. I assert that finding ways to listen to women matters. Indeed, activists like Tarana Burke have demonstrated just how powerful such listening can be. The founder of what became the #MeToo Movement, Burke began using the phrase "me too" in the early 2000s. She gave workshops throughout the US, showing "how the exchange of empathy between survivors of sexual violence could be a tool to empower us toward healing and into action."[47] In 2017, after actress Alyssa Milano urged those who had been sexually harassed or assaulted to speak up by posting the words "me too" on their social media accounts, the #MeToo Movement gained wider

---

42 Ibid., 367–68.
43 Ibid., 368.
44 After publishing *Sex and the Single Girl*, Brown served as editor-in-chief of *Cosmopolitan Magazine* from 1965 to 1997.
45 Scanlon, *Bad Girls Go Everywhere*, 94.
46 Ibid., 94–95.
47 Burke, *Unbound*, 7.

visibility.[48] In both of its manifestations—Burke's pioneering work centering Black and Brown women and girls and the broader social media campaign encouraged by Milano—#MeToo has encouraged women to give voice to their experiences.[49]

Along with these contemporary resonances, this book also revives some of the discussions that emerged in the late 1980s and early 1990s. This was when Americans began to look back and critically examine the 1950s.[50] Interestingly, this was also the moment when feminist musicology came of age. Marcia J. Citron has highlighted the significance of the 1988 annual meeting of the American Musicological Society and the "critical mass of feminist contributions that debuted" there.[51] In the years that followed, a flurry of groundbreaking publications appeared, including, of course, Susan McClary's *Feminine Endings: Music, Gender, and Sexuality*.

Women in American Operas of the 1950s is indebted to the work of early feminist musicologists. It is also indebted to some of the early engagement with Clément's *Opera*, which, not coincidentally, was published in English during this pivotal moment in musicology.[52] As Mary Ann Smart pointed out in 2000, musicologists who responded to Clément were eager to "make room for what is *different* about opera," namely "the centrality of performers to the experience."[53] Thus, they were quick to scrutinize Clément's decision to focus solely on opera plots.[54] In 1993, Carolyn Abbate famously asserted the tremendous power of what women *sing* in opera, suggesting that opera be understood as "a genre that so displaces the authorial musical voice onto female characters and female singers that it largely reverses a conventional opposition of male (speaking) subject and female (observed)

---

48   Milano was called to action after she and more than a dozen women accused film producer Harvey Weinstein of sexual assault and harassment. On February 24, 2020, Weinstein was convicted of two of five criminal charges: one count of criminal sexual assault in the first degree and one count of rape in the third degree.

49   To be clear, however, there are importance differences between Burke's work and Milano's. Burke lays these out in *Unbound*.

50   For example, see Oakley, *God's Country* and Eisler, *Private Lives*, both published in 1986. See also Urbanska, "Book Review: Ike's '50s and Reagan's '80s: Decades Apart and Yet …"

51   Citron, "Feminist Approaches to Musicology," 15.

52   It is telling that McClary wrote the foreword to Clément's *Opera, or the Undoing of Women*.

53   Smart, "Introduction" in *Siren Songs*, 7.

54   See Ellen Rosand's assessment of Clément's book in "Review: Criticism and the Undoing of Opera." Rosand argued that it was impossible to understand how opera treats women without considering the music.

object."[55] Smart's own work from the 1990s also speaks to the importance of singers and of looking beyond opera plots.[56] In an article entitled "The Lost Voice of Rosine Stoltz," Smart tackled the nineteenth-century biographical practice of reading singers' lives through the roles they played: "Perhaps more than that of any other nineteenth-century soprano, Stoltz's biography falls into familiar patterns, endless rehearsals: of her outbursts and the people she offended, the powerful men she married and had affairs with, the analogies between her life and the roles she played."[57] As Smart admitted, she collected a body of evidence that "might reinforce the view that women, both real and fictional, are silenced by opera."[58] But then she pivoted, briefly examining the "image of Stoltz and Donizetti collaborating on her music."[59] Smart explained that "the collaboration of singer and composer" was "not uncommon in the pragmatic world of nineteenth-century opera."[60] Nor was it uncommon in the US in the 1950s, when composers interested in writing new operas in English relied on singers to be their allies and partners. In this book, I extend Smart's notion that "we owe some of the individuality and vigour of opera's female characters to the humanizing touch of the demanding, fallible, sopranos who were their 'creators.'"[61] I also investigate the line between the lives of sopranos and the roles they played and created. I look for overlaps between the opera stage and singers' lived experiences, but I look for divergences as well. Both help to illuminate that when we consider the perspectives of the women who helped to move

---

55   Abbate, "Opera; or, the Envoicing of Women," 228–29.
56   See Smart, "The Silencing of Lucia." Smart challenges Clément's liberatory reading of the famous mad scene from *Lucia di Lammermoor*, examining three musical dimensions that might "be interpreted both in terms of liberation and confinement" and ultimately asserting that Lucia is "defeated both by the forces of musical language and by the oppressive power of the plot" (pp. 140–141).
57   Smart, "The Lost Voice of Rosine Stoltz," 34. See also Smart, "The Queen and the Flirt," 126–36. At the beginning of this article, Smart briefly touches on the way two popular audio-visual excerpts of Maria Callas in performance seem to "mesh fictional enactment with some of the more painfully exposed aspects of the singer's own life" (p. 126). Callas's biographers have been quick to read her biography both as an opera and through the roles she played. For example, see Levine, *Maria Callas* and Edwards, *Maria Callas*.
58   Smart, "The Lost Voice of Rosine Stoltz," 50.
59   Ibid.
60   Ibid.
61   Ibid. In her work on seventeenth-century opera, Rosand has also emphasized the role of singers. See *"I più canori cigni e le suavissime sirene*: The Singers" in *Opera in Seventeenth-Century Venice*, 221–244.

American operas into the spotlight, we can locate a piece of feminist history lurking just beneath the seemingly placid surface of the 1950s.

In Chapter 1 ("American Opera at Mid-Century"), I establish the framework for this book by briefly exploring the stunning success of Gian-Carlo Menotti's *The Consul* (1950). This opera, or "musical drama," as Menotti referred to it, centers on the plight of Magda Sorel, a desperate wife and mother from an unnamed totalitarian country in Europe. Menotti modeled the character of Magda after a woman named Sofia Feldy whose death had been reported in the *New York Times* in 1947. Portrayed by soprano Patricia Neway (1919–2012), Magda pulled at the heartstrings of US audiences, for Magda represented a broken wife and mother from a broken family. When Neway brought her to life and death night after night at the Ethel Barrymore Theatre on Broadway, she embodied the women, families, and way of life many Americans believed to be at stake during the early Cold War.

Ultimately running for eight months on Broadway, *The Consul* was an unprecedented commercial success for a homegrown opera in the US. As a point of comparison, when *Porgy and Bess* opened on Broadway in 1935, it ran for approximately three and a half months.[62] Of course, *Porgy and Bess* has been revived on Broadway on numerous occasions, while *The Consul* has never been revived there. In this chapter, I illuminate how *The Consul*'s initial success was intimately tied to the conditions of the 1950s, as new venues for opera sprang up across the country and Americans attended a variety of opera performances in record numbers.[63] It was during this decade, for example, that Maria Callas (1923–1977) reached the height of her fame in the US. As Robert Levine writes, "in an era captivated by popular culture personalities like Marilyn Monroe and Elvis Presley" Callas commanded attention as well, helping to expand the audience for opera in the US.[64] Yet, because Callas devoted herself to the operas of the European canon, her name is largely absent from this book. Interestingly, Menotti's biographer John Gruen asserts that Menotti asked Callas to sing the role of Magda at La Scala in 1951.[65] Gruen writes that La Scala's general manager Antonio Ghiringhelli believed "no one in his company … could compare to Patricia

---

62 *Porgy and Bess* ran for 124 performances, opening at the Alvin Theatre on October 10, 1935, and closing on January 25, 1936. *The Consul* ran for 269 performances, opening at the Ethel Barrymore Theatre on March 15, 1950, and closing on November 4, 1950.

63 Several scholars have emphasized the 1950s as a period of growth for opera in the US. See Waleson, *Mad Scenes and Exit Arias*, 5–46; Wierzbicki, *Music in the Age of Anxiety*, 127–130; Kirk, *American Opera*, 272; Dizikes, *Opera in America*, 485–491.

64 Levine, *Maria Callas*, 91.

65 Gruen, *Menotti*, 100–101.

Neway in dramatic intensity."⁶⁶ As Neway was busy touring with *The Consul* in the US, Ghiringhelli suggested that Menotti look for an Italian soprano from outside his company for the role of Magda. When Menotti chose Callas, the soprano and the general manager—who reportedly hated one another—found that they could not agree on the terms of Callas's appearance, and Menotti settled on a singer named Clara Petrella.⁶⁷ In addition to possibly revealing a characteristically dramatic moment in Callas's life and career, this episode speaks to the power of Neway's performance as Magda. This is one of the focal points of Chapter 1, as I emphasize that as the possibilities for opera in the US began to expand, a composer-librettist and singer demonstrated together that American operas could be profitable, as well as culturally and politically relevant, seemingly inspiring a generation of composers, singers, and audience members alike.

In Chapter 2 ("A Conniving Gold Digger: Elizabeth 'Baby Doe' Tabor"), I turn to the first of two operas that pick up where *The Consul* left off, featuring a family under attack. To a certain extent, both *The Ballad of Baby Doe* and *Lizzie Borden* are based, like *The Consul*, on "real" women. Just as Menotti modeled Magda Sorel after Sophia Feldy, Douglas Moore claimed to have begun thinking, at least casually, about writing an opera about Elizabeth "Baby Doe" Tabor after reading the sensational account of her death in a New York newspaper.

During the late nineteenth and early twentieth centuries, Elizabeth Tabor was popularly known by the nickname Baby Doe, and she was notorious. She brazenly defied the sanctity of the family, divorcing her first husband and, worse yet, taking up with another woman's husband before her divorce was finalized. Baby Doe died alone and in poverty. Her body was discovered frozen to death in an old miner's shack in Leadville, Colorado, a dismal but deserved fate, according to many Americans. I argue that when Moore and his librettist John Latouche revived Baby Doe in the 1950s, they punished her anew, portraying her first as a gold digger and homewrecker and then as a doomed reincarnation of the Victorian "Angel in the House."⁶⁸ As I intimated earlier, however, soprano Beverly Sills did not exactly sing along to this approach to the paradigm of the virgin or the whore.

In Chapter 3 ("A 'Really Vicious Monster': Lizzie Andrew Borden"), I examine Jack Beeson, Kenward Elmslie, and Richard Plant's *Lizzie Borden*,

---

66 Ibid., 100.
67 In a special to the *New York Times*, Arnaldo Cortesi reported that *The Consul* was received "with mixed feelings" at La Scala. See "La Scala Offers Menotti's 'Consul' with 2 Members of Original Cast."
68 The phrase "Angel in the House" refers to the feminine ideal inspired by Coventry Patmore's 1854 narrative poem by the same title.

conceived in 1954 as Moore and Latouche started to bring Elizabeth "Baby Doe" Tabor back to life. In 1892, after the mangled bodies of Andrew Jackson Borden (1822–1892) and his wife Abby Durfee Borden (1828–1892) were discovered in their home in Fall River, Massachusetts, Andrew's eldest daughter found herself accused of the axe murders. Lizzie Andrew Borden (1860–1927) was tried and acquitted the following year, but in the court of public opinion, she remained guilty. Beeson, Plant, and Elmslie certainly believed in her guilt, and with their opera, they sought to pinpoint just what would drive a woman to murder her parents. Like *The Ballad of Baby Doe*, *Lizzie Borden* is about the punishment and penance of an unruly woman. Beeson, Plant, and Elmslie constructed their title heroine as a repressed spinster driven to commit murder because of a psychosexual complex and an unbearable domestic situation. At the end of the opera, Lizzie appears as a grotesque woman-turned-man of the house, something of a reincarnation of psychiatrist Richard Freiherr von Krafft-Ebing's "Mannish Lesbian."[69] In contrast to *The Ballad of Baby Doe*, the title heroine's transformation in *Lizzie Borden* is written so completely into the opera's libretto and score that, as singers such as Phyllis Pancella (b. 1963) and Lauren Flanigan (b. 1958) have suggested, resistance through performance seems impossible. The only way to "undo" the paradigm of the virgin or the whore in *Lizzie Borden* is to lay it out in the pages of this book for critique.

In Chapter 4 ("A Chaste White Woman: Laurie Moss"), I analyze the first of two operas about young single women. I read Aaron Copland and Erik Johns's *The Tender Land* (1954, rev. 1955) alongside James Agee and Walker Evans's *Let Us Now Praise Famous Men* (1941) and Erskine Caldwell's *Tragic Ground* (1944), the primary literary texts that informed the opera's libretto, and I show how Copland and Johns molded their eighteen-year-old heroine Laurie Moss into a chaste white woman whose virginity must be protected. As Laurie approaches her high school graduation, her mother and grandfather worry obsessively that she *could* be raped or seduced. She isn't, but their anxiety colors the entire opera and constricts her life. Finally, Laurie resists her mother and grandfather's attempts to protect and control her. She sets off at the end of the opera, determined to make her own way in the world. I conclude this chapter by examining the limits of the sexual and political autonomy that Copland and Johns seemed to want to suggest for Laurie at the end of *The Tender Land*, reflecting on the lives and careers of Rosemary Carlos (1925–2005),

---

69 Richard Freiherr von Krafft-Ebing (1840–1902) was an Austro-German psychiatrist best known for his work *Psychopathia Sexualis* (1886). He coined the term "Mannish Lesbian" in the 1880s.

Alice Hotopp (b. 1932), and MaVynee Betsch (1935–2005), three of the women who sang the role of Laurie in the 1950s.

In Chapter 5 ("A Dangerous Jezebel: Susannah Polk"), I turn to Carlisle Floyd's *Susannah*, an opera that has the potential to illuminate the history of rape in the US as well as the longstanding tradition of violence against women in opera. Like Laurie Moss, Susannah Polk is an eighteen-year-old virgin, yet the people in her community regard her as an unchaste and dangerous single woman, perhaps, I argue, because they suspect her of having African American ancestry. Soprano Phyllis Curtin (1921–2016) began singing the role of Susannah in 1955. It was she who helped bring Floyd's opera to the attention of the New York City Opera (NYCO) in 1956, and she continued to sing the title role well into the 1960s. I maintain that just as Sills identified with Baby Doe, Curtin saw herself in Susannah. Born in Clarksburg, West Virginia, Curtin admitted that she grew up in an Appalachian community not entirely unlike Floyd's fictional New Hope Valley, Tennessee. As she asserted, she "understood Susannah right to the ground."[70] Curtin also had some experience with being shamed for her sexuality. Floyd notes that when photographs of the soprano performing the "Dance of the Seven Veils" in *Salome* were published in *Life* magazine, a preacher in Clarksburg responded by denouncing her from the pulpit. Curtin brought this experience to *Susannah*, and Floyd took that experience seriously. Over the course of his life, he repeatedly referred to Curtin's perspective on *Susannah*, affirming that his perspective on the opera entwined with hers. In fact, along with soprano Renée Fleming (b. 1959), Curtin convinced Floyd to stop using the word "seduction" as a euphemism for "rape" in *Susannah*.

Undoing Gendered Archetypes

At the end of *Opera, or the Undoing of Women*, Clément imagines a feminist future for opera: "Beautiful and alive, the women will continue to sing in a voice that will never again submit to threat. They will say something entirely different than the words breathed in delirium and pain. They will ask no more than that they finally be permitted to die."[71] According to Susan McClary, Clément longs for "a sisterhood that can sing freely and who cannot, *will not*, be driven underground."[72] With the exception of Magda Sorel, all the heroines featured in this book are alive but transformed at the end of their operas. For Baby Doe and Lizzie Borden, there appears to be

---

70 Duffie, "Soprano Phyllis Curtin."
71 Clément, *Opera, or the Undoing of Women*, 180.
72 McClary, "Foreword" in Clément, *Opera, or the Undoing of Women*, xvii.

little hope. In the eyes of Moore, Latouche, Beeson, Plant, and Elmslie, they might as well be dead, for they appear doomed to endure a sad, solitary existence of more than thirty years. The futures for Laurie Moss and Susannah Polk are less clear. Neither *The Tender Land* nor *Susannah* locks its heroine into place in the manner of *The Ballad of Baby Doe* or *Lizzie Borden*. Laurie sets off on her own, less optimistic than she appeared at the beginning of *The Tender Land*, yet still apparently ready to embrace whatever life has to offer. Susannah, on the other hand, is bitter and angry. One can imagine her growing old and remaining on her property, ostracized from the rest of her community like Baby Doe and Lizzie Borden, but one can also imagine her picking up her shotgun and leaving, as though following in Laurie's footsteps.

I am not convinced that Baby Doe, Lizzie, Laurie, or Susannah could ever be construed as explicitly "feminist" operatic heroines, but they did suggest that something new might be afoot in the US. Just as important, while it would be difficult to label either Beverly Sills or Phyllis Curtin as "feminist" singers, they found their voices in American opera and, with their voices, sought to change American opera and American culture more broadly. Sills's and Curtin's efforts to undo the binary of the virgin or the whore demonstrate how over the course of the 1950s, women in the US increasingly questioned the moral and political dimensions of the postwar domesticity. They worked to sing freely and above ground. It is time for us to listen to their voices.

Chapter One

American Opera at Mid-Century

On March 16, 1950, New York's music and drama critics reported on the premiere of Gian-Carlo Menotti's *The Consul*, presented the previous evening at the Ethel Barrymore Theater. Everyone had something to say about Patricia Neway (1919–2012), the soprano who sang the role of Magda Sorel. Neway "stands out as a singing actress of unusual power," wrote Virgil Thomson in the *New York Herald Tribune*.[1] Olin Downes was more voluble, describing to readers of the *New York Times* how Neway's "warm, brilliant voice and spirit, and feeling for her role, enabled her to give the fullest interpretive value to every note and every word, whether it was of sustained melody or graphic recitative. The climax of her nobly fashioned aria ... at the end of the second act simply stopped the show for minutes, and overwhelmed the audience."[2] With Neway at the helm, *The Consul* did indeed "overwhelm" audiences. It ran on Broadway for eight straight months, racking up a total of 269 performances and winning both the 1950 Pulitzer Prize for Music and New York Drama Critics' Circle Award for Best Musical.[3]

The year 1950 proved to be a strange and difficult one in the US. As historian J. Ronald Oakley pointed out, "never had the nation been more powerful, but not since the early dark days of World War II had the American people felt so puzzled and so threatened by world events."[4] "Everywhere," Oakley continued, "there was talk of Joseph Stalin and the Russians, of the 'loss of China,' of a communist plot to rule the world, of the Cold War and World War III, of subversives in the State Department, colleges and

---

1 Thomson, "The Music: Pathos and the Macabre."
2 Downes, "Menotti 'Consul' Has Its Premiere."
3 See *The Consul*, Internet Broadway Database. *The Consul* ran for two weeks at the Shubert Theatre in Philadelphia before transferring to Broadway.
4 Oakley, *God's Country*, 6.

universities, entertainment industry, and no telling where else."[5] *The Consul* spoke to US audiences during this uncertain time—and interestingly, it managed to do so across what many perceived to be a longstanding cultural divide. Menotti was anxious about billing *The Consul* as an opera, and he ultimately chose to call the piece a "musical drama" to avoid the stigma that he believed accompanied the word "opera" in the US.[6] Yet despite Menotti's trepidation, many viewers immediately and enthusiastically understood *The Consul* to be an opera. Downes proudly invoked the "o" word when he congratulated Menotti, stating that the "opera" had "eloquence, momentousness, and intensity of expression unequaled by any native composer."[7] Drama critic Robert Garland insisted: "Don't let the 'musical drama' printed in the program fool you. What Mr. Menotti, the composer-librettist, has written is a grand opera."[8] Garland encouraged viewers, moreover, to embrace the luxury, "make the most of it," and have "a grand opera time."[9] In 1952, the NYCO added *The Consul* to its repertory, continuing to produce the opera regularly into the 1960s and adding to the work's enduring status as an opera.

The Consul centers on Magda Sorel, a struggling wife and mother who lives in "the present ... somewhere in Europe."[10] Magda's husband John is a political dissident; hounded by secret police, he is forced to abandon his family and go into hiding during the opening scene of the opera. Just before he leaves, John advises Magda to seek help from the foreign—presumably US—consulate. Day after day, Magda dutifully visits the consulate. There, she encounters a wall of impenetrable bureaucracy, personified by the consul's secretary, a callous woman who refuses to do anything but push an endless pile of paperwork. Magda becomes increasingly desperate as she realizes that her family's future is doomed. She watches, for example, as her baby dies of malnutrition and her mother-in-law of sorrow. Finally, Magda resorts to the most extreme of measures, gassing herself to death in her family's apartment because she believes that John will remain in hiding only if he

---

5   Ibid.
6   In March 1950, Menotti's publisher at G. Schirmer made coy reference to *The Consul* in an article in *Opera News*, suggesting that the composer regarded the term "opera" as something of a "naughty word" in the US. See Heinsheimer, "The Future of Opera in America," 11.
7   Downes, "Menotti 'Consul' Has Its Premiere."
8   Garland, "Patricia Neway Great in Fine Musical Drama."
9   Ibid.
10 See Menotti, *The Consul: Musical Drama in Three Acts, Libretto*. After the list of characters, Menotti included the following: "Time—the present. The action takes place somewhere in Europe."

knows that she too is dead. In a final tragic twist, John comes back anyway and is arrested. At the opera's conclusion, his fate remains unknown.

In 1973, Chandler Cowles, the man responsible for commissioning and producing *The Consul*, recalled in an interview with Menotti's biographer that "Gian Carlo struggled hard with that opera. The premise was a good one, the characters were real."[11] To a certain extent, the characters were "real." Menotti found his inspiration from a notice that had appeared in the *New York Times* on February 12, 1947.[12] According to the notice, a thirty-eight-year-old Polish woman named Mrs. Sofia Feldy had come to the US to reunite with her husband, who had successfully immigrated to Chicago some years prior. Mr. Feldy, however, claimed that he had divorced his wife back in November of 1940 and agreed only to accept his daughter, who had accompanied her mother. Mrs. Feldy was "refused admission" to the country, and she "committed suicide by hanging in the Ellis Island detention room."[13] Menotti crafted his music and libretto around the story of Sofia Feldy's abandonment, both personal and political, shifting the Ellis Island location to a police state in Europe.[14]

The Consul's bleak European setting proved particularly poignant to US audiences, playing on their fears and sympathies. As historian Tara Zahra writes, in the wake of World War II, there was "widespread consensus" that

---

11 Chandler Cowles, interview with John Gruen, September 8, 1973, John Gruen collection of Gian Carlo Menotti research (MSS 23), Box 1/Folder 32, Curtis Institute of Music Archives. Cowles (1917–1997) was an actor and producer, active both on Broadway and in Hollywood. He was very supportive of Menotti's work during the 1940s and 1950s.
12 See "Immigrant a Suicide." See also Gruen, *Menotti*, 78.
13 "Immigrant a Suicide."
14 In fact, Menotti had been interested in the plight of displaced European immigrants for some time. As Gruen reports, Menotti spent some of 1947 living in Hollywood, where he attempted several film scripts. *The Bridge*, for example, was based in part on a newspaper story about a group of Austrian refugees who lived on a bridge between Austria and Hungary for an entire week, because neither country was willing to assume responsibility for them as citizens. Gruen writes that Arthur Freed (of Metro-Goldwyn-Mayer) found *The Bridge* "too depressing" and unlikely to "appeal to the majority of moviegoers, who were tired of sad war pictures" (see *Menotti*, 77). Menotti subsequently abandoned *The Bridge* and began a new script entitled *A Happy Ending*. Unfortunately, this too was deemed unsuitable for Hollywood. Gruen maintains that Menotti's Hollywood experience and *The Bridge* in particular "proved invaluable," leading the composer to his next major work, *The Consul* (see *Menotti*, 78). For the newspaper article that may have inspired *The Bridge*, see "Refugees Dodge Trains on Border Bridge As Both Austria and Hungary Bar Entry."

the war "had destroyed the family as completely as Europe's train tracks, factories, and roads."[15] Historian Laura A. Belmonte argues that with Europe in shambles and the Soviet Union poised to exert and expand its influence, the US sought to define itself as "an attractive alternative to life behind the Iron Curtain."[16] Belmonte explains how US information officials worked to portray the US as a place where "men were able to take care of their wives and children," "women devoted themselves to their families and their communities," and "the state protected families."[17] Much of *The Consul*'s early reception suggests that it was understood within this culture of propaganda because in *The Consul*, it would seem that Menotti defined the US and the American family through opposition. As Howard Taubman wrote in the *New York Times*: "The country [the Sorels] wish to leave is never designated; you are at liberty to make your own guess. The country to which they wish to go is not designated either, but to any one who knows Europe today and the yearning of many of its people to come to the United States, only one guess seems necessary."[18] Robert Coleman of the *Daily Mirror* was more partisan, gleefully exclaiming that Menotti had delivered "a slashing operatic blow at totalitarianism," which he went on to define as "Nazism, Black Fascism and Red Fascism, or Communism, if you prefer."[19] He urged "all the local comrades who think life behind the Iron Curtain is just dandy" to "see 'The Consul,'" arguing that "it might help to open the eyes of these dim-witted dupes, and it will certainly make good Americans proud of their democratic Republic."[20] Coleman touted a similar message in 1957, asserting that Menotti's opera would "be timely as long as there are totalitarian states and people with the courage to seek escape from them."[21] He concluded that while many refugees would be unsuccessful, "their love of freedom is moving, indeed."[22]

Reviewers generally did not dwell on the fact that Menotti's portrayal of the bureaucratic hoops at the consulate could be seen as painting an unflattering portrait of the US and its policies. Richard Watts Jr. said only that *The Consul* "dramatiz[ed] at once the horror of a police state and the unfeeling

---

15 Zahra, *The Lost Children*, 4. See also Bailey, *The Problem of the Children in the World Today*.
16 Belmonte, *Selling the American Way*, 137.
17 Ibid.
18 Taubman, "Labeling 'The Consul.'"
19 Coleman, "'Consul' a Dramatic Blast at Brutalitarian Rule."
20 Ibid.
21 Coleman, "'Consul' in Park Real Spellbinder."
22 Ibid.

inhumanity of diplomatic red tape."[23] He noted how the opera "shifts back and forth between a home shadowed by the secret police and the consulate of some happier land."[24] Yet Watts refused to explicitly name that "happier land" or hold it accountable. In this, Watts followed Menotti's lead, for Menotti's libretto referred only vaguely to a totalitarian country "somewhere in Europe."[25]

At least one exception occurred in 1953, when Zechariah Chafee Jr., a university professor at Harvard, contributed a review of a 1952 bulletin entitled *American Visa Policy and Foreign Scientists* to the *University of Pennsylvania Law Review*. Chafee summarized the periodical's findings, explaining how scientists from both inside and outside the country were being prevented "from crossing the frontiers of the United States in either direction for the purpose of furthering the advance of knowledge."[26] He charged: "It is high time that thoughtful American citizens knew what our country is actually doing because of its fear of communism."[27] A few pages later, he made reference to *The Consul*: "The Bulletin shows how often these great foreign scientists have been subjected by our consuls and other officials to the run-around. Anybody who has been shocked by Menotti's opera 'The Consul' will see its scenes re-enacted in these pages."[28] Chafee clearly did not regard *The Consul* as pro-US propaganda; indeed, he used the opera to make a statement about the detrimental impact of the anti-communist sentiment enveloping the US. Yet Chafee appears to have been in the minority. Moreover, although he offered this reading just three years after *The Consul*'s premiere, his words resonated within a vastly different political context. By March 1953, the Korean War, which had begun during *The Consul*'s Broadway run, was coming to its conclusion, and Senator Joseph R. McCarthy was well into his anti-communist crusade in Washington. Chafee may have gained some political perspective by 1953, but most viewers in 1950 appear to have been swept away by the notion that the opera proved the US's superiority.

In this respect, the women whom Menotti created for *The Consul*, Magda and the Secretary, were crucial. They both stood apart from the mid-century feminine ideal, contributing to pro-US readings of the opera. Magda strives but fails to conform to the image of the beautiful and capable American

---

23 Watts, "A Police State in Musical Drama."
24 Ibid.
25 Menotti, *The Consul: Musical Drama in Three Acts, Libretto*.
26 Chafee, "Book Reviews: American Visa Policy and Foreign Scientists," 703.
27 Ibid., 705.
28 Ibid., 711.

housewife that was littered throughout popular media of the 1950s.[29] Over the course of the opera, Magda gradually loses her poise. Finally, she loses both her family and her sanity, demonstrating that she simply cannot cope with her domestic situation. When Patricia Neway performed the role in a 1960 film for television, she darted around the stage frantically, repeatedly raking her hands through her disheveled hair; just before the climax of Magda's mad scene, Neway sang with eyes wide with fear and lack of sleep, lamenting the death of her child and the endless paperwork that is to blame (Fig. 1.1).[30] Nine years before US Vice President Richard M. Nixon and Soviet First Secretary Nikita Khurshchev would engage in the "kitchen debate," Magda served as a foil for the American wife and mother whose life was made easy by her government, her husband the breadwinner, and all the modern conveniences available in a Capitalist society.[31]

If Magda strives to conform to the role of the good wife and mother, the Secretary does not even care to try. Throughout *The Consul*, the Secretary acts as the primary antagonist. We never learn the Secretary's name, but it is she who appears to bar Magda's escape. In 1950, a writer for *Newsweek* referred to her as a "mistress of red tape," a characterization aided by Menotti's own rather misogynistic depiction of the character.[32] The Secretary is the epitome of the dispassionate working girl, a popular stereotype following World War II. As Elaine Tyler May notes, while working women were celebrated in American popular media during the 1930s and to some extent during the 1940s, "the emancipated heroine did not survive in peacetime," and "after the war, less positive images of women began to appear in films."[33]

---

29   See Friedan, "The Happy Housewife Heroine" in *The Feminine Mystique*, 33–68.
30   See Menotti and Dalrymple, *The Consul*. Dalrymple produced this production of *The Consul* for television in 1960.
31   On the "kitchen debate," see May, *Homeward Bound*, 19–22.
32   "Opera's Heir Presumptive," 82. Misogynistic characterizations are not unusual in Menotti's operas. In his opera blog, Patrick Hansen, director of Opera McGill, described *The Telephone* (1947) as a "terrible, slightly misogynistic look at a woman obsessed with her telephone." Hansen charged: "It's not an uncanny pre-cursor op-ed on why social media is disconnecting all of us from each other. It's an un-funny look at a woman who lies, chatters about without any thoughts in her head, and then is asked for her hand in marriage by a loser named Ben." See "Patrick's Opera Blog: Why Menotti Operas Are Flawed."
33   May, *Homeward Bound*, 62. See also Haskell, *From Reverence to Rape*, 90–152, 189–230.

Figure 1.1. Patricia Neway playing Magda Sorel in *The Consul* (1960).

The Secretary is impatient and barely cares to look at the people who seek her assistance in the waiting room. Throughout the opera, she sings primarily in an angular, perfunctory recitative, and she is unmoved by the emotional outpourings that the other characters sing. In Act I, Scene 2, she mocks a woman who approaches her desk but speaks no English: "Oh, dear! You ... you 'non capisco,' eh?"[34] Then she sighs and asks in exasperation: "Is there anyone in this room who can understand her?"[35] Later in the scene, Magda comes up to the desk, but the Secretary ignores her, flirting instead with someone over the phone. According to Menotti's stage directions, the Secretary answers the phone and "laughs coquettishly."[36] After she hangs up, she turns to Magda, "with cold efficiency again," and asks: "Yes?"[37] The Secretary regards Magda as little more than a nuisance. In a 1963 production, televised in Austria, director Rudolph Cartier highlighted the Secretary's aloof and detached nature by having Gloria Lane play the role in dark sunglasses (Fig. 1.2).[38] Commentators who wanted to approach *The Consul* as pro-US propaganda were therefore aided by Menotti's play on the paradigm of the virgin or the whore. Importantly, by vilifying the Secretary, more so than the Consul or his country, Menotti was able to shift away any blame that might fall on the US, mapping it instead onto an unnamed female body.

Americans were certainly moved by Menotti's music and subject matter, but they were also moved by Patricia Neway's performance and portrayal of Magda Sorel. At the time of *The Consul*'s premiere, Neway was thirty years

---

34 Menotti, *The Consul: Musical Drama in Three Acts, Libretto*, 15.
35 Ibid.
36 Ibid., 17.
37 Ibid.
38 See Menotti and Cartier, *Der Konsul*. Gloria Lane played the secretary in the original Broadway production of *The Consul* as well.

Figure 1.2. Gloria Lane playing the Secretary in *Der Konsul* (1963).

old and largely unknown. Born in Brooklyn and raised on Staten Island, she earned her BA from Notre Dame College (now part of St. John's University) in 1939. After college, she became interested in music and studied voice with Morris Gesell, whom she later married. In 1946, she appeared in a production of Mozart's *Così fan tutte* at the Chautauqua Opera, and in 1948, she shared the role of the Female Chorus with Brenda Lewis (the singer who would go on to create the role of Lizzie Borden) in Benjamin Britten's *The Rape of Lucretia* at the Ziegfeld Theatre on Broadway.[39] Magda ultimately proved not only to be Neway's big break, but also the role that defined her career. In 1962, music critic John Ardoin reported on the NYCO's new production of *The Consul*, confessing that it was "impossible to think of anyone but Patricia Neway as Magda."[40] When Neway died in 2012, *Opera News* described her as "a dramatic soprano whose singing was invested with pathos as well as power," recalling that in *The Consul*, "Neway stopped the show cold with Magda's principal aria."[41] Similarly, Margalit Fox noted in her obituary for the *New York Times* that "it was as Magda in 'The Consul' that she made her reputation" as she "brought down the house nearly every night."[42] After playing Magda, Neway played two more European mothers; in 1958, she took on "the mother" in Menotti's *Maria Golovin*, and in 1959, she appeared as the Mother Abbess in Rodgers and Hammerstein's *The Sound of Music*.

In 1974, Neway discussed the role of Magda with John Gruen, at work on his biography of Menotti. Neway described Magda as a "fabulous" role with "all the great qualities of a human being, with the exception of the

---

39   See Zolotow, "Patricia Neway Talks of Magda Sorel."
40   Ardoin, "The Consul," 25.
41   "Patricia Neway, 92, the First Magda Sorel in *The Consul*, Has Died."
42   Fox, "Patricia Neway, Operatic Soprano Who Won a Tony, Dies at 92."

fact that Magda commits suicide."[43] Neway stumbled somewhat as she reflected on Magda's final act: "You know that the story of THE CONSUL was inspired by a notice in the newspaper that [Menotti] had read, about a woman committing suicide. But, as it turned out, Magda became stronger as a character ... and then to have such a monument of strength commit suicide became something of a sticky thing."[44] Neway did not expand on her discomfort with *The Consul*'s conclusion, but she may have suspected how in this characteristically operatic act Menotti sought to render Magda and, by extension, "somewhere in Europe," inherently powerless. In fact, in 1950, Richard Watts Jr. described Magda as "both an appealing human being and a moving symbol of the unhappy womanhood of a tortured continent."[45]

Neway's perspective on Magda is fascinating given that what she was suggesting was that Menotti, the composer and librettist, did not actually understand the character he had created. By 1974, Neway had accessed the role of Magda through the act of performance over a period of more than ten years and in her estimation, "about 550" performances, and she claimed a superior understanding of Magda's character.[46] She simply was not convinced that Magda would have lost her mind and killed herself. As musicologist Susan McClary has pointedly argued, operatic madwomen are "first and foremost male fantasies of transgression dressed up as women," noting that "real women—mad or otherwise—do not enter into this picture at all."[47] Yet in the case of *The Consul*, Neway increasingly sought to enter into the picture, and Menotti sought to sideline her.

Neway admitted to Gruen that by the 1960s, she and Menotti were often "at odds" with each other over the role of Magda.[48] Describing her final two performances with the NYCO in 1966, she explained that "there were things that I needed desperately to get emotionally out of the role" whereas

---

43 Patricia Neway, interview with John Gruen, April 8, 1974, John Gruen collection of Gian Carlo Menotti research (MSS 23), Box 1/Folder 9, Curtis Institute of Music Archives.
44 Ibid.
45 Watts, "A Police State in Musical Drama."
46 Neway, interview with Gruen.
47 McClary, *Feminine Endings*, 110. Musicologist Ralph P. Locke approaches this issue from another angle, suggesting that perhaps women in opera "are not really women at all." As Locke explains, "audiences—and the (male) composers themselves—use women characters in opera partly as a means of searching for a way to restore emotional wholeness, to find or construct the 'missing pieces,' that is to say, the pieces that men, especially, tend to be missing or rather cannot acknowledge having." See "What Are These Women Doing in Opera?", 74.
48 Neway, interview with Gruen.

Menotti "had been used to training people anew."[49] Neway recalled that Menotti directed the first performance of the 1966 NYCO production, and she characterized it as a complete disaster. A few months later, she sang in the second and final performance, this time directed by Frank Rizzo. According to Neway, the results of the performance under Rizzo were much better. For his part, Menotti complained about Neway to Gruen, charging that the soprano "became terribly didactic ... teacherish and very set in her ways."[50] Thoroughly dismissing the "interpretive arts," he balked at Neway taking ownership of what he regarded as solely his work.[51] Yet Neway's complete commitment to the role of Magda contributed enormously to *The Consul*'s success. Neway grew to regard Magda as more than a role and more than a character. She described being so touched, for example, when after performances of *The Consul*, audience members would appear "backstage with tear-stained faces to thank me for telling their story."[52] Aided no doubt by Cold War propaganda, Neway believed Magda's experience was real, and it was that belief and dedication to it that allowed her to embody the desperate European wife and mother so completely that many audience members believed as well, mapping aspects of their own stories onto Neway's body and voice.

※ ※ ※

In 1991, composer Ned Rorem, who studied briefly with Menotti, argued that his mentor had "singlehandedly revitalized the concept of living opera in the United States."[53] Rorem was exaggerating, yet he was right to highlight Menotti's stature and perhaps even influence during the 1940s and 1950s. When *The Consul* opened on Broadway, Menotti was featured on the cover of *Time* magazine, a clear marker of his popular appeal.[54] In October 1951, approximately one year after *The Consul* closed on Broadway, the

---

49 Ibid.
50 Menotti, quoted in Gruen, *Menotti*, 227.
51 Menotti told Gruen: "I've never been very fascinated by interpretive artists ... I'm much more fascinated by writers, or painters, or poets. It's the creative process that fascinates me." Quoted in ibid.
52 Neway, quoted in Fox, "Patricia Neway, Operatic Soprano Who Won a Tony, Dies at 92." Menotti's own biographer saw elements of his family history in Magda's struggle. Gruen recalled in his 2008 memoir that he was "very moved" by *The Consul*, "with its story echoing my own experiences in war-torn Europe, when my parents had to flee Germany and Italy." He explained how "their efforts were met with the same sort of bureaucratic red tape" that Magda encountered. See *Callas Kissed Me ... Lenny Too!*, 223.
53 Rorem, "In Search of American Opera," 10.
54 See "Composer on Broadway."

magazine *Opera News* suggested "Menotti mania" as "a possible slogan for current operatic taste in the United States."[55] Even musicologist Joseph Kerman, who considered Menotti "an entirely trivial artist," could not deny Menotti's popularity when he first published *Opera as Drama* in 1956.[56] Menotti's success demonstrated that opera in the US could be more than an artistic and financial liability. As Rorem explained in 2007, "every composer in America, and in by extension, the world, said if he can hit the jackpot, so can I."[57] Once again, Rorem was exaggerating but as I demonstrate below, there is a kernel of truth to his statement.

The first half of Menotti's career can be viewed as something of a microcosm of the development of American opera in the twentieth century, and tracing Menotti's successes and failures illuminates much about a quickly changing landscape. Born and raised outside Milan, Menotti (1911–2007) arrived in Philadelphia in 1928 to study at the Curtis Institute of Music.[58] With the Great Depression on the horizon, the time was not exactly ripe for investment in expensive ventures like opera. Still, by 1937, several years before World War II would help to bring the US out of the Depression and spur the development of opera, Menotti had begun to make his mark. That year, Curtis gave the premiere of his first mature opera, *Amelia Goes to the Ball*, and in 1938, the Met mounted seven acclaimed performances of the one-act opera buffa in New York City.[59] On the heels of this success, the National Broadcasting Company (NBC) commissioned Menotti to

---

55 "Menotti Mania ...," 19. In this article, *Opera News* estimated that at least 357 performances of operas by Menotti had taken place throughout the year.
56 See Kerman, *Opera as Drama*, 264. In 1988, Kerman published a revised edition of *Opera as Drama*, and as he explained in the preface to it, he had deleted "many of the spot judgments" from the original edition. He even went so far as to delete the entire final chapter from the original "so as to omit *inter alia* an unduly shrill attack on the operas of Gian-Carlo Menotti and a gratuitous wisecrack about Benjamin Britten." Kerman justified his decision by noting that he had been "hoping for a long time to be able to remove these *péchés de jeunesse* from public view." Menotti's name is entirely absent from the revised edition. See *Opera as Drama, New and Revised Edition*, x.
57 Rorem, quoted in Safo, "Menotti, Cultural Giant, Dies at 95."
58 At Curtis, Menotti studied composition with the Italian composer Rosario Scalero (1870–1954). In addition to Menotti, Scalero's students included Marc Blitzstein, Samuel Barber, Nino Rota, Hugo Weisgall, Lukas Foss, and Ned Rorem.
59 Menotti wrote the libretto for *Amelia Goes to the Ball* in Italian, translating it into English prior to the Curtis premiere. In 1938, the original *Amelia al ballo* was presented in San Remo. After *Amelia*, Menotti wrote most of his librettos in English.

write a radio opera. The result, a one-act comedy entitled *The Old Maid and the Thief*, was broadcast on April 22, 1939. It was soon picked up and staged by professional opera companies, as well as by college and community opera groups.[60] Thus by the end of the 1930s, Menotti's operas had been successfully produced in the opera house, as well as in more experimental venues.

Menotti suffered his first major setback in 1942, when the Met gave four performances of his new opera *The Island God*. Neither Menotti nor New York's music critics were pleased with the performances. Menotti initially complained that he did not have enough control over the production. Later, he referred to the opera as being "made up of very bad Italian music" and removed it from his oeuvre.[61] In the wake of this setback, Menotti swore off the Met, claiming that the company was not interested in mounting new works. Admittedly, the Met did not have a great track record for successfully producing new operas.[62] By the 1940s, it was firmly established as a repertory company, specializing primarily in nineteenth-century European operas.

Menotti's next major success came in 1946, when he directed the premiere of his eerie new melodrama *The Medium* at Columbia University. One year after the Columbia premiere, *The Medium* appeared on the Ballet Society's one-act opera season, sponsored by Lincoln Kirstein; several months later, it opened on Broadway.[63] In the case of these latter two pro-

---

60 In 1941, the Philadelphia Opera Company produced the first staged production of *The Old Maid and the Thief*. In 1948, the NYCO presented the first staged production in New York City.

61 Menotti, quoted in Gruen, *Menotti*, 45.

62 During Giulio Gatti-Casazza's tenure as general manager (1910–1935), the Met mounted fourteen American operas, but none of these operas were particularly successful. Indeed, in his 1969 history of the Met, music critic John Briggs included a rather dismal chapter entitled "The Search for the Great American Opera," noting that "the long, unbroken string of failures at the Metropolitan almost made it seem as if the house were under an evil spell as far as new works were concerned." See *Requiem for a Yellow Brick Brewery*, 137. Moreover, as cultural historian John Dizikes and musicologist Davide Ceriani argue, Gatti-Casazza may not have been particularly interested in nurturing American opera. As Dizikes put it, "Gatti-Casazza's Metropolitan" had to avoid being "identified as an American institution run by foreigners for foreign interests," for "the snobbery which led Americans to favor European names and reputations easily turned into jingoistic xenophobia." In other words, Gatti-Casazza's seeming commitment to American opera may have been for show. See *Opera in America*, 377. See also Ceriani, "Italianizing the Metropolitan Opera House."

63 *The Medium* and *The Telephone* opened together on February 18, 1947 at the Heckscher Theatre in New York during the Ballet Society's one-act opera season. The double bill then played at the Ethel Barrymore Theatre from May 1,

ductions, because Kirstein desired a double bill, Menotti paired *The Medium* with a comic curtain raiser entitled *The Telephone*.[64] *The Medium* and *The Telephone* ran for six months at the Ethel Barrymore Theatre, only to be surpassed by *The Consul*'s eight-month run in 1950. Once again, by the end of the decade, Menotti was back on top. This time, however, he cashed in on Broadway instead of bowing to the cultural authority of the Met.

After *Amahl and the Night Visitors*, Menotti's highly successful television opera that premiered on NBC on December 24, 1951, Menotti struggled to write another hit.[65] Yet he remained a household name in the US throughout the 1950s and into the 1960s because of the continued appeal of *The Old Maid and the Thief*, *The Medium*, *The Telephone*, *The Consul*, and *Amahl and the Night Visitors*, all of which were staged routinely by the NYCO, as well as by colleges and smaller professional opera companies. By the 1970s, Menotti's reputation had clearly begun to wane. He continued to write operas into the 1990s, but he was increasingly regarded as something of a hack.[66] Menotti's heyday during the 1940s and 1950s, however, suggested that finally the time had come for American opera. The Met, with its focus on European repertory, was no longer the sole purveyor of opera. Following in Menotti's footsteps, composers working in the US could consider other opera companies, and they could look to universities, Broadway, and television. In the end, no composer would, as Rorem put it, make "the grade the way [Menotti] did," but they certainly found more room to work.[67]

    1947 to November 1, 1947, totaling 212 performances. *The Medium* and *The Telephone* were revived on Broadway in 1950, this time at the Arena Theatre (later renamed the Edison Theatre and now a ballroom at the Hotel Edison).

64 See Ardoin, *The Stages of Menotti*, 49.

65 *Amahl and the Night Visitors* was widely hailed during the 1950s and 1960s. See Bauch, "Amahl and the Night Visitors." See also Barnes, *Television Opera*, 15–41. *Amahl* continues to be a holiday favorite, on television and on stage, particularly among school and community opera theater programs. According to Opera America, *Amahl* consistently ranks among the ten most-produced American operas. See "North American Works Directory."

66 Menotti was also regarded as someone utterly incapable of meeting a deadline. When Beverly Sills recalled her experience starring in the premiere of Menotti's *La Loca* at the San Diego Opera in 1979, she explained that the opera "wasn't finished when we started rehearsing it," and it "wasn't finished when we *performed* it." Labeling some of Menotti's text "just plain silly," Sills claimed that she and Tito Capobianco had to construct much of the opera's mad scene themselves. See Sills and Linderman, *Beverly*, 287–288. Sills's copy of the vocal score, clearly copied and pasted together, attests to her description of the score's status in San Diego. See Gian-Carlo Menotti, *La Loca, Vocal Score*, in Beverly Sills Scores, Music Division, New York Public Library, New York, NY.

67 Rorem, quoted in Safo, "Menotti, Cultural Giant, Dies at 95."

The institution most devoted to the cause of advancing American opera immediately after World War II was the NYCO. Founded in 1943, the NYCO began in the spirit of the New Deal when New York City Mayor Fiorello H. La Guardia lent his name and support to a campaign to make opera performances in the city more affordable for the broader public.[68] The NYCO launched its first season in 1944, presenting three operas: Puccini's *Tosca*, Flowtow's *Martha*, and Bizet's *Carmen*.[69] As opera critic Heidi Waleson reports, "a sold-out, enthusiastic crowd greeted the [opening night] performance [of *Tosca*] with bravos. So did the press."[70] The NYCO eventually earned the moniker "the people's opera," and during the 1950s and 1960s, the company increasingly positioned itself as the American people's opera, often providing greater opportunities to American singers and composers than the Met. In fact, the Met mounted just one American opera (Samuel Barber's *Vanessa*) in the 1950s, whereas the NYCO, as Waleson writes, "carve[d] out its niche by focusing on contemporary and American repertoire."[71]

The NYCO presented its first American premiere in the spring of 1949, mounting three performances of William Grant Still and Langston Hughes's *Troubled Island*.[72] The following decade, the company continued to present a steady stream of American works, some old and some new. In 1952, it staged *Amahl and the Night Visitors* (1951) and *The Consul* (1950). In

---

68 The campaign to found the New York City Center Opera (later called the New York City Opera) was spearheaded by Morton Baum and Newbold Morris. Baum was a lawyer. He became chair of the New York City Center's finance committee in 1943, continuing in that position until his death in 1968. Morris, also a lawyer, was a member of the New York City Planning Commission. He served as president of the New York City Council from 1938 to 1945 under La Guardia. Martin L. Sokol documented the early history of the NYCO in his 1981 book *The New York City Opera: An American Adventure*.

69 Sokol, *The New York City Opera*, 225.

70 Waleson, *Mad Scenes and Exit Arias*, 8.

71 Ibid., 148. The Met gave the premiere of *Vanessa*, its music by Barber, its libretto by Menotti, on January 15, 1958. Five years earlier, the Met gave the American premiere of Igor Stravinsky's *The Rake's Progress* (1951). I am not convinced, however, that it makes sense to count *The Rake's Progress* as an American opera. To be sure, Stravinsky and his librettist W. H. Auden wrote the opera in English while living in the US, but the premiere took place at the Teatro La Fenice in Venice. Another early performance, before the Met's production in 1953, occurred at the Opéra-Comique in Paris.

72 A historical drama, *Troubled Island* loosely chronicles the life of Haitian Revolutionary, Jean-Jacques Dessalines. See Kernodle, "Arias, Communists, and Conspiracies."

1954, it premiered *The Tender Land* (1954) and revived Jerome Kern and Oscar Hammerstein II's *Show Boat* (1927). In 1956, it presented the first professional performances of *Susannah* (1955). Then, in 1957, the Ford Foundation gave the company, now under the direction of Julius Rudel, $105,000 for an entire season of American opera the following year. The first American season made enough of a splash that the NYCO presented a second Ford-funded season of American opera in 1959 and a third in 1960. Such efforts cemented the NYCO's reputation, in the words of John Dizikes, as "the most American of opera companies."[73]

After the final all-American opera season, Rudel tackled another idea, asking the Ford Foundation to support a season devoted to twentieth-century operas. As Waleson explains, Rudel wanted to feature American works alongside European ones, "to see if the American product could hold its own next to Poulenc, Prokofiev, and Shostakovich."[74] The Ford Foundation agreed to the project, ultimately funding the NYCO's 1965 and 1966 spring seasons of contemporary operas. As musicologist Tedrin Blair Lindsay points out, the NYCO routinely presented *The Ballad of Baby Doe*, *Street Scene*, *The Consul*, and *Susannah*, four operas from the three all-American seasons, over later seasons including these twentieth-century ones, thereby ensuring that American operas "attained real repertoire status in the company."[75]

Throughout his twenty-two-year tenure as general director of the NYCO (1957–1979), Rudel produced a total of thirty-five American operas, and when he looked back on his efforts in his 2013 memoir, he proudly asserted that the NYCO's seasons "of new and unusual fare paved the way for regional companies to begin to explore twentieth-century American works."[76] In 1980, Beverly Sills took over as the NYCO's director. She had begun singing with the NYCO in 1955, and she had helped to solidify the company's identifiably American status during the 1950s and 1960s. When the NYCO added *The Ballad of Baby Doe* to its repertory it was Sills who starred in the title role. Like Neway in *The Consul*, Sills was key in bringing American opera to life. Moreover, no matter the role she sang, Sills proved enormously popular with audiences, and her popularity directly contributed to the stature of the NYCO. When Sills starred in the NYCO's 1966 production of Handel's *Giulio Cesare in Egitto*, for example, she helped the NYCO to temporarily upstage the Met.[77] As ethnomusicologist Nancy Guy

---

73   Dizikes, *Opera in America*, 489.
74   Waleson, *Mad Scenes and Exit Arias*, 24.
75   Lindsay, "The Coming of Age of American Opera," 483.
76   Rudel and Paller, *First and Lasting Impressions*, 85.
77   In 1966, the Met and the NYCO moved from their previous locations to Lincoln Center Plaza for the Performing Arts. To mark the openings of their

points out, by 1975, the year Sills finally made her debut at the Met, the soprano "had been singing to sold-out houses regularly for nearly a decade … only a hundred feet across Lincoln Center Plaza from the Met."[78]

Despite its importance and centrality, the NYCO was not the only mover and shaker during this critical period in which the landscape for American opera began to broaden, particularly in New York City. Menotti, for example, initially planned for the NYCO to premiere *The Consul*, but according to Morton Baum, chair of the New York City Center's finance committee, when NYCO director Laszlo Halasz "sought to drive too hard a bargain with Chandler Cowles … negotiations collapsed," and Menotti turned to Broadway.[79] There, he found a ready audience, for as musicologist Larry Stempel writes, Broadway in the 1940s and 1950s featured "a brief flowering of American stageworks that challenged many of the most cherished notions associated with opera as a highbrow enterprise."[80] Stempel categorizes *Porgy and Bess* (first revived on Broadway in 1942), *Street Scene* (1947), *Lost in the Stars* (1949), *Regina* (1949), and *West Side Story* (1957) as "Broadway operas," works developed in terms of songs or separate musical numbers; he categorizes *Carmen Jones* (1943), *The Medium* (1947), *The Consul* (1950), *The Saint of Bleecker Street* (1954), *Trouble in Tahiti* (1955), and *Maria Golovin* (1958) as "operas on Broadway," works that tended toward a more through-composed music drama.[81]

Admittedly, opera's moment on Broadway was short-lived. In 1955, Carlisle Floyd looked briefly to Cowles as he shopped around for a production of *Susannah* in New York. A Floyd family friend, Cowles deemed *Susannah* too dark for Broadway in 1955. According to Floyd's biographer Thomas Holliday, Cowles described Floyd's opera as "so grim, so bleak,

---

new opera houses, both companies planned celebratory productions. In a rare move, the Met decided to commission and premiere an American opera. In another rare move, the NYCO chose to revive an opera from the Baroque era. The Met's premiere of Samuel Barber's *Antony and Cleopatra* was a disaster. Two weeks later, the NYCO's revival of *Giulio Cesare* was a smashing success. As Nancy Guy writes, "the coloratura tour de force of Cleopatra … fit [Sills's] voice perfectly" and the soprano "skyrocketed to fame." See *The Magic of Beverly Sills*, 44.

78 Ibid., 13.
79 See Morton Baum, History, Folder 6, Box 3 (History, 1949–50), pp. 230–231, Heddy Baum Papers, Music Division, New York Public Library, New York, NY. Laszlo Halasz (1905–2001) was a Hungarian-born director, conductor, and pianist. Appointed in 1943, he was the first director of the NYCO. He left the NYCO in 1951.
80 Stempel, *Showtime*, 373.
81 Ibid.

unrelieved."[82] Holliday noted that this was "a strange judgment from a backer of Menotti, whose *Consul* heroine ends by putting her head in a gas oven."[83] Thus just five years after *The Consul*'s premiere, Broadway was no longer as hospitable to opera. The following year, Douglas Moore and John Latouche also failed to secure a Broadway production of *The Ballad of Baby Doe*. Even Menotti's *The Saint of Bleecker Street* and *Maria Golovin*, while mounted on Broadway in 1954 and 1958, respectively, were far less successful than *The Medium* or *The Consul* had been. *The Saint* ran for ninety-two performances at the Broadway Theatre, while *Maria Golovin* lasted just five performances at the Martin Beck Theatre.[84] In 1974, when Neway looked back on opera's moment on Broadway, she remarked that "1950 was a very special time."[85]

Even so, opera on Broadway was not a fluke, and it ought not be read in isolation. As different as such institutions might appear, theaters on Broadway, universities, and radio and television broadcast companies were all willing to consider the possibility of presenting American operas at midcentury, and performances under one set of institutional conditions often nurtured and encouraged performances under another set. *The Medium*, for example, made its way to Broadway, paving the path for *The Consul* three years later, largely because of an opportunity Menotti found at Columbia University. The school began championing opera shortly after Douglas Moore, who had been on the music department faculty since 1926, became chair of the department in 1940. That very year, three years before the establishment of the NYCO, Moore began advocating that contemporary opera move into the university. Frustrated by the reality that the American opera house (i.e., the Met) had "dedicated" itself "to the greatness of the past," Moore suggested a new way forward in an essay in *Modern Music*.[86] "If the opera house must continue to be a museum and the movies and theatre to be timid," he wrote, "there is one more possible field for experimentation in opera, our schools, universities and conservatories."[87] Moore

---

82   Cowles, quoted in Holliday, *Falling Up*, 131.
83   Holliday, *Falling Up*, 131.
84   See *The Saint of Bleecker Street*, Internet Broadway Database; *Maria Golovin*, Internet Broadway Database.
85   Neway, interview with Gruen.
86   Moore, "Our Lyric Theatre," 3.
87   Ibid., 6. Similarly, in his 1951 appeal *Opera for the People*, stage director Herbert Graf emphasized that "the growth of a truly American opera" was being "fostered in decisive fashion by the development of music schools throughout the country." Graf wrote that by the end of World War II, "the number of music schools in the United States had risen from fewer than twenty-five to some three hundred." See *Opera for the People*, 187.

noted that opera departments at Juilliard, Curtis, and Eastman had already begun to make progress, "experiment[ing] to some extent with productions of operas by contemporary Europeans and Americans."[88] Thus, during the early 1940s, he worked to make Columbia a similarly hospitable institution.

Under Moore's guidance, Columbia's operatic ventures featured neglected operas of the past and new works. These included Giovanni Battista Pergolesi's *The Music Master* and *The Jealous Husband*, Johann Schenk's *The Village Barber*, André Grétry's *The Two Misers*, and Giovanni Paisiello's *The Barber of Seville* (all given in English).[89] In terms of new works, there were Benjamin Britten's *Paul Bunyan* (1941), Ernst Bacon's *A Tree on the Plains* (1942), Normand Lockwood's *The Scarecrow* (1945), Menotti's *The Medium* (1946), Virgil Thomson's *The Mother of Us All* (1947), Otto Luening's *Evangeline* (1948), Jan Meyerowitz's *The Barrier* (1950), and Moore's own *Giants in the Earth* (1951).[90]

In April 1945, Moore boasted about Columbia's recent operatic activities in an article in *Opera News*: "Opera at Columbia is small scale, experimental, and not a bit grand but it is opera, it is American, and it is exciting because its concern is with the future."[91] Moore highlighted the Alice M. Ditson Fund, asserting its role in furthering American opera on and beyond Columbia's campus. Established in 1940 with a bequest of $400,000 from Alice M. Ditson, widow of Boston music publisher Oliver Ditson, the Alice M. Ditson Fund supported an annual commission of "an American composer and librettist for an opera designed for production at [Columbia's] Brander Matthews Hall," Moore explained.[92] He pointed out that "American operas generally have been regarded with a fishy eye by the public and by the critics."[93] Admitting that there would be no magical or instantaneous solution to this dismal state of affairs, he argued, "we can hardly expect a full blown masterpiece to roll along until there has been a lot of trail blazing along the road."[94] Thus Moore identified his "trail blazing" mission at Columbia. *The Medium* represented one particularly successful result of Ditson funding, and regardless of whether one considers *The Consul* a

---

88   Moore, "Our Lyric Theatre," 6.
89   Programs for these productions can be found in the collection of the Columbia Theater Associates, 1893–1958, University Archives, Rare Book & Manuscript Library, Columbia University Libraries.
90   Programs for these productions can also be found in the collection of the Columbia Theater Associates, 1893–1958.
91   Moore, "Opera Productions at Columbia University," 13.
92   Ibid.
93   Ibid.
94   Ibid.

"full blown masterpiece," Menotti's experience with *The Medium*, both at Columbia and on Broadway, certainly contributed to his subsequent ability to tackle a full-length tragic opera.

In his 1945 article for *Opera News*, Moore also highlighted the importance of Columbia's Opera Workshop, organized in 1943. Led primarily by stage director Herbert Graf, music director Willard Rhodes, and conductor Otto Luening, the Opera Workshop provided a training ground of sorts for not-yet-established performers, composers, and librettists.[95] In 1951, Graf asserted that "such a workshop is really a little experimental opera theater, designed to fill the gap that exists in America between school training and engagements with major professional companies."[96] He continued: "In this respect, opera workshops are the American substitutes for the Middle European 'Stadtheaters.'"[97] Luening spoke similarly of the workshop, explaining that it was "like a provincial German repertory theater."[98] In addition to providing rigorous training, the Opera Workshop appears to have helped to impart Columbia's values. The conductor John Crosby (1926–2002), who went on to found the Santa Fe Opera in 1956, participated in the Opera Workshop in 1952 and 1953.[99] Like Columbia, the Santa Fe Opera demonstrated a commitment to rigorous training and a decided interest in new works, particularly those by composers based in the US.[100] In its first summer season (1957), the company premiered Marvin David Levy's *The Tower*. The following year, it premiered Carlisle Floyd's *Wuthering Heights*. To this day, Santa Fe maintains this commitment, alternating almost every season between premieres and revivals of American operas.[101]

---

95   Ibid., 12.
96   Graf, *Opera for the People*, 187.
97   Ibid.
98   Luening, *The Odyssey of an American Composer*, 457.
99   See Smith, *A Vision of Voices*, 32. See also Dizikes, *Opera in America*, 510–511.
100 The Santa Fe Opera currently defines its mission as follows: "to advance the operatic art form by presenting ensemble performances of the highest quality in a unique setting with a varied repertoire of new, rarely performed, and standard works; to ensure the excellence of opera's future through apprentice programs for singers, technicians and arts administrators; and to foster an understanding and appreciation of opera among a diverse public." See "Our Mission," Santa Fe Opera, https://www.santafeopera.org/company/our-mission/ (accessed August 23, 2022).
101 In 2015, for example, the company unveiled Jennifer Higdon's *Cold Mountain*. The following year, it revived Samuel Barber's *Vanessa* (1958). In 2017, it premiered Mason Bates's *The (R)evolution of Steve Jobs*, and in 2018, it revived John Adams's *Doctor Atomic* (2005).

✶ ✶ ✶

The 1950s marked an exciting decade for American opera, one in which composers, performers, and audiences believed that something new was underway. New opera companies and festivals sprang up across the country. Opera increasingly made its way outside the confines of the traditional opera house, and new repertory seemed to flourish. The four operas featured in the following chapters of this book benefitted from the broadening of the landscape for opera in the US in the 1950s. They also benefitted, to varying degrees, from dedicated sopranos. When I interviewed Carlisle Floyd in 2015, I was struck by the way he looked back on *Susannah*, repeatedly referring to the insights he had gained from sopranos who sang the title role. He spoke at length, for example, of Phyllis Curtin's perspective, and he encouraged me to speak with Sharon Daniels, who began singing the role of Susannah in the 1970s. Unlike Menotti, who balked at Neway taking ownership of *his* opera, Floyd seemed pleased that so many women had taken custody of *Susannah*.[102] According to performance statistics gathered by the service Opera America, *Susannah* is currently the most-performed American opera overall.[103] In other words, it is the centerpiece of the American-opera canon. Along with *The Tender Land*, *The Ballad of Baby Doe*, and *Lizzie Borden*, *Susannah* demonstrates that just as the feminist movement began its gradual reawakening in the US, several American sopranos found their voices on the opera stage, sometimes singing in tandem with and sometimes singing against their assigned roles.

---

102 *Susannah* was Floyd's first major success, and as of this writing, it remains his most popular opera. Still, it is worth noting that Floyd continued to work successfully as an opera composer well into the twenty-first century. In 2016, the Houston Grand Opera (founded in 1955, as new opera companies sprouted across the country) premiered his twelfth opera, *Prince of Players*, demonstrating that as the Met has continued in its role as the standard bearer of the European opera canon, generally eschewing new works as well as US composers, composers of contemporary opera have looked for performance opportunities elsewhere.

103 See "North American Works Directory."

Chapter Two

A Conniving Gold Digger: Elizabeth "Baby Doe" Tabor

In 1954, Douglas Moore (1893–1969) and John Latouche (1914–1956) began working on an opera about the infamous "gold digger" and "home-wrecker" Elizabeth "Baby Doe" Tabor (1854–1935). Two years later, the Central City Opera premiered the result, *The Ballad of Baby Doe*, a work wedded to the age-old binary of the virgin or the whore.[1] The second wife of Colorado silver king Horace Tabor (1830–1899), Baby Doe was known for her beauty and for her ability to wrest Tabor away from his first wife, the devoted and long-suffering Augusta Pierce Tabor (1833–1895). At the outset of *The Ballad of Baby Doe*, Augusta appears as the respectable woman (the virgin), and Baby Doe as the sexualized other (the whore). Yet as Moore asserted in 1958, *The Ballad of Baby Doe* is "unusual" because "the golddigger who should be the villain is not"; over the course of the opera, Baby Doe "grows from a little nitwit into a wonderful woman."[2] Baby Doe transforms, impossible as it may seem, from a whore into a virgin.

The Ballad of Baby Doe has proven Moore's most enduring work. According to Opera America, it is currently the eighth most-performed American opera.[3] *The Ballad of Baby Doe* also remains closely associated with the voice and career of Beverly Sills (1929–2007), the soprano who helped to popularize the opera and who made the title role her own. When I first began listening to *The Ballad of Baby Doe* and to Sills, I could not help but wonder from my vantage point in the twenty-first century what had

---

1   Founded in 1932, the Central City Opera in Central City, Colorado, is the fifth-oldest opera company in the US. The company's annual summer opera festival typically revolves around two operas and one musical theater piece.
2   "Composer Is an Admirer of 'Baby Doe.'" In 1961, Moore acknowledged that although Baby Doe "had been suspected of being *only* a gold-digger," she "turned out to be [Horace Tabor's] main reliance." See Moore, "Something about Librettos," 11. Italics mine.
3   "North American Works Directory."

drawn Sills to the title role. Was this soprano, who would go on to have a sensational career, as both an opera singer and administrator, all while raising a family, really so attached to such simplistic narratives of women's experiences and identities? Did Moore's music somehow make up for or gloss over the opera's narrative? To both questions, I think the answer is no. Sills was clearly drawn to Moore's music, but a close examination of her perspective on Baby Doe reveals how she sought to dismantle the dualistic paradigm embedded in *The Ballad of Baby Doe*. Sills identified with Baby Doe, and she worked, as she put it, to turn her back into "a real woman."[4]

This was no easy task. As historian Judy Nolte Temple has documented, by the 1950s, the "legend of Baby Doe" was firmly established in American history and lore.[5] Approximately one hundred years earlier, Horace Tabor had made his way out to Colorado in search of gold. Accompanied by his wife Augusta, he was unsuccessful. Then, in 1878, two of the prospectors that he had grubstaked—meaning outfitted with provisions in return for a share of future profits—discovered a silver mine. Tabor made a fortune overnight, and in the following years, he continued to add to his wealth and prestige. He financed major developments in Leadville and Denver, including two opera houses.[6] He served as Colorado's first lieutenant governor and apparently even dreamed of running for president.

In the early 1880s, Tabor met Elizabeth Doe (born Elizabeth Nellis McCourt), recently separated from her husband Harvey Doe. Elizabeth had become rather famous in Colorado's mining camps; she was known to be quite beautiful, and miners had taken to calling her by the nickname "Baby Doe." When Horace divorced Augusta in 1883 and married Baby Doe in a lavish ceremony in Washington, DC. (attended by President Chester A. Arthur), scandal ensued. As Moore pointed out, Baby Doe was never "accepted by Denver society."[7] Musicologist Howard Pollack put it more bluntly, writing that Baby Doe was regarded as "a mercenary Irish-Catholic homewrecker."[8]

When the US embraced the gold standard, causing silver to collapse in 1893, many Coloradans expected Baby Doe to run off with another man.

---

4   Sills and Linderman, *Beverly*, 123.
5   Temple, *Baby Doe Tabor*, 3.
6   He financed the Tabor Opera House in Leadville (1879) and the Tabor Grand Opera House in Denver (1881).
7   Untitled document, dated June 2, 1958, Douglas Moore Papers (Box 11, Folder "Ballad of Baby Doe (General Corr.) 3"), University Archives, Rare Book & Manuscript Library, Columbia University Libraries. An edited version of these remarks appears in Moore, "Something about Librettos," 10. See also Hardee, "The Perils of Baby Doe," 3.
8   Pollack, *The Ballad of John Latouche*, 430.

Yet she stood by Horace, who lost just about everything he had ever owned. Horace died in 1899, and still, Baby Doe appeared to remain faithful to his memory. Seemingly abandoned by her two daughters, she lived out the rest of her life alone in Leadville in a shack next to what had been Horace's most profitable mine. Coloradans came to regard her as a spectacle and a madwoman. She rarely went out in public, and when she did, her tattered half-masculine, half-feminine dress garnered attention, as did the heavy cross she wore around her neck. Some understood this cross to be a symbol of the solace she sought in her faith, others, of the penance required for her sins. In 1950, a self-proclaimed expert on Baby Doe named Caroline Bancroft described Baby Doe's 1935 death in lurid detail:

> The formerly beautiful and glamorous Baby Doe Tabor, her millions lost many years before, was found dead on her cabin floor at the Matchless Mine ... Her body, only partially clothed, was frozen with ten days' stiffness into the shape of a cross. She had lain down on her back on the floor of her stove-heated one room home, her arms outstretched, apparently in sure foreboding that she was to die.[9]

Temple recalled reading Bancroft's words years later and wondering "what great wrong Baby Doe had done that she was not only crucified but deserted in poverty and frozen as well."[10] Temple concluded that Baby Doe had committed a number of "distinctly female sins: beauty, gold digging, husband stealing, poor mothering."[11]

Along with his librettist John Latouche, Moore was certainly swayed by the tropes of Baby Doe the homewrecker and gold digger. In 1958, he recalled that when he read about Baby Doe's death in the newspaper in 1935, he immediately thought that the story had "all the elements of a moving and effective story for the lyric theater."[12] Perhaps he meant something along the lines of a tragic nineteenth-century opera like *La Traviata* or *Carmen*, for similar to both Violetta and Carmen, Baby Doe (the actual woman and the character on the opera stage) existed outside the bounds of "proper" womanhood. As a homewrecker and gold digger, she appeared to deserve punishment, or, to use Catherine Clément's terminology, "undoing." Yet at the same time, Moore grew increasingly ambivalent about such tropes. As Lewis J. Hardee Jr. explains, Moore took a particularly "active

---

9   Bancroft, *Silver Queen*, 5.
10 Temple, *Baby Doe Tabor*, ix.
11 Ibid., ix.
12 Untitled document, dated June 2, 1958, Douglas Moore Papers (Box 11, Folder "Ballad of Baby Doe (General Corr.) 3").

role in the writing of The Ballad of Baby Doe libretto."[13] Moore urged Latouche to soften Baby Doe's character, and ultimately, he and Latouche turned Baby Doe into something of a reincarnation of the Victorian "Angel in the House," that feminine ideal inspired by Coventry Patmore's 1854 narrative poem by the same title.[14] Virginia Woolf described the Angel in the House as "intensely sympathetic," "immensely charming," and "utterly unselfish," a woman who "sacrificed herself daily."[15] Most importantly, "she was pure."[16] At the end of Moore and Latouche's opera, Baby Doe undergoes a critical transformation, finally becoming a "good" and "proper" woman, wholly devoted to her husband no matter the personal cost. She becomes the angel in the shack next to the Matchless Mine.

Beverly Sills began singing the role of Baby Doe in 1958, when the NYCO presented *The Ballad of Baby Doe* as part of its first all-American season. As *New York Times* music critic Anthony Tommasini wrote after the soprano's death, "Sills was America's idea of a prima donna."[17] She "demystified opera—and the fine arts in general—in a way that a general public audience responded to."[18] Indeed, in her 2015 book *The Magic of Beverly Sills*, ethnomusicologist Nancy Guy examined the extraordinary impact of Sills's artistry, emphasizing how "Sills's fan base reached across socioeconomic borders."[19] Guy argued that "the components of Sills's performative magic all worked toward one key goal—communication," explaining how "as Sills entered deeply into the drama and took on her characters' personae completely, she communicated their thoughts and feelings through the total expression of her voice and body."[20] Sills's portrayal of Baby Doe serves as a case in point. Seeking to humanize Baby Doe's character, Sills worked to further dilute the homewrecker and gold-digger stereotypes that remained in Moore and Latouche's text. She also embraced Baby Doe in all

---

13   Hardee, "The Musical Theatre of Douglas Moore," 78. Hardee continues: "During the entire two-year period of planning and writing, he was largely in charge of the project, and it was he who kept it alive when it threatened to die."

14   *The Angel in the House* was published in four installments: first in 1854, then in 1856, 1860, and finally 1862.

15   Woolf described the Angel in the House in "Professions for Women," a 1931 speech for the Women's Service League, a version of which she published in a 1942 collection of essays. See "Professions for Women" in *The Death of the Moth and Other Essays*, 235–242.

16   Ibid., 237.

17   Tommasini, "Beverly Sills."

18   Ibid.

19   Guy, *The Magic of Beverly Sills*, 8.

20   Ibid., 149.

her potential complexities, rejecting the notion that Baby Doe could only be a homewrecker and gold digger *or* an angel by de-emphasizing the heroine's transformation over the course of the opera.

Sills invested quite personally in this project. The second wife of Peter Greenough, she knew what it was like to be painted as the "other" woman; moreover, as a Jew who married into a wealthy White Anglo-Saxon Protestant family and social circle, she knew what it was like to be scorned and punished for her status as an ethnic outsider. Sills's memoirs suggest the extent to which she identified with Baby Doe, as well as how the role of Baby Doe provided a literal and theatrical escape from all the anti-Semitism she experienced while living in Cleveland, Ohio. Through singing the role of Baby Doe, Sills gained the confidence she needed to make it through a difficult juncture in her personal and professional life. Whereas Moore and his librettists—influenced by the culture of the 1950s and by the existing literature on the Tabors—largely sought to contain and constrain Elizabeth Tabor through *The Ballad of Baby Doe*, Sills used those constraints to better understand and break free from those that she faced in her own life. In the process, she resisted the longstanding tradition of opera as a form that culminates in the "undoing of women," and she began to "redo" Baby Doe as a more fully human and sympathetic heroine. I maintain that Sills *began* to redo Baby Doe because I am not convinced that Sills or anyone else could ever be entirely successful on this front. Without a substantial revision to the opera's final scene, which presents Baby Doe's solitary retreat as a kind of sacrifice in honor of her husband, the soprano who plays Baby Doe can never "kill the angel in the house" as a fully autonomous woman writer such as Virginia Woolf could.[21] Still, Sills's experience, perspective, and performance as Baby Doe illuminate how resistance to the paradigm of the virgin or the whore, so often employed as a means to limit women's options, was possible.

The Legend of Baby Doe

Moore never specified where he read the 1935 notice of Elizabeth Tabor's death, but if he read it in the *New York Times* (as Lewis J. Hardee Jr. believes he did), he might have been struck by another story that ran on the very same page.[22] According to the newspaper, Augusta Pinza, wife of the famous bass Ezio Pinza, was suing Elisabeth Rethberg, one of the Met's principal

---

21   Woolf, "Professions for Women," 237–238. See also Showalter, "Killing the Angel in the House."
22   Hardee, "The Perils of Baby Doe," 3.

sopranos, for seeking "to break up the marital relationship existing between my husband and myself."[23] The *New York Times* invoked the charge of "homewrecking" in a blaring headline: "RETHBERG IS SUED BY WIFE OF PINZA; Prima Donna Is Accused of Wrecking Basso's Home—$250,000 Damages Asked." Did Moore read this story in 1935? Did he make note of the similarities between it and the Tabor saga? Rethberg's attorney argued that Augusta Pinza's charge was "ridiculous," asserting that the Pinzas had been estranged for years.[24] Elizabeth Tabor also claimed that Horace and Augusta Tabor's marriage had fizzled long before she moved to Colorado. I am not convinced that it really matters whether Moore took note of these uncanny similarities. What matters is that the similarities demonstrate the threat to the home and family that women like Elizabeth Tabor in the 1880s and Elisabeth Rethberg in the 1930s were thought to pose. However "ridiculous," perceptions of that threat remained alive and well in the 1950s.

As a legend that continued to live and breathe in Colorado, Baby Doe also remained alive and well in the 1950s. When Moore introduced readers of the *New York Times* to *The Ballad of Baby Doe* six days before the opera's Central City premiere, he noted that although it was often difficult to bring historical figures "to life on the stage," he faced no such problem when it came to *The Ballad of Baby Doe*.[25] People in Leadville and Denver "still remember Horace Tabor, his wife Augusta and the young woman who caused the trouble between them," he explained.[26] Moore's perspective was hardly unique. Americans had long been fascinated by Baby Doe and her relationship with Horace Tabor. During her lifetime, Baby Doe's name and reputation preceded her throughout the country, amplified through newspaper and magazine articles, books, and movies. An Associated Press report, published in the *New York Times* on August 14, 1935, demonstrates how in the months after Baby Doe's death, "travelers from all over the United States" flocked to her last place of residence, "scrawl[ing] their names on the cabin walls."[27] Baby Doe's "rude cabin" was soon nearly "demolished" by these treasure hunters and souvenir seekers so eager to capture a piece of Baby Doe for themselves.[28]

In 2007, Judy Nolte Temple published one of the most complex and nuanced assessments of Elizabeth Tabor's life and legacy to date. Temple worked to separate the "real" Elizabeth Tabor from the "cautionary gender

---

23 "RETHBERG IS SUED BY WIFE OF PINZA."
24 Ibid.
25 Moore, "True Tale of West."
26 Ibid.
27 "Treasure Hunters Wreck Cabin of 'Baby Doe' Tabor."
28 Ibid.

tale" that she regarded as the "legend" of Baby Doe: "Don't be too beautiful or other women will hate you; don't challenge social norms or you'll be shunned; don't raise a daughter too sexually independent or she'll break your heart; don't show your face when your beauty fades or you'll become a spectacle; don't age without the protection of a man."[29] Analyzing the impact of several mid-twentieth-century depictions of Elizabeth Tabor's character and relationship with Horace Tabor, Temple also drew on Elizabeth Tabor's own writings, seeking to allow her subject to "speak" for herself for the first time since her retreat from society in the early 1900s.[30] Temple's careful and recuperative work is significant because much of the previous literature on Baby Doe—including some of the literature that inspired *The Ballad of Baby Doe*—was so highly sensationalized. In 1932, for example, David Karsner published *Silver Dollar: The Story of the Tabors*, one of the sources that influenced Moore and his librettists. A writer and socialist activist, Karsner wrote numerous biographies over the course of his career, including several about socialist leaders such as Eugene V. Debs and Horace Traubel.[31] Before turning to the Tabors, he also wrote a biography of Andrew Jackson. Karsner tended to write his biographies with an imaginative touch; rather than always presenting carefully researched and impartial accounts of his subjects' lives, he often put his own words directly into his subjects' mouths.[32]

Karsner's story of the Tabors demonstrates this very tendency. Divided into three parts, *Silver Dollar* reads like something of an adventure novel. Part I, entitled "Gold," focuses on Horace and Augusta Tabor's fortitude as they made their way from Vermont to Colorado. By the end of Part I, Horace had made his fortune. In Part II, "Silver," Karsner introduces Elizabeth McCourt, the woman who would become Baby Doe. Born in Oshkosh, Wisconsin, McCourt had married the relatively wealthy Harvey

---

29 Temple, *Baby Doe Tabor*, xvi.
30 Ibid., ix–x.
31 David Karsner (1889–1941) began his career in Chicago, where he became interested in socialism through his association with Upton Sinclair. He eventually moved to New York City, where from 1908 to 1923 he worked as managing editor of *The New York Call*, a daily socialist newspaper. After the *Call* folded, Karsner worked as a copyreader for the *New York Post*.
32 As Hermione Lee explains, while a "biographer has a responsibility to the truth," there are many ways of getting around the truth. She points out that "plenty of biographers dramatize their narratives with descriptions of emotions, highly coloured scene-setting, or strategies of suspense. Some go further, and deploy full-scale fictional methods: invented meetings between author and subject, imaginary episodes, musings of the identity of the biographer, hypothetical conversations." In short, "some biographies read more like fiction than history." See *Biography*, 6–7.

Doe, and like Horace and Augusta Tabor, Harvey and Elizabeth Doe traveled to Colorado to seek their mining fortune. Karsner devoted considerable ink to Elizabeth Doe's beauty, writing that she "was so seductive that she could have revived the imagination of a dying hermit."[33] He explained how miners began to refer to her by the name Baby Doe because her "face was as fair as a baby's, and her figure—they were sure of it."[34] According to Karsner, Elizabeth embraced the name because "it testified to her beauty and her popularity."[35] "Dross," Part 3 of *Silver Dollar*, takes up after Tabor's downfall and centers on the sad fate of his youngest daughter, Rose Mary Echo Silver Dollar (known simply as Silver). According to Karsner, Silver grew up without a moral compass, becoming a drug addict and alcoholic:

> Haw Tabor's daughter thought nothing of sitting up half the night and emptying a bottle of whisky with her lover ... When drunk, she delighted in receiving callers in the nude ... Perhaps she had plucked that twig of exhibitionism from her ancestral tree. Maybe it was a flareback to Haw and Baby Doe themselves, parading before Presidents and displaying their millions in theaters, mansions, public offices, silks, broadcloth, jewels, and plug hats. Silver had never had the benefit of any of these things, but she was cursed with a princess complex from birth.[36]

In 1925, Silver was found in a dingy Chicago apartment, her body apparently scalded to death. An aunt identified her at the morgue; Baby Doe, however, refused to acknowledge that the body was that of her daughter.[37]

Most crucial to Karsner's portrayal of Baby Doe was his suggestion that Baby Doe intentionally set out to trap Horace Tabor, his fame, and his fortune. Karsner wrote that after moving to Central City with Harvey, Baby Doe began fantasizing about Horace some eighty miles away in Leadville.[38] Baby Doe eventually traveled to Leadville on her own, and according to Karsner, "she registered at the Clarendon [Hotel] ... because she had been told by the stagecoach driver that Tabor lived there, and she did not want to miss seeing him."[39] When he appeared, Baby Doe supposedly "caught her breath" for "she saw a man who was really handsome, with a spring in his step, and youth in his eyes, despite his fifty years ... She scrutinized him and decided that she liked Haw Tabor. She had no doubts as to his

---

33 Karsner, *Silver Dollar*, 139.
34 Ibid., 146.
35 Ibid..
36 Ibid., 332.
37 Temple, *Baby Doe Tabor*, 35.
38 Karsner, *Silver Dollar*, 148.
39 Ibid., 149.

greatness."⁴⁰ Baby Doe wondered briefly about Mrs. Tabor "What did she look like? 'She isn't pretty like me, nor as young, nor as fair,' Baby Doe's mind whispered."⁴¹ Karsner reported that after a performance at the opera house, Baby Doe followed Tabor to a restaurant and sat at a table near him: "Was it a design, or merely curiosity? Who knows?"⁴² Thus Karsner more than planted the suggestion that Baby Doe was a conniving gold digger. In fact, when discussing Baby Doe's initial attraction to Harvey Doe, Karsner took pains to emphasize all that Baby Doe stood to gain through marriage to a wealthier man, thereby establishing something of a pattern for gold digging.⁴³

Karsner may have been motivated by political disdain for Horace and Elizabeth Tabor, as well as for the capitalist enterprise more broadly, yet the sexist threads that characterize his treatment of Baby Doe are more pronounced than any potential political critique. It is worth noting, moreover, that as he researched his subject, Karsner drew on a variety of sources, yet he never made any effort to interview Elizabeth Tabor herself.⁴⁴ This practice was not in keeping with Karsner's usual approach to biography. He had, for example, interviewed Eugene V. Debs and Horace Traubel when he wrote about them. But at the end of *Silver Dollar*, Karsner dismissed Elizabeth Tabor as an unreliable and insane interlocutor, explaining that to interview her "would have been folly."⁴⁵ By relying on the partial perspectives of those who knew (and often despised) Baby Doe, Karsner ultimately portrayed Baby Doe, according to Temple, as something of "a sexual predator."⁴⁶

In 1938, six years after the publication of Karsner's book and three years after Elizabeth Tabor's death, Caroline Bancroft published a new account of Baby Doe's scandalous life. "Silver Queen: Baby Doe Tabor's Life Story as Told to Sue Bonnie" appeared in the serial *True Story*, and according to Temple, it "became the mother lode of the evolving legend."⁴⁷ Temple argues that it was through "Silver Queen" that the "mythic elements" of

---

40   Ibid.
41   Ibid., 150.
42   Ibid.
43   Ibid., 140–142.
44   As Temple explains, "Karsner drew on newspaper articles, general histories of the mining West, and on his relationships with journalists, an academic, a curator at the Colorado Historical Society, and the heirs of Tabor's first wife, Augusta." See *Baby Doe Tabor*, 4.
45   Karsner, *Silver Dollar*, 347.
46   Temple, *Baby Doe Tabor*, 90.
47   Ibid., 49.

Baby Doe's life story coalesced around "the eternal issues" of "seduction, adultery, riches, ruin, and redemption."[48] Like *Silver Dollar*, "Silver Queen" was factually weak. It too was written in a rather imaginative fashion, and, in a new twist, from the first-person perspective, masquerading as a transcription of Baby Doe's own words, as told to a woman named Sue Bonnie. When Bancroft republished "Silver Queen" as a book in 1950, now under the title *Silver Queen: The Fabulous Story of Baby Doe Tabor*, she admitted that she had purchased Sue Bonnie's name "to meet the editorial requirements of *True Story*."[49] "Of course," she continued, "the serial was actually written by me."[50] Bancroft also acknowledged that she, similar to Karsner before her, had imagined at least some of Baby Doe's words.[51] Like *Silver Dollar*, *Silver Queen* was immediately popular. Bancroft was a persuasive writer, and as Temple explains, her "highly illustrated eighty-page 'autobiography' in the voice of Baby Doe went through many editions, each endorsed in the fore matter by subsequent governors of Colorado."[52] To this day, *Silver Queen* remains in print.

From the very beginning of her account of Baby Doe's life, Bancroft established Baby Doe, by dint of her beauty and Irish-Catholic heritage, as an outsider.[53] She noted that trouble arose in Oshkosh when Elizabeth McCourt began seeing Harvey Doe, a Protestant *and* the most eligible young man in town. According to Bancroft/Elizabeth, "The Does were the sort of Protestants who thought of Catholics almost as heathen idol-worshipers. Harvey never said anything to me about their attitude, but I had heard from the neighbors that his mother wasn't a bit pleased with his seeing so much of a 'Romanist and Papist.'"[54] Things worsened as Harvey and Elizabeth's relationship became more serious. Bancroft wrote that Elizabeth recalled how "more and more I knew girls were saying catty things behind my back, insinuating I was fast."[55] Bancroft/Elizabeth attributed these words to jealousy colored by xenophobia, commenting on "the

---

48 Ibid., 51.
49 Bancroft, *Silver Queen*, 8.
50 Ibid.
51 At the end of her introduction, Bancroft proclaimed: "So let us have Baby Doe Tabor tell us of her life in nearly her own words—many she actually used in talking to Sue Bonnie and others I have imagined as consonant with her character and the facts of her story." See *Silver Queen*, 9.
52 Temple, *Baby Doe Tabor*, 52.
53 Bancroft, *Silver Queen*, 10.
54 Ibid., 18–19.
55 Ibid., 21.

snobbish girls who said I was just the common daughter of an Irish tailor."[56] After Harvey and Elizabeth were married, much to the chagrin of Harvey's mother, the young Does left for Central City, where Harvey was to inherit some of his father's mining property.

In Central City, however, Elizabeth (now Baby Doe) discovered "what Harvey was really like."[57] According to Bancroft/Baby Doe, she found that "his shyness was just weakness" and that "he was lazy and procrastinating."[58] When Harvey learned that the property he had inherited from his father likely did not contain high-grade ore, he gave up on the dream of mining his own land. Baby Doe was devastated, particularly when she learned that Harvey was considering going to work in one of the big mines. She was horrified at the idea of being "the wife of a common miner—working for a few dollars a day."[59] The young couple began to quarrel and fight on a regular basis. At one point, Bancroft/Baby Doe recalled that Harvey referred to her as a "common Irish hussy!"[60] Bancroft/Baby Doe admitted that although her church "did not sanction divorce," she longed to be free of Harvey.[61]

In Bancroft's account, it was Baby Doe who hatched the plan to extricate Horace Tabor from Augusta. After she divorced Harvey, Baby Doe moved to Leadville, where she became Horace's mistress. Bancroft/Baby Doe maintained that Augusta knew all about Baby Doe's relationship with her husband but refused to grant Horace a divorce because "she considered divorce a lasting disgrace and stigma."[62] According to Bancroft, Baby Doe suggested the following plan to Horace: "With all your influence, couldn't you get a divorce in some other county than Arapahoe where you also own property? Maybe it wouldn't be entirely valid. But we could act like it was, and get married. If Augusta knew she was married to a bigamist, maybe she would consider that a worse disgrace than being a divorcee!"[63] It would seem that Baby Doe got what she wanted, and she and Horace traveled to Washington, DC, for an elaborate wedding ceremony, where Horace paid off the priest who officiated.[64] Baby Doe's joy, however, was short-lived. Back in Denver, she was immediately ostracized. Bancroft/Baby Doe recalled that she was "disturbed and vexed" for years; she "made no real friends" and

---

56   Ibid.
57   Ibid., 29.
58   Ibid.
59   Ibid., 32.
60   Ibid., 37.
61   Ibid., 47.
62   Ibid., 80.
63   Ibid., 83.
64   Ibid., 89–90.

"received no invitations" as the "society women of Denver remained steadfastly aloof."[65]

After Horace Tabor's demise and death, Bancroft asserted that Baby Doe retreated not only to the Matchless Mine in Leadville but to her Catholic faith. Bancroft writes that Baby Doe prayed repeatedly for God to help her "save the Matchless."[66] She also sought to pay for the sins of her youth: "In some ways, my plain bedraggled habit, my make-shift rosary, my legs strapped in gunny sack and twine and my grey shawl over the black dress seemed only a just penance for the clothing extravagances and sins of my youth ... Those rags were a chosen punishment for former vanity."[67] In a 1962 postscript, first published in the seventh edition of *Silver Queen*, Bancroft argued that "in the other histories Baby Doe had been given the brush-off; as a floosy, when young, and a freak, when old."[68] She suggested that her account of Baby Doe's life was more nuanced, yet Bancroft's Baby Doe is essentially still a floosy who becomes a freak, wedded to the trappings of the Catholic faith. She is hardly more sympathetic than Karsner's Baby Doe, and the outlines of her character—the beautiful, brash, dangerous, and daring young woman who must be punished in and through old age—remain highly stereotypical.

Transferring the Legend of Baby Doe to the Opera Stage

In the early 1950s, not long after Baby Doe completed the transformation from woman to legend, Frank Ricketson Jr., president of the Central City Opera House Association, began thinking about commissioning an American opera.[69] On January 11, 1954, Ricketson and the other Association board members formally agreed that Douglas Moore and Paul Green, both Pulitzer Prize winners, should each receive $5,000 for an opera about the Tabors of approximately two hours in length to be premiered in the summer of 1955.[70] It took a little longer for what would become *The Ballad of Baby Doe* to make it to the stage in Central City, and the history of

---

65 Ibid., 96.
66 Ibid., 118.
67 Ibid.
68 Bancroft, "Postscript to Seventh Edition," ibid., 127.
69 Smith with Moriarty, *The Ballad of Baby Doe*, 2.
70 Ibid., 2–3. According to Hardee, before teaming up with Green, Moore attempted to collaborate with "his friend Pearson Underwood." Hardee explained that "Underwood had poetic talents but lacked a strong dramatic sense" and "the project went nowhere." See "The Perils of Baby Doe," 4.

the opera's commission, composition, performance, and revision reveals the highly contested nature of the legend of Baby Doe.

Moore and Green were brought together by their mutual friend Donald Oenslager, and on paper, the composer and librettist may have appeared a perfect match. Moore had long been interested in the story of Elizabeth Tabor, and he had an established reputation within the world of American opera.[71] Chair of the department of music at Columbia University, Moore had worked diligently to promote opera at Columbia.[72] He had also succeeded as an opera composer himself, having written two operas based on American subject matter: a "folk opera" entitled *The Devil and Daniel Webster* (1938) and the Pulitzer Prize–winning *Giants in the Earth* (1951), a story about Norwegian American settlers in the Dakota Territory. Similarly, because of his reputation as a playwright and his interest in the Tabor material, Paul Green (1894–1981) must have seemed an ideal choice for librettist. Green received the Pulitzer Prize for Drama for his 1927 play, *In Abraham's Bosom*, and in 1932, he worked as a story writer for a film about the Tabors.[73] That film, entitled *Silver Dollar*, was based on Karsner's book, and as he began his work on the libretto for Moore, Green would continue to be influenced by Karsner's approach to Baby Doe.[74]

Yet despite how well matched Moore and Green may have initially appeared, by March 1954, their collaboration had stalled.[75] When Lewis J. Hardee Jr. interviewed Green in 1967, the playwright explained that he was "more interested in a drama, Moore in an opera." [76] He also complained about Moore's "modern" musical style.[77] For his part, Moore told Hardee that although he "admired Paul Green very much in [his libretto for Kurt Weill's] *Johnny Johnson*," when Green sent Moore an outline for the first scene of their opera about the Tabors, Moore thought it "was just *awful*."[78] According to Jerry L. McBride, because "Green wanted to write a play with

---

71 For a biographical portrait of Moore, see "Chronological Biography" in McBride, *Douglas Moore*, 1–81.
72 For a discussion of Moore's efforts to promote opera at Columbia, see Chapter 1.
73 Pollack, *The Ballad of John Latouche*, 428.
74 Green also had some experience working with composers; in 1936, he collaborated with Kurt Weill, writing the book and lyrics for the musical *Johnny Johnson*.
75 Hardee, "The Perils of Baby Doe," 4.
76 Green, quoted in ibid.
77 Green, quoted in ibid.
78 Moore, quoted in ibid., 4–5. Moore continued: "And I showed it to John Latouche who had been wanting to do something with me, and he said, 'This sounds as if it were translated from a foreign language.'"

accompanying music rather than an opera," the text "was impossible for Moore to set musically."[79] Moore admitted to Hardee that he quickly "torpedoed the project."[80] As historian Duane A. Smith writes, Frank Ricketson Jr. responded by "hurr[ying] off to New York in late March [of 1954]" to meet with Moore and his lawyer, who suggested that the Central City Opera pay Green off with a few hundred dollars.[81] According to Smith, Moore planned to "arrange for another librettist with an advance of $1,000."[82] Matters became more complicated, however, when Green told Ricketson that he wanted to continue work on the commission, perhaps with a composer other than Moore.[83] At this point, fearing legal difficulties, Ricketson and the Central City Opera House Association backed out. Ricketson wrote to Moore on April 6, 1954, explaining that Green would not be bought off with a few hundred dollars and expressing his displeasure with both Moore's and Green's behavior: "I know that you are all fine gentlemen, but I do feel that the one that has really been damaged in this entire matter is the Central City Opera House Association, by the unfortunate publicity that has been given to a project that will never materialize."[84] Ricketson concluded: "I also am personally depressed by the entire experience because I didn't have the foresight to perceive that there might be such a misunderstanding. Be assured though that I do not want any part of this story or this production."[85] Just three months after the Central City Opera House Association had formalized their plan to commission an opera about Horace and Elizabeth Tabor, the project appeared dead in the water.

To a certain extent, Ricketson was justified in his frustration with Moore and Green. Why had the composer and librettist agreed to work together without first learning about the other's approach to the project? Yet there was at least one other key player in the story of the opera's commission, and she may have been partially responsible for the way things unraveled between Moore and Green. When the Central City Opera House Association commissioned the opera about the Tabors, it named Caroline Bancroft as historical advisor to Moore and Green.[86] By the 1950s, Bancroft was *the* keeper of

---

79 McBride, *Douglas Moore*, 43.
80 Moore, quoted in Hardee, "The Perils of Baby Doe," 5.
81 Smith with Moriarty, *The Ballad of Baby Doe*, 5.
82 Ibid., 5.
83 Pollack, *The Ballad of John Latouche*, 432; Smith with Moriarty, *The Ballad of Baby Doe*, 5.
84 Letter, F. R. Ricketson to Douglas Moore, April 6, 1954, Douglas Moore Papers (Box 77, Folder 3).
85 Ibid.
86 Smith with Moriarty, *The Ballad of Baby Doe*, 3.

Baby Doe, and as McBride explains, she became "a curious and querulous character in the story of the creation of the opera."[87] She falsely claimed, for example, to have copyrighted the name "Baby Doe."[88] On January 21, 1954, Moore's lawyer Lewis M. Isaacs Jr. wrote to Ricketson, expressing concern "as to whether Messrs. Moore and Green will be willing to accept the proposition that [Bancroft] act as historical advisor to them."[89] Isaacs explained that "the author and composer might resent interference by a third person who had legal rights, although I suppose they would welcome any suggestions."[90]

Isaacs was right to predict difficulties for as it turned out, Bancroft wanted to serve as more than historical advisor, and Green was not welcome to the idea. In February, Ricketson received a barrage of complaints. Bancroft wrote to him on February 17, explaining that she sought "to be a collaborator in the project, lesser in degree to Green and Moore, but nonetheless making a creative contribution to the project and entitled to a share in billing and royalties."[91] On February 18, Green wrote to Ricketson, stating that he was "very much disturbed" by a letter Bancroft had sent to Oenslager that suggested Bancroft "seem[ed] to expect something out of me as author."[92] Green explained that he did "not intend to encroach upon any of her work" and that "if Miss Bancroft wants me to give her a percentage of my earnings on my own original libretto I must reply that I cannot do that."[93] Green also claimed he wanted to be able to take creative liberties in his telling of the Tabor story; he did not want to be tied down by Bancroft's facts. Green concluded his February 18 letter by pointing to the ramifications of a legal battle with Bancroft. Before signing off, he begged Ricketson: "Can't your association please work out a legal agreement with Miss Bancroft so that Moore and I can proceed unhampered and secure? I am anxious to hurry

---

87   McBride, *Douglas Moore*, 43.
88   Temple, *Baby Doe Tabor*, 61. See also letters, Caroline Bancroft to Douglas Moore and John Latouche, c/o Central City Opera House Assoc., January 18, 1956; Davis W. Moore to Douglas Moore, February 14, 1956, Douglas Moore Papers (Box 11, Folder "Ballad of Baby Doe (Central City Opera House Association)").
89   Copy of letter, Lewis M. Isaacs Jr. to F. H. Ricketson Jr., January 21, 1954, Douglas Moore Papers (Box 65, Folder 1).
90   Ibid.
91   Copy of letter, Caroline Bancroft to F. H. Ricketson Jr., February 17, 1954, Douglas Moore Papers (Box 65, Folder 1).
92   Letter, Paul Green to F. H. Ricketson Jr., February 18, 1954, Douglas Moore Papers (Box 65, Folder 1).
93   Ibid.

right along with the job and do something you all will be proud of. As you know, my time is short, and Moore is besieging me, bless his heart."[94]

On March 1, Green wrote to Moore, "enclosing the prologue for our opera" and noting his plan to telephone Ricketson and report back on Central City's progress with Bancroft.[95] "We just mustn't have any lawsuit on our hands," he concluded.[96] Seven days later, Green wrote to Moore again, explaining that he was still waiting to hear from Ricketson. Green also noted that the difficulties with Bancroft had sent his "inspiration down below freezing," for by this point, Green was concerned that he might in fact be infringing on Bancroft's intellectual property.[97] He explained to Moore:

> As an instance of what thin ice we are walking on—I have in the first scene when Baby Doe tells her story her statement that her husband deserted her. Now in the Denver Post historical account it looks as if Baby Doe deserted him. So I realize that I have absorbed the Bancroft account without being conscious of it. This is the sort of thing she would wreck me on.[98]

Bancroft's perspective on Baby Doe was so ubiquitous that it was almost impossible to escape, and by March, Green realized that he might be in trouble. Hampered by his struggle with Bancroft, Green may simply not have been able to produce writing of his usual quality. This may have been a contributing factor to the project's unraveling, when on March 21 Green sent Moore "the first forty some pages of the script," and Moore found the material unusable.[99]

After things fell apart with Ricketson and the Central City Opera, Moore and Green gave each other permission to use the scenario they had devised together as they each saw fit.[100] Without any performance prospects in sight, Moore formally reached out to Latouche.[101] Like Moore (and like Green), Latouche had been interested in the story of the Horace and Elizabeth Tabor

---

94 Ibid.
95 Letter, Paul Green to Douglas Moore, March 1, 1954, Douglas Moore Papers (Box 65, Folder 1).
96 Ibid.
97 Letter, Paul Green to Douglas Moore, March 8, 1954, Douglas Moore Papers (Box 65, Folder 1).
98 Ibid.
99 Letter, Paul Green to Douglas Moore, March 21, 1954, Douglas Moore Papers (Box 65, Folder 1).
100 Pollack, *The Ballad of John Latouche*, 432.
101 Latouche had ample experience in musical theater. Best known for his work on musicals such as Vernon Duke and Lynn Root's *Cabin in the Sky* (1940) and Jerome Moross's *The Golden Apple* (1954), he also contributed lyrics to Leonard Bernstein's *Candide* (1955).

for some time. As Latouche recalled in *Theatre Arts Magazine* in 1956, he had previously considered collaborating with Jerome Kern on a musical about the Tabors, but Kern died before the project could materialize.[102]

When Latouche agreed to come on as Moore's librettist, Moore succeeded in convincing the Serge Koussevitzky Music Foundation to sponsor the work's composition.[103] Moore also succeeded in mending fences with Ricketson and the Central City Opera, who agreed to mount the premiere of *The Ballad of Baby Doe* in the summer of 1956. Latouche began with the scenario that Moore and Green had completed together, and thus like Green—and despite Bancroft's claims—Latouche relied heavily on the story of the Tabors as passed down in the press and by Karsner. In 1961, Moore noted that he and Latouche could easily have written three operas about Baby Doe: "one on the early years, one (the one we wrote) about the romance of Baby and Tabor and one about the tragic end of their daughter, Silver Dollar."[104] This three-part understanding of Baby Doe's saga maps fairly well onto the three parts of Karsner's *Silver Dollar*, a copy of which exists in Moore's personal papers at Columbia University.[105] Moore and Latouche relied mostly on Part II of Karsner's book, completely ignoring Part I and offering only a glimpse of Part III.

Latouche consciously worked to steer clear of Bancroft's work. On April 10, 1955, in a letter she sent to Moore and Latouche, Bancroft had fired something of a warning shot, accusing Green of plagiarism.[106] On April 20,

---

102 Latouche, "About the Ballad of Baby Doe," 83.
103 In the summer of 1953, Moore learned that the Koussevitzky Foundation had awarded him a $1,500 commission for an orchestral work in honor of the bicentennial of Columbia University. Moore petitioned the foundation in the spring of 1954, asking for permission to write an opera rather than an orchestral work. The foundation agreed, and shortly thereafter, Moore and Latouche got to work and Moore reached out to Ricketson again, asking if the Central City Opera might be interested in mounting the premiere. See letter, Harold Spivacke, Chief, Music Division, Library of Congress, to Douglas Moore, August 19, 1953, Douglas Moore Papers (Box 11, Folder "Ballad of Baby Doe (M. S. & I. S. Isaacs, Lucy Kroll, Michael Myerberg et. al.) 3").
104 Moore, "Something about Librettos," 11.
105 See Douglas Moore Papers (Box 100).
106 Letter, Caroline Bancroft to Douglas Moore and John La Touche, April 10, 1955, Douglas Moore Papers (Box 11, Folder "Ballad of Baby Doe (General Corr.) 1"). Bancroft claimed that when she met Green for lunch in Central City in the summer of 1953, he "had the effrontery to tell me, the Tabor authority of the world, what was significant in the Tabor legend." She continued: "In telling me, he quoted my writings verbatim, much better than I could myself, and said these were significant, and also in the public domain." Green did indeed travel to Colorado in August 1953. He sent Moore a packet of

Moore's lawyer urged Moore not to respond to Bancroft's letter, explaining that Moore and Latouche would be "better off" not engaging Bancroft; Moore's lawyer also cautioned Latouche to scour the newspapers as he worked on the libretto and to be careful to avoid "Miss Bancroft's bright imaginings."[107] Still, Bancroft later asserted with pride that Latouche had drawn directly from *Silver Queen*.[108] She stated that Latouche admitted as much in *Theatre Arts Magazine* and that "his lyric telling of the story follows fairly closely the same line" as her own.[109] In fact, what Latouche admitted was that he had read an amusing anecdote in *Silver Queen*. He pointedly lamented, however, that he had read "Miss Bancroft's work too late to include this episode in my script."[110]

The Ballad of Baby Doe begins in Leadville in 1880. The opera traces Horace and Baby Doe's encounter, their illicit affair, Horace's messy divorce from Augusta, his lavish marriage to Baby Doe, and his financial demise. The opera's final scene begins in 1899, the year of Horace's death. Horace visits the Tabor Grand Theater, marveling at the wealth he once had. He falls ill and suffers hallucinations. First, he sees Augusta, who warns him that his eldest daughter "will run away, will change her name so none will call her Tabor."[111] Then he sees his youngest daughter, Silver. She appears half naked, dancing and singing drunkenly with two men.[112] Just before Horace dies, Baby Doe rushes to his side to comfort him. The opera concludes with Baby Doe alone on stage. Gradually, the lighting reveals her to be in the

---

his research findings, dated August 29, 1953. All of the materials included in this packet appear to have come from newspaper clippings. See "Baby Doe—Horace Tabor Material," Douglas Moore Papers (Box 65, Folder 1).

107 Letter, Lewis M. Isaacs Jr. to Douglas Moore, April 20, 1955, Douglas Moore Papers (Box 11, Folder "Ballad of Baby Doe (General Corr.) 1"). On this point, as Hardee reports, the headline that appeared in the *New York Times* on March 8, 1935, announcing the discovery of Baby Doe's body, inspired the opera's final scene. The headline read: "WIDOW OF TABOR FREEZES IN SHACK; Famed Belle Dies at 73 Alone and Penniless, Guarding Old Leadville Bonanza Mine. FORTUNES THROWN AWAY Fought to Last for Husband's Dying Belief That Matchless Would Come Back." See "The Perils of Baby Doe," 3.

108 Bancroft, "Postscript to Seventh Edition" in *Silver Queen*, 127.

109 Ibid.

110 Latouche, "About the Ballad of Baby Doe," 82.

111 See Moore and Latouche, *The Ballad of Baby Doe*, 239.

112 Moore and Latouche hint only briefly at the struggle with drugs and alcohol that led to Silver's premature death, but because members of the press had so greatly sensationalized the story of her death in 1925, any hint at Silver's debauchery was likely to be plenty potent.

shaft of the Matchless Mine. She pushes back her hood; her hair, now stark white, shows the passage of time.[113] She sings:

> Death cannot divide my love
> All we sealed with living vows
> Warm I'll sleep beside my love
> In a cold and narrow house.[114]

Finally, she concludes:

> Still the old song will be sung.
> I shall change along with him,
> So that both are ever young,
> Ever young.[115]

Thus Baby Doe gives herself over to Horace's memory, promising to remain in the shack by the Matchless Mine, per his supposed last request, for the rest of her life.[116] With her white hair, Baby Doe gives the audience a brief but crucial glimpse of her future—her beauty gone, snow falling around her, as though burying her, the angel in the shack, in her final resting place.

The Ballad of Baby Doe: The Premiere and the Revisions

In February 1956, Robert J. Brown, general manager of the Central City Opera House Association, was upbeat about audience interest in the coming season. Along with *The Ballad of Baby Doe*, Central City was featuring *Tosca*, and Brown pointed out excitedly that although it was "too early to sense a trend," *The Ballad of Baby Doe* was "outselling *Tosca* by a wide margin."[117] In the end, *The Ballad of Baby Doe* proved a smashing success. Central City initially scheduled sixteen performances, but due to audience demand,

---

113 According to the stage directions, "[Baby Doe] puts back her hood revealing her hair which is white." See Moore and Latouche, *The Ballad of Baby Doe*, 248.
114 Ibid., 248–249.
115 Ibid., 250.
116 According to Karsner, on his deathbed, Tabor told Baby Doe: "Whatever happens, hold on to the Matchless. It will give you back all that I have lost." See *Silver Dollar*, 283. Throughout *Silver Queen*, Bancroft repeats this rumor as well. See *Silver Queen*, 105, 124.
117 Letter, Robert J. Brown to Douglas Moore, February 23, 1956, Douglas Moore Papers (Box 11, Folder "Ballad of Baby Doe (Central City Opera House Association)").

it added three more.[118] Emerson Buckley, who had been one of Moore's students at Columbia, conducted the performances. Donald Oenslager designed the production, and Hanya Holm and Ed Levy served as co-directors. Singers from the Met starred in the lead roles; soprano Dolores Wilson played Baby Doe, baritone Walter Cassel played Horace Tabor, and mezzo-soprano Martha Lipton played Augusta Tabor.

Music critics from across the country were invited to Central City for the premiere, and in general, they congratulated the composer and librettist, as well as the performers. Writing in the *New York Times*, Howard Taubman described Moore's score as "filled with an old-fashioned sentiment redolent of the era of crinolines, bustles, antimacassars, and the innocent Western urge for respectability and 'culture.'"[119] Similarly, a writer for *Time* characterized Moore's score as "clean" and "melodious ... conveying strong period flavor without being condescendingly folksy."[120] Critics remarked fondly, albeit vaguely, on Wilson's Baby Doe. John Chapman wrote in the *New York Daily News* that "none could be more beautiful than Miss Wilson," who "sang most sweetly of love."[121] *Denver Post* critic Allen Young described Wilson as "radiantly beautiful ... match[ing] her looks with singing that is memorable."[122] Looking back on *The Ballad of Baby Doe* in 1993, however, Young remembered Wilson somewhat differently, writing that while she "sang the arias beautifully," she "lacked the ability to quicken hearts through her acting ability" and "walked through some scenes like an automaton."[123] It is possible that Wilson's portrayal left something to be desired in 1956, for several critics at the premiere focused much more on Lipton's portrayal of Augusta. According to Taubman, Lipton "dominated the opening-night cast" with her "steely, intense and finally tragic" characterization of Augusta.[124] He argued that Lipton's "acting and singing were indivisible in a brilliant achievement that had the impact of living rather than

---

118 Pollack, *The Ballad of John Latouche*, 452. According to Duane A. Smith, the treasurer of the Central City Opera House Association had worried about the cost of producing a new opera. Davis Moore's 1956 treasurer's report demonstrated the financial side of *Baby Doe*'s triumph, as Davis Moore explained that to his knowledge, *The Ballad of Baby Doe* "was the only major original Opera ever undertaken on a professional level to which every ticket to every performance was sold before the curtain rose." See Smith with Moriarty, *The Ballad of Baby Doe*, 20.
119 Taubman, "Opera: Rooted in West."
120 "Baby Doe," *Time*, 42.
121 Chapman, "'Baby Doe,' a Superb Opera."
122 Young, "Central City Triumph."
123 Young, *Opera in Central City*, 40.
124 Taubman, "Opera: Rooted in West."

performance."[125] Somewhat similarly, Chapman raved that while the entire cast was "splendid," it was Lipton who "took the honors, vocally and dramatically, for a matchless impersonation of a proud, embittered wife who has been put aside for a younger and much more beautiful one."[126] Both the *New York Times* and *New York Post* chose to run photos of Lipton, rather than Wilson, alongside Taubman's and Chapman's reviews. This is interesting, particularly because prior to the Central City premiere, photos of Wilson had been the subject of some controversy. On June 1, 1956, approximately one month before Wilson stepped out on stage as Baby Doe, Ricketson wrote to Moore to complain about her weight: "I think, Douglas, that you should mention to this young lady that she should go on a diet before coming to Colorado. Baby Doe was a petite, doll-like beauty ... Miss Wilson is too plump to have the appeal that made Baby Doe a glamorous figure, particularly on our intimate stage."[127] Ricketson became aware of Wilson's size when *The Denver Post*, which had committed itself to a full-color cover of Wilson for its Sunday supplement magazine, decided that all the photographs it had received of Wilson were unusable. According to Ricketson, *The Denver Post* "was shocked at the proportions" of the soprano, lamenting that "a substitute cover" would need to be developed.[128]

Rather predictably, Wilson was not the only woman who struggled to live up to the legendary appeal of Baby Doe. For a while during the 1950s, it looked as though no contemporary soprano would quite be able to embody Baby Doe's "glamorous figure," as Ricketson put it, and meet the opera's vocal demands.[129] Moore noted that he had written the role of Baby Doe such that it needed "a top-flight lyric soprano who can do coloratura."[130] He was initially interested in Mimi Benzell, explaining to Ricketson that she was

---

125 Ibid.
126 Chapman, "'Baby Doe,' a Superb Opera."
127 Letter, F. H. Ricketson Jr. to Douglas Moore, June 1, 1956, Douglas Moore Papers (Box 11, Folder "Ballad of Baby Doe (Central City Opera House Association)).
128 Ibid.
129 On November 23, 1955, Ricketson wrote to Moore, announcing that "as a publicity and promotional effort, the Association would like to ask the one hundred most important music critics and opera sponsors in the United States to suggest a beautiful, young, coloratura soprano for the role of Baby Doe." See letter, F. H. Ricketson Jr. to Douglas Moore, November 23, 1955, Douglas Moore Papers (Box 11, Folder "Ballad of Baby Doe (Central City Opera House Association)").
130 Letter, Douglas Moore to F. W. Ricketson Jr., November 17, 1955, Douglas Moore Papers (Box 11, Folder "Ballad of Baby Doe (General Corr.) 1").

"a good actress" and "pretty, gay and sexy, which is highly important."[131] Benzell was a no-go for Ricketson, and Moore convinced himself that Wilson "would probably sing [the role] better."[132] In 1976, Beverly Sills recalled that as the NYCO prepared for its 1958 spring season, rumors flew that Moore, Julius Rudel, and Emerson Buckley "had auditioned scores of women singers for the role of Baby Doe but none had met with the approval of all three men."[133] Sills also noted that she almost refused to audition for the role because she knew that both Moore and Buckley had "this preconceived notion that [she was] too tall."[134] When Sills ultimately agreed to audition, she did so defiantly. As she remembered:

> I wore the highest-heeled pair of new shoes I could find at Bergdorf's and a white mink hat of my mother's—I must have looked nine foot three. "Mr. Moore," I said to the composer, "this is how tall I am before I begin to sing for you and I'm going to be just as tall when I'm finished. We could save your time and my energy if you'd tell me now that I'm too big to play Baby Doe."
>
> Douglas was such a dear sweet man, such a perfect gentleman, that I think he was thoroughly taken aback. He walked down the aisle to the stage and in a gentle voice said: "Why, Miss Sills, you look just perfect to me." I sang The Willow Song. Douglas walked down to the stage again. "Miss Sills," he said, "you *are* Baby Doe."[135]

Finally, it appeared that a soprano had succeeded in bringing Baby Doe back to life. Indeed, New York's music critics were generally blown away by Sills's portrayal of Baby Doe.[136]

---

131 Letter, Douglas Moore to F. W. Ricketson Jr., November 22, 1955, Douglas Moore Papers (Box 11, Folder "Ballad of Baby Doe (General Corr.) 1").

132 Ibid. Ricketson had not been pleased with Benzell's 1954 appearance in Central City, when she performed in *Ariadne auf Naxos*. He admitted, however, that Benzell was "a pretty little girl." See letter, F. H. Ricketson Jr. to Douglas Moore, November 17, 1955, Douglas Moore Papers (Box 11, Folder "Ballad of Baby Doe (Central City Opera House Association)").

133 Sills, *Bubbles*, 83.

134 Ibid.

135 Ibid., 84.

136 As Sills recalled in *Bubbles*, "the morning after opening night I grabbed the *New York Herald Tribune* from Peter before he had a chance to look at it. But there was no review on the regular review page. 'Look at that,' I said to Peter, 'they didn't even cover it, can you imagine?' 'Well,' Peter said, 'do you mind if I read the rest of the paper?' He turned to the front page and there—on the front page!—was the review." (p. 85). See Harrison, "American Opera Hailed Here." See also Biancolli, "'Baby Doe' Gets City Premiere"; Eyer, "Ballad of Baby Doe"; Kastendieck, "Tip Your Hat, America"; Sargeant, "Musical Events: Bonanza"; Taubman, "Opera: 'Baby Doe' Here."

Moore and Latouche began revising *The Ballad of Baby Doe* during Central City's summer festival.[137] Working in consultation with Broadway producer Michael Myerberg, they condensed Scenes 1 and 2 from Act I. They replaced Horace Tabor's Act I, Scene 2 aria "Out of the darkness" with "Warm as the autumn light"; they replaced Baby Doe's Act II, Scene 1 aria "Wake snakes" with "The fine ladies walk." They added a new scene (Act II, Scene 2) in which Horace plays poker with four of his friends, and they condensed Act II, Scene 3.[138] Throughout July 1956, various news outlets reported that *The Ballad of Baby Doe* might make it to Broadway that fall.[139] On July 18, Arthur Gelb commented on the plans in the *New York Times*; playwright and librettist James A. Goldman sent Moore a cutout of the notice, writing "To hell with the Metropolitan," a pointed jab at the Met's longstanding indifference to American opera.[140] On July 19, Moore and Latouche entered into a formal contract with Myerberg, who planned to produce *The Ballad of Baby Doe* at the Mansfield Theatre (now the Brooks Atkinson Theatre).[141] Unfortunately, the Broadway production never materialized.[142] As Pollack explains, the opera's failure "to make it to Broadway helped signal the end of the rialto's more-than-twenty-year reign as a preeminent showcase for new American opera, a role that the New York City Opera steadily had been assuming."[143] To be sure, it was the NYCO that presented the revised version of *The Ballad of Baby Doe* in 1958.

---

137 In retrospect, it was fortunate that Moore and Latouche were so quick to attend to revisions because on August 7, 1956, Latouche died from a heart attack.
138 In his production notes, Myerberg also argued that Scenes 1 and 2 of Act I should be collapsed into a single scene, something Moore and Latouche (or possibly just Moore) ultimately did. See "Production Notes: 'The Ballad of Baby Doe,'" Douglas Moore Papers (Box 11, Folder "Ballad of Baby Doe (General Corr.) 1").
139 See "Baby Doe," *Time*, ; Chapman, "'Baby Doe,' a Superb Opera."
140 Gelb, "FOLK MUSIC PLAY MAY BE DONE HERE." See Douglas Moore Papers (Box 68, Folder 3).
141 On September 6, 1956, Myerberg sent Moore his first set of production notes, referring frequently to his viewing of *The Ballad of Baby Doe* in Central City, as well as to the discussions he had engaged in there with Moore and Latouche. Myerberg asserted "that basically the plan of production used [in Central City] was sound and effective; however, in need of expansion and refinement for New York." See letter, Michael Myerberg to Douglas Moore, September 6, 1956, Douglas Moore Papers (Box 11, Folder "Ballad of Baby Doe (M. S. & I. S. Isaacs, Lucy Kroll, Michael Myerberg et. al.) 3"). See also "Production Notes."
142 According to Pollack, Myerberg struggled to find investors for the Broadway production. See *The Ballad of John Latouche*, 455.
143 Ibid., 455.

One of the revisions that Moore and Latouche made as they revamped *The Ballad of Baby Doe* had particularly significant consequences. When Moore and Latouche replaced the aria "Wake snakes" with "The fine ladies walk" in Act II, Scene 1, they began to soften as well as refine Baby Doe's character, gradually toning down the image of Baby Doe the gold digger and homewrecker and preparing audiences for her ultimate, angelic transformation. Act II opens outside the Windsor Hotel in Denver in 1893. Baby Doe, happily married to Horace, is at the Governor's Ball along with her mother. Mama McCourt is incensed by the way Augusta's friends shun her daughter. When Baby Doe attempts to speak to them, they turn their backs on her.[144] Mama McCourt notes:

> Those stuck up old things.
> I'd like to slap their faces.
> Who do they think they are?
> One step from a miner's shanty
> And they act like duchesses.[145]

Baby Doe, however, laughs the women off, unperturbed: "Who cares what they think?"[146] At the Central City premiere, she then launched into the following aria:

> Wake, snakes. Moon's arisin
> Kadydid's fiddling loud and shrill
> Bring a glow worm for your lamp
> Hie to the hoe-down
> Dance to a show-down
> Wake up the dead in Leadville.[147]

In Moore's copy of the Central City libretto, next to Baby Doe's "Wake snakes," someone had written simply that this aria "must be a dance or cut."[148] Moore's setting, jaunty and upbeat, in tandem with Latouche's text, made Baby Doe out to be something of a back-country hick, completely unaware of and/or unbothered by the fact that the women of Denver hate her (Fig. 2.1).

---

144 The "first woman" notes that "if it weren't for [Horace's] money she would leave him in a minute like she did the last one." Together, all four women conclude: "Baby Doe will leave him, leave him when something better comes along." See *The Ballad of Baby Doe*, typescript libretto, 2-1-3, Douglas Moore Papers (Box 93, Folder 2).
145 Ibid., 2-1-4.
146 Ibid.
147 Ibid., 2-1-4 and 2-1-5.
148 Ibid.

In "The fine ladies walk," on the other hand, Baby Doe is keenly aware of the women who shun her. She explains, as she begins the aria:

> The fine ladies walk with their heads held high
> As they look down their noses at me.
> They sit in the parlors of their proud chilly houses
> And sharpen their tongues with my name.

Her tone shifts dramatically as she proclaims:

> But deep in themselves they know what I've got;
> Something they never will have,
> A love that walks beside me, morning and midnight,
> Guarding each moment tenderly.

Most importantly, Baby Doe asserts that her love for Horace is true:

> Maybe when I first met Horace, Mama,
> I thought of the money and the power that was his.
> But the moment he kissed me all that was forgotten.
> I only knew that the other part of me,
> Lost for so long, had come home.

Baby Doe concludes her aria by admitting the price of her love:

> So let them sneer and pass me by,
> As they look down their noses at me.
> I have a love that will keep me aglow
> As the world grows gray and cold.[149]

Moore begins his setting of "The fine ladies walk" in a matter-of-fact style. The vocal line sits in the middle of the soprano register and moves primarily by step. As the aria progresses and as Baby Doe becomes increasingly impassioned, Moore writes larger and larger leaps, moving into the soprano's upper register. For example, he emphasizes Baby Doe's epiphany of how her life changed "the moment he kissed me" with a leap of a minor seventh ($b\flat^1$ to $a\flat^2$). Through "The fine ladies walk," Baby Doe begins to sound sincere, like a woman deeply committed to her husband. She no longer appears so blithe, unsophisticated, or conniving. She admits, of course, to initially being attracted to Tabor's wealth and success but demonstrates that her commitment has grown much deeper.

At first glance, Baby Doe's gradual transformation is compelling. It is refreshing to see the gold-digger and homewrecker stereotypes fade away. It is disappointing, however, to see Baby Doe quickly adhere to another stereotype. As I noted at the beginning of this chapter, Moore believed that

---

149 Moore and Latouche, *The Ballad of Baby Doe*, 147–151.

Figure 2.1. Beginning of "Wake snakes," from *The Ballad of Baby Doe*, Act II, Scene 1, Manuscript Piano/Vocal Score from Central City. Douglas Moore Papers (Box 43, Folder 3).

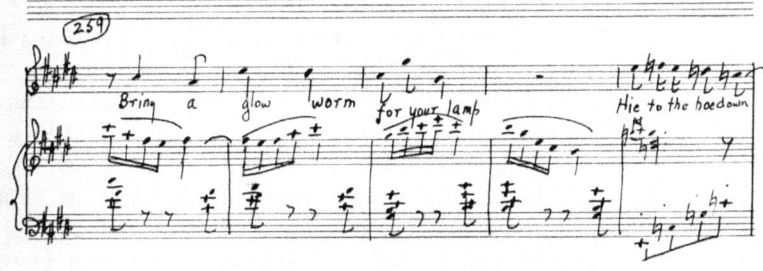

over the course of the opera, Baby Doe grew "from a little nitwit into a wonderful woman."[150] Similarly, composer and music critic Herbert Elwell argued that Baby Doe's "true character" was revealed in the opera's conclusion, when it became clear that the "alleged strumpet ... was more like an angel of devotion and loyalty."[151] In suggesting that Baby Doe could either be a "nitwit" or a "wonderful woman," a "strumpet" or an "angel," Moore and Elwell demonstrated that in *The Ballad of Baby Doe*, there was very little room for any complexity in Baby Doe's character. Augusta's character did not fare much better. In 1956, Howard Taubman described Augusta as the "hard core for the story," explaining how "she emerges as the central figure—a woman, no longer young, who is torn between love and bitterness at being tossed aside after years of loyalty and endless labor at her husband's side."[152] Likewise, Elwell commented on Augusta's "integrity," noting that she was "not merely a meddling, jealous wife, but one who senses tragedy in the whole situation."[153] Whereas Baby Doe, through her commitment to Horace, transforms into a good and devoted woman in *The Ballad of Baby Doe*, Augusta, also through her commitment to Horace, proves to be a good and devoted woman all along. Neither woman exists as more than a virgin or a whore. Neither exists on her own, apart from Horace, even after Horace is gone.

Moore admitted as much when he described in the *New York Times* how he and Latouche had struggled over the opera's conclusion, writing that "when the dying Tabor tells [Baby Doe] that she has been the only real thing in his life the drama is over."[154] Thus *The Ballad of Baby Doe*, although it is populated by strong women, revolves around a man. Moore drove this point home, explaining that while "Baby Doe's actual death is deeply touching and must somehow be indicated ... it seemed an anti-climax, even in a short epilogue."[155] It would appear that Moore and Latouche chose to allude to Baby Doe's death, rather than stage it, because for them, the apparent sacrifice that Baby Doe made leading up to her death was more important than either her life or her death. Indeed, it was through sacrifice, through remaining "beside [her] love," that Baby Doe became worthy. In being willing and even eager to hole up inside her husband's last remaining piece of property, she finally became good. Thus despite the changes that Moore and Latouche made to *The Ballad of Baby Doe* between the 1956 premiere in Central City

---

150 See "Composer Is an Admirer of 'Baby Doe.'"
151 Elwell, "'Baby Doe' Best in Last Scenes."
152 Taubman, "Opera: Rooted in West."
153 Elwell, "'Baby Doe' Best in Last Scenes."
154 Moore, "True Tale of West."
155 Ibid.

and the 1958 performance in New York City, the opera ultimately traps Elizabeth Tabor—first as a gold digger and homewrecker and finally as an angel.

Beverly Sills and Baby Doe

Beverly Sills, however, sought to sing and act her way out of the trap. Sills largely rejected the legend of Baby Doe, and she worked to turn Baby Doe back into "a real woman."[156] Sills wrote about Baby Doe at length in all three of her autobiographies: *Bubbles: A Self-Portrait* (1976), *Bubbles: An Encore* (1981), and *Beverly: An Autobiography* (1987). In *Bubbles: A Self-Portrait*, Sills embraced the style of a glossy coffee-table book, narrating the story of her rise to fame through witty anecdotes and photographs. *Bubbles: An Encore* is a revised edition of this book. Six years later, with the help of Lawrence Linderman, Sills published her definitive autobiography, *Beverly*, which differs from both editions of *Bubbles* in important ways. Although it includes some photographs, *Beverly* is decidedly not a coffee-table book. It is less fun and froth. Sills is more candid, settling old scores and refusing to skim over the various obstacles she faced in her career.

Taken together, *Bubbles* and *Beverly* illuminate the extent to which Sills shaped and was shaped by the role of Baby Doe. Sills argues that in the early 1960s, she began using opera to "escape" from reality.[157] Yet in the late 1950s, when she first began singing *The Ballad of Baby Doe*, she approached opera as a way to cope with her lived experience. The shift in Sills's approach seems to have coincided with the soprano's experience as a biological mother. Sills gave birth to her daughter, Meredith Holden Greenough, in 1959, and to her son, Peter Bulkeley Greenough Jr., in 1961. Just before Meredith turned two, Sills and her husband discovered that she was deaf; around the same time, six-month-old Peter was diagnosed with epilepsy and significant developmental and cognitive disabilities. Sills was initially overwhelmed, and she took some time away from opera. When she returned in February 1962, she sang the role of Manon with the NYCO and she noted that she "had a curious reaction."[158] As she recalled, she enjoyed *Manon* because "for three hours a night I forgot about my own troubles and concentrated on hers. It was a great source of escape—that's what opera became for me."[159] Thus,

---

156 Sills and Linderman, *Beverly*, 123. Sills's performance mission was not entirely unlike Temple's scholarly mission.
157 Ibid., 144.
158 Ibid.
159 Ibid.

Sills began to see opera as a way to take a break from her personal life. Yet as Sills admitted, prior to the 1960s, she looked for herself in the roles she took on. When she recalled her portrayal of the role of Queen Elizabeth in *Roberto Devereux* in 1970, she explained how the role differed from those she had played in the past: "Until then, in every opera I'd sung, I'd played a young woman, and I'd always looked like myself ... For *Devereux*, I had to become Queen Elizabeth in the autumn of her life."[160] Because of the acting and characterization involved, Sills described Queen Elizabeth as "the most ambitious undertaking" of her career, perhaps acknowledging that in playing Queen Elizabeth, she was finally not playing a version of herself.[161]

Throughout *Bubbles*, Sills described her commitment to inhabiting her parts, crediting soprano Lily Pons with sparking her interest "in characterization on stage."[162] Sills recalled seeing Pons in *Lakmé* at the age of eight, enthusing that "not only was her voice remarkable; she also *looked* all her roles."[163] In the early 1950s, while on a tour organized by Charles Wagner, Sills learned still more about the importance of characterization from stage director Désiré Defrère. He encouraged the soprano, when playing a role based on a figure in literature, "to read the literature first," and as Sills asserted, she "always followed that advice—going back to the original Lucia, the original Traviata, the original Manon" because it was "the ideal way of gaining insight into a character that is perhaps not so obvious in the treatment given it by the composer."[164] In fact, Sills would apply Defrère's advice to the historical roles she performed as well. As she recalled, when she took on the role of Baby Doe, "I read everything that had ever been written about her. I copied her hairdos from whatever photographs I could find. I absorbed her so completely in those five weeks of studying the opera that I knew her inside and out. I *was* Baby Doe."[165] According to Sills, Baby Doe became "an integral part" of her "operatic experience."[166] She elaborated: "It was difficult to shake her off even after I left the opera house. If I have ever achieved definitive performances during my career thus far, Baby Doe is one of them. The other three would be Manon, Cleopatra in *Julius Caesar*, and Queen Elizabeth in *Roberto Devereux*."[167] Interestingly, three out of the four roles that comprised Sills's "definitive performances" were historical

---

160 Ibid., 214.
161 Ibid., 213–214.
162 Sills, *Bubbles*, 23.
163 Ibid., 22.
164 Ibid., 44.
165 Ibid., 84.
166 Ibid., 85.
167 Ibid.

roles, and in each of these cases, Sills recalled engaging in significant research as she became the role. For example, she described her "enormous" preparations for the role of Queen Elizabeth, explaining how she "read extensively about Elizabeth's life, about her physical appearance ... She was a multifaceted lady and consequently, fascinating to play."[168] Sills's approach to Queen Elizabeth very nearly recalls her approach to Baby Doe.

Sills's description of her research process demonstrates how she sought to access the roles she embodied and portrayed without the "permission" of a composer or librettist. Indeed, Sills asserted that the insights she gleaned about a character might not be "so obvious" in the hands of the composer. Like Patricia Neway in *The Consul*, Sills held fast to her right to examine and mold a character as she saw fit.[169] With Baby Doe, Sills did occasionally refer to what she believed to be Moore's perspective, yet for the most part, she relied on her research and perhaps on the way her research served as a mirror to her own life experience, something that becomes increasingly apparent upon a close reading of *Beverly*.

Sills was careful when it came to discussions of her personal life in *Bubbles*. She described her courtship with Peter Greenough, the man who would become her husband, in rosy terms, glossing over the fact that when she met him, Greenough was in the midst of divorce proceedings. Similarly, she acknowledged differences in their religious and socio-economic backgrounds in a matter-of-fact manner: "The announcement that a nice middle-class Jewish girl from Brooklyn named Beverly Sills was engaged to a rich Boston Brahmin named Peter Bulkeley Greenough must have puzzled a good many people."[170] When she discussed her biological children, Sills made note of some of the challenges she faced, yet throughout *Bubbles*, she maintained a fairly cheerful facade. Her plucky, can-do attitude and sense of humor always seemed to prevail, and as she later acknowledged in *Beverly*, when she "wasn't cheerful at all," pretending to be cheerful became "a way of life."[171]

With *Beverly*, Sills brought readers more fully into the painful parts of her personal and professional life. She wrote at length about familial and societal opposition to her marriage, much of which, she asserted, was

---

168 Ibid., 159.
169 For a discussion of Patricia Neway's perspective on *The Consul*, see Chapter 1.
170 Sills, *Bubbles*, 71. In a similar vein, she wrote that when she asked her father-in-law what his reaction had been when he learned that his son planned "to marry a Jewish opera singer," her father-in-law had responded: "'Well, I'll tell you, dear. Peter and I were off Martha's Vineyard at the time, fishing in my boat, and I had two choices—I could throw myself overboard or I could go on fishing. Being the intelligent man that I am, I went right on fishing and said to Peter, 'Tell me about her.'" Ibid., 74.
171 Sills and Linderman, *Beverly*, 203.

informed by anti-Semitism. Sills met Greenough in Cleveland, Ohio, in 1955, while on tour with the NYCO. A descendant of John Alden (who had come to America on the *Mayflower*), Greenough was Associate Editor of the *Cleveland Plain Dealer*, which Greenough's very wealthy family owned.[172] According to Sills, Greenough's first wife also "ranked very high in Cleveland social circles."[173] Sills explained that when Greenough filed for divorce and had "the nerve to fight for custody of his children," Cleveland's "rinky-dink version of high society" retaliated: "In the 1950s, a husband couldn't get custody of his children unless he proved their mother guilty of either moral turpitude or gross neglect of duty. Peter chose gross neglect of duty and eventually won, but it was a costly victory."[174] She soon discovered that reactions to Greenough's divorce offered just a preview of reactions to his second marriage.

Before moving to Cleveland, Sills admitted to being very "naïve about anti-Semitism."[175] As she put it:

> I thought Peter's family and friends would avoid me at first because I was Jewish, but I was sure they'd become my friends once they got to know me. It never occurred to me that they wouldn't *allow* themselves to get to know me ... it wasn't anything personal. I wasn't Beverly; I was a Jew. For me, Cleveland was a five-year freeze-out in more ways than one.[176]

Like the Irish-Catholic Elizabeth Tabor in Denver, shunned because of her class, religion, and ethnicity, and because she supposedly "stole" someone else's husband, Sills struggled to find a place for herself in Cleveland. When conductor Jean Morel came to town with the Met, Sills attempted to throw a party in his honor. As she explained, she "did the whole bit— formal invitations, caterers, florists, musicians" and "invited forty people." Only two people attended.[177] Sills concluded: "I'd put up with some hard times since coming to Cleveland, but this was the worst. Forget little emotions like anger, fury, or rage. After that night, and for all the rest of the nights I lived in Cleveland, I was a bitter woman. I felt utterly trapped."[178] By the spring of 1958, Sills was eager to get out of Ohio. In April, she returned to New York, where she sang the role of Baby Doe with the

---

172 See "Peter B. Greenough."
173 Sills and Linderman, *Beverly*, 92.
174 Ibid., 94.
175 Ibid., 117.
176 Ibid.
177 Ibid., 118.
178 Ibid.

NYCO for the first time, immersing herself completely in the role.[179] Two years later, Sills and Greenough left Cleveland for good, moving to Milton, Massachusetts, so that Greenough could take a job as financial columnist for *The Boston Globe*.[180]

In addressing *The Ballad of Baby Doe* in *Beverly*, Sills focused less on her preparation going into the opera and more on how she sought to humanize Baby Doe's character. Referring to Baby Doe as "the classic Other Woman," she explained that her "biggest challenge was to make her a real woman and a woman the audience would like."[181] In 2011, Jerry L. McBride described Baby Doe as "the most complex character to play" in *The Ballad of Baby Doe* because she "is both a strong and a tender character."[182] As he elaborated, he suggested that he had absorbed Sills's perspective on the character: "If she is not played strongly enough, the audience's sympathies will tip toward Augusta, and yet she must be tender enough that the audience will believe she really loves Horace and is not just after his money."[183] Sills argued that although "a lot of singers play Baby Doe as a fortune hunter who deliberately set out to snare Tabor," she "saw that interpretation as a trap."[184] She preferred to play Baby Doe, from the beginning of the opera, in less starkly defined terms. At the end of the first scene of Act I, for example, Sills was careful in how she portrayed Baby Doe during her first exchange with Horace.

When Baby Doe arrives in Leadville, she finds Horace outside the opera house. She asks him for directions to the Clarendon Hotel and Horace obliges. As he bids farewell to Baby Doe, he says, "I hope we'll meet again," to which Baby Doe responds, "I'm sure we'll meet again, Horace Tabor. Indeed we'll meet again."[185] A singer could toss off Baby Doe's lines in a flirtatious or conniving matter. When Howard Taubman reviewed the premiere of *The Ballad of Baby Doe*, he described Dolores Wilson as "just vulgar enough at the outset to remind you that [Baby Doe] was no angel,"

---

179 Sills, *Bubbles*, 84.
180 Sills and Linderman, *Beverly*, 134. Sills recalled that "years later, when I went back to sing in Cleveland as Mrs. America Superstar, all of a sudden people were remarkably friendly to me. I was invited to be a houseguest here and to a party in my honor there—and I said no to everything. Except for my few buddies in town, I saw no one, and I went nowhere. And I made a point of not recognizing anybody … I really let Cleveland have it. The five years I lived there were the angriest, bitterest period of my life."
181 Ibid., 122–123.
182 McBride, *Douglas Moore*, 47.
183 Ibid.
184 Sills and Linderman, *Beverly*, 123.
185 Moore and Latouche, *The Ballad of Baby Doe*, 30.

suggesting that Wilson played up the gold-digger/homewrecker angle.[186] A singer could choose, however, to make much less of Baby Doe's early lines. Sills preferred this approach, for she sought to portray Baby Doe "as very reluctant to get involved with Tabor."[187]

Sills's portrayal clearly convinced some audience members. In 2004, psychologist Beth Hart published a tribute to Sills in *The Opera Quarterly*, explaining that she had first heard Sills when at the age of twelve, she attended the NYCO's 1958 *Ballad of Baby Doe* production. Hart recalled Sills's vivid entrance: "How lovely and friendly she was when she stepped onstage and sang exactly what I had been feeling: 'I've just arrived from Central City and I don't know my way about. Cousin Jack there knows so little English, I have to find the way by myself.' I would have done anything to make her feel at home."[188] Sills, moreover, believed she had this "leeway to portray Baby as a more likable woman."[189] She did not think Baby Doe was "wicked," and citing Moore's score as evidence, she argued that the composer did not think so either.[190] "Moore wrote exquisitely beautiful, simple music for her—and you just don't do that for a scheming woman," she explained.[191] *The Ballad of Baby Doe* does indeed include "beautiful" and "simple" arias for the soprano cast as Baby Doe. Her first aria, an onstage number called the "Willow Song," is particularly poignant. In a 1955 letter to Ricketson, Moore compared this number to "The Last Rose of Summer" (which Friedrich von Flotow famously included in his 1847 opera *Martha*).[192] Like "The Last Rose of Summer," the "Willow Song" is nostalgic and sentimental, garnering sympathy for its singer. Interestingly, it was Moore himself, rather than Latouche, who wrote the lyrics for the "Willow Song."[193]

Accompanying herself on a piano inside the Clarendon Hotel, Baby Doe sings the "Willow Song" in Act I, Scene 2. Tabor overhears and is smitten. The song begins and ends with an arresting vocalise, drawing Horace, and listeners more broadly, to Baby Doe (Ex. 2.1). Hart recalled that "with the melancholy "Willow Song," [Sills] etched Baby Doe's gentle romantic soul

---

186 Taubman, "Opera: Rooted in West."
187 Sills and Linderman, *Beverly*, 123.
188 Hart, "What Becomes a Legend Most?," 624.
189 Sills and Linderman, *Beverly*, 123.
190 Ibid.
191 Ibid.
192 See letter, Douglas Moore to F. W. Ricketson Jr., November 22, 1955, Douglas Moore Papers (Box 11, Folder "Ballad of Baby Doe (General Corr.) 1").
193 McBride, *Douglas Moore*, 44. In addition to writing the lyrics for the "Willow Song," Moore wrote the lyrics for Baby Doe's famous "Letter Aria" and Augusta's aria from Act I, Scene 3.

in floating pianissimos and lustrous arching phrases."[194] According to the stage directions, as soon as Baby Doe completes the last majestic phrase, Horace, "in the darkness, applauds and Baby Doe comes to the window."[195]

A few moments after the "Willow Song," Horace sings his first aria, "Warm as the autumn light," one of the arias that Moore and Latouche added after the Central City premiere. Addressing Baby Doe directly, Horace attests to the power of "the sound of [her] singing," emphasizing its rejuvenating qualities:

> And while I was list'ning
> I was recalling
> Things that once I had wanted so much
> And forgotten as years slipped away ...
> But only tonight came again in your singing
> That feeling of wonder
> Of longing and pain[196]

With her youth, beauty, and voice that is "warm as the autumn light, soft as a pool at night," Baby Doe makes an aging Horace feel young and free. Augusta, on the other hand, seems only to remind Horace of his old way of life and responsibilities. Moore and Latouche underlined the tension between the old wife and the young soon-to-be mistress by breaking Baby Doe and Horace's exchange with Augusta's voice. After Horace kisses Baby Doe's hand, Augusta calls to him: "Horace, are you still down there?"[197] When Horace fails to respond, she repeats her question. Finally, Horace responds, and Augusta admonishes him: "Ar'nt you coming up? It's getting on to midnight."[198]

Working in tandem, the "Willow Song" and "Warm as the autumn light" serve to establish the foundation for Horace and Baby Doe's relationship, and when a soprano like Sills takes the "Willow Song" at face value, the song helps to paint a picture of an innocent young woman who is about to find herself in a compromising situation. A soprano who wanted to establish Baby Doe as a conniving gold digger might imply that Baby Doe knows she is performing for Horace in this scene. Sills, however, held fast to Baby Doe's innocence. In 1962, when she sang the "Willow Song" before a studio audience on television, she appeared in a simple dress that fell just below the knee and featured a modest neckline.[199] She played Baby Doe as an ordi-

---

194 Hart, "What Becomes a Legend Most?," 631.
195 Moore and Latouche, *The Ballad of Baby Doe*, 43.
196 Ibid., 45–47.
197 Ibid., 49.
198 Ibid., 50.
199 "Profile of Douglas Moore."

Example 2.1. Moore and Latouche, *The Ballad of Baby Doe*, mm. 747–756. Words and music by John Latouche and Douglas Moore. © 1958 (Renewed) Chappell & Co., Inc. All Rights Reserved. Used by Permission of Alfred Music.

nary young woman, not someone who needed to transform from a "strumpet" into an "angel."

Sills's commitment to her character's complexity and humanity, however, was not entirely unique to Baby Doe. In *Beverly*, Sills noted how she sought to portray Massenet's Manon as "a fifteen-year-old farm girl, not a slut," explaining that although some sopranos played Manon as "the village whore," she did not.[200] Sills's work in characterization can be understood as a conscious effort to push back against the sexism and misogyny embedded not only in the opera tradition but in society more broadly. Indeed, I wonder if Sills was hesitant to reduce the women she played to the paradigm of the virgin or the whore because like many women, she knew just how much that paradigm hurt. Hart acknowledged this possibility in her 2004 tribute to Sills, delving into some of the tension between Sills and her father, who died when Sills was just twenty years old. As Hart pointed out, Sills's "arguments with her own father, while not about virgins and whores, were nonetheless about his split representation of Woman."[201] Sills's father was uncomfortable with Sills pursuing a career on stage because it conflicted with his ideas of her eventual role as a wife and mother. As Sills put it in *Beverly*, to her father, "singing simply wasn't a respectable profession."[202]

To my knowledge, Sills never commented on the similarities between her life in Cleveland in the 1950s and Baby Doe's life in Colorado in the 1890s. Yet Sills certainly had an acute understanding of what it meant to be perceived as the "other" woman or the less "respectable" woman. Sills may have been drawn to Baby Doe precisely because her character, predicament, and punishment, however historically removed, were familiar. *The Ballad of Baby Doe*, even as it turns Baby Doe into a "good woman," punishes its title heroine—as so many operas do—for being a "bad woman," at the same time as Sills and many other women in the US were dealing with another wave of impossible and punishing expectations.

Beverly Sills as Baby Doe

Baby Doe figures prominently in all three of Sills's memoirs, and Sills is, without a doubt, the soprano most associated with the role, so much so that historians sometimes overstate the fame that *The Ballad of Baby Doe* brought Sills.[203] As Nancy Guy rightly points out, Sills did not catapult to stardom until she sang the role of Cleopatra in the NYCO's 1966 production of Handel's *Giulio Cesare*.[204] Yet even if it was the role of Cleopatra

---

200 Sills and Linderman, *Beverly*, 68.
201 Hart, "What Becomes a Legend Most?," 639.
202 Sills and Linderman, *Beverly*, 16.
203 In 1970, for example, Lewis J. Hardee Jr. falsely claimed that *The Ballad of Baby Doe* was "the only American opera in the history of American opera by which an opera singer has risen to stardom." See "The Musical Theatre of Douglas Moore," 73.
204 Guy, *The Magic of Beverly Sills*, 43.

that made Sills's career, I suspect that it was the role of Baby Doe that gave Sills the confidence she needed to get there. As Sills explained in *Beverly*: "Nothing compared to the magic of my opening night performance in *The Ballad of Baby Doe* ... I usually left theaters feeling a bit disappointed or angry with parts of my performance. Not *that* night. I felt I'd performed flawlessly ... No other soprano in the world could have matched my performance that night. I believed it then, and I believe it now."[205] Sills made those who heard her "believe it" as well. Taped inside the front cover of a copy of *The Ballad of Baby Doe* in Sills's collection of scores at the New York Public Library is a Christmas card, inscribed by Moore, "to Beverly whose voice and beauty will always remain a part of Baby Doe."[206]

Sopranos who later came to *The Ballad of Baby Doe* had to contend, therefore, not only with the legend of Baby Doe, but also with the legend of Sills. Whereas Sills seems to have relished the opportunity to seek within *The Ballad of Baby Doe* a new kind of operatic heroine—one who might begin to resist being undone by her composer, her librettist, and the world at large—other sopranos were not always so enticed by the challenge. Elizabeth Futral (b. 1963) starred in *The Ballad of Baby Doe* at the NYCO in 2001, and in interviews surrounding the production, she sounded somewhat conflicted about the title role. She told Freeman Gunter of *Classical Singer* that Baby Doe was "perhaps ... not the most interesting character I've ever played."[207] "The singer has to fill in a lot," she explained.[208] Futral spoke more highly of *The Ballad of Baby Doe* in the *New York Times*. According to David Mermelstein, Futral "found that Baby Doe wasn't nearly as one-dimensional a part as she had assumed."[209] Futral told Mermelstein that *The Ballad of Baby Doe* had "substance," providing "a real sense of Baby Doe's maturing as the opera proceeds, musically as well as dramatically."[210] In offering her perspective on *The Ballad of Baby Doe* in the *New York Times* in the midst of the opera's run at the NYCO, Futral was certainly trying to help the NYCO sell tickets, yet it is also possible that as she prepared for the NYCO production with Sills's voice and perspective in her ears, she began to see Baby Doe in a new light.

---

205 Sills and Linderman, *Beverly*, 124.
206 See Douglas Moore and John Latouche, *The Ballad of Baby Doe: Opera in Two Acts, Piano-Vocal Score* in Beverly Sills Scores, Music Division, New York Public Library, New York, NY. Nancy Guy also discovered this inscription. See *The Magic of Beverly Sills*, 32.
207 Futral, quoted in Gunter, "An Exclusive Interview with Elizabeth Futral."
208 Ibid.
209 Mermelstein, "MUSIC; Vocalism in Her Soul, Drama in Her Blood."
210 Futral, quoted in ibid.

In fact, during her interview with Gunter, Futral referred to a meeting with Sills. She explained that when she had arrived in New York City to begin rehearsals with the NYCO, Sills had invited her to have coffee. According to Futral, the pair "spent an hour together, just chatting and talking about the role [of Baby Doe] and my career."[211] Futral noted that Sills "really loved the character [of Baby Doe], and loved singing it."[212] Perhaps it was Sills who helped Futral see the "substance" in Baby Doe, so fleetingly visible in Moore and Latouche's text. Music critic Anne Midgette, however, remained unconvinced. When she reviewed the NYCO's 2001 production in the *New York Times*, she argued that although *The Ballad of Baby Doe* had "been hailed as an American classic, largely on the strength of Moore's pretty melodies and Beverly Sills's quasi-legendary 1958 performance," the opera "lacks some basic dramatic and musical qualities."[213] Midgette also took issue with several of Colin Graham's production decisions, complaining, for example, that he had "removed some of the title figure's piquancy by casting her not as an ambitious gold-digger but simply a nice woman in a difficult position."[214] Thus Midgette, presumably for the sake of the drama, wanted Baby Doe to adhere to a starkly defined stereotype.

When Sills died in 2007, she was buried alongside her mother and father and husband in Sharon Gardens Cemetery in Valhalla, New York. The epitaph on her headstone reads "Loving Wife and Mother, 'Always and Forever,'" the last three words a reference to Horace and Baby Doe's final exchange in *The Ballad of Baby Doe*.[215] At face value, the epitaph might seem to relegate Sills to the 1950s role of wife and mother, wholly devoted, like Moore and Latouche's Baby Doe, no matter the personal cost. Yet Sills believed that the final exchange between Horace and Baby Doe revealed something else—Horace's eventual understanding and deep love for Baby Doe as a person. Sills believed her own husband loved her in this way too. As she explained in *Beverly*:

> One of the things I've always loved about Peter is that he really never gave much of a damn about my singing. Yes, he's very proud of me, and he loves my voice, and he's always respected my art and my enthusiasm for it. But with Peter, I never had to worry that he was attracted to me because he liked

---

211 Futral, quoted in Gunter, "An Exclusive Interview with Elizabeth Futral."
212 Ibid.
213 Midgette, "OPERA REVIEW." For a contrasting perspective on the NYCO's 2001 production of *The Ballad of Baby Doe*, see Davis, "Rocky Mountain High."
214 Midgette, "OPERA REVIEW."
215 See Guy, *The Magic of Beverly Sills*, 80.

the idea of going out with an opera singer.[216]

In an interview with Lewis J. Hardee Jr., Sills lingered on the significance of Horace's last words: "You were *always* the real thing, Baby. The only real thing."[217] Sills explained to Hardee that these words seemed to have the power to "destroy" her on stage.[218] The tears would begin to flow, and she would wonder: "how will I ever get through the last aria?"[219] She told Hardee: "I really don't know why that line always gets me."[220] By the time she wrote *Bubbles*, Sills seemed to have figured it out. She described how she and baritone Walter Cassel "lived those roles when we were on stage; there was never a moment during the performances when I didn't believe he was Horace Tabor. And even offstage he never called me Beverly or anything else, just 'Baby.'"[221] In seeking to take on Baby Doe and to portray her, from the very beginning of the opera, as a "real woman," Sills foreshadowed Horace's realization at the opera's conclusion. Sills's Baby Doe never transformed from whore to virgin. She "always" was who she was, and she bawled when Horace finally saw her.

---

216 Sills and Linderman, *Beverly*, 91.
217 Sills, tape recorded interview, New York City, June 20, 1969, quoted in Hardee, "The Musical Theatre of Douglas Moore," 84. Italics mine. See also Moore and Latouche, *The Ballad of Baby Doe*, 245–246.
218 Sills, tape recorded interview, quoted in Hardee, "The Musical Theatre of Douglas Moore," 84.
219 Ibid., 84–85.
220 Ibid., 85.
221 Sills, *Bubbles*, 84.

Chapter Three

A "Really Vicious Monster": Lizzie Andrew Borden

In the middle of Jack Beeson, Kenward Elmslie, and Richard Plant's 1965 opera *Lizzie Borden*, a woman sits at a harmonium, accompanying herself as she performs what sounds like a nineteenth-century parlor song. The woman's name is Abbie, and she is Lizzie Borden's ill-fated stepmother.[1] The song she sings, which Beeson referred to as the "Bird Song," recalls the "Willow Song" that Douglas Moore included in *The Ballad of Baby Doe*. Indeed, both songs sound back to nineteenth-century ideas about gender and domesticity—and the operas to which both songs belong suggest that such ideas are under attack.

※ ※ ※

In 1954, the very same year in which Douglas Moore and John Latouche began working on *The Ballad of Baby Doe*, Jack Beeson and Richard Plant began writing an opera about Lizzie Borden, the alleged axe-murderess from Fall River, Massachusetts. In contrast to Elizabeth "Baby Doe" Tabor (1854–1935), Lizzie Andrew Borden (1860–1927) appeared not merely to threaten the American family but to violently obliterate it. On August 11, 1892, seven days after her father and stepmother were found hacked to death in their home, the thirty-two-year-old Lizzie was arrested.[2] She was tried and eventually acquitted, yet in the court of public opinion, she remained

---

1   Lizzie Borden's stepmother spelled her first name as "Abby." Throughout this chapter, when referring to the historical figure, I use the name Abby; when referring to the character in the opera, I use the name Abbie.
2   Andrew Borden's body was found slumped across the sofa in the living room of his home in Fall River, Massachusetts on August 4, 1892; he appeared to have suffered ten or eleven hatchet blows, one of which sliced his left eyeball cleanly in half. Abby Borden was found face down on the floor in one of the upstairs bedrooms. She appeared to have suffered nineteen direct blows to the

guilty. Since 1892, Lizzie the hatchet-swinging murderess has loomed large in New England lore—in newspaper stories and exposés, books, plays, a ballet, a children's rhyme, a television miniseries, and numerous movies.[3]

Lizzie Borden has almost always prompted the same question: why? Why would a "lady" pick up a hatchet and wield it, first against her stepmother, and then against her father, striking each one not just once but over and over again? Beeson and Plant were particularly drawn to the idea of writing an opera that would answer this question, and in its final form, *Lizzie Borden* suggested that the title heroine was a repressed spinster, driven to commit murder because of a psychosexual complex and an impossible domestic situation. Beeson, Plant, and Kenward Elmslie (who took over as librettist in 1961) turned Lizzie's stepmother into a cruel and conniving woman, and they turned her father into a physically abusive miser. They encouraged their audience to initially sympathize with Lizzie's plight against her parents, yet when Lizzie finally grabs her hatchet and rushes up the stairs to commit the first murder, letting out a savage, guttural cry, she demonstrates that she is no longer a "lady," and she no longer elicits sympathy. She strikes fear. In the opera's final scene, Lizzie appears utterly transformed. Alone in her father's house, counting the family money and assets like her father before her, Lizzie is the spitting musical and visual image of her father. If at the beginning of the opera, Lizzie was trapped in her father's house, Lizzie is now trapped in his body and voice. She is a grotesque woman-turned-man of the house. As Elmslie put it, she is "a frightening, really vicious monster."[4]

If not for this final scene, Lizzie might be construed as a symbol of "women's liberation." In fact, when I first began examining the opera, I wanted, somewhat desperately perhaps, to regard Lizzie as an operatic heroine with the power to literally hack patriarchal oppression to death. My perspective on *Lizzie Borden* has changed, and as I argue through musical and historical

---

back of her head. For a concise and impartial retelling of Borden murders, see Chaney, *New England Remembers Lizzie Borden*.

[3] In 2014, the Lifetime television network aired the movie *Lizzie Borden Took an Ax*. The next year, Lifetime continued the story in a miniseries entitled *The Lizzie Borden Chronicles*, set in the days following Lizzie's acquittal. Both the movie and the miniseries starred Christina Ricci. In 2018, the movie *Lizzie*, starring Kristen Stewart and Chloë Sevigny, opened in theaters throughout the US. These recent retellings demonstrate how Lizzie Borden remains alive and well in the early twenty-first century. In fact, to this day, Lizzie Borden enthusiasts can spend the night at the Lizzie Borden Bed & Breakfast Museum in Fall River, sleeping in one of the rooms where the murders took place.

[4] Elmslie also noted: "The first time I saw *Lizzie Borden* on television, it scared me shitless!" See "Winston Leyland Interviews Kenward Elmslie" in Leyland, *Gay Sunshine Interviews*, vol. 2, 98.

analysis, there are profound limits to Lizzie's operatic liberation. Instead of a celebration of women's lib, she is a male-generated fantasy of the anxieties that surrounded the movement.[5]

This becomes increasingly clear when one situates *Lizzie Borden* in the broader context of both Beeson's and Moore's operatic outputs. Over the course of the 1950s and 1960s, Beeson and Moore each wrote two operas about unconventional, rebellious women from the past. At the same time as Beeson began working with Plant on what would become *Lizzie Borden*, he was engaged in work with Elmslie on *The Sweet Bye and Bye*, an opera about Aimee Semple McPherson (1890–1944), the Pentecostal evangelist and media celebrity famous for founding the Foursquare Church. As it turned out, Moore had introduced Beeson to Elmslie, who was a protégé (and the partner) of Latouche. Moore had also suggested McPherson as the subject for *The Sweet Bye and Bye*.[6] Elmslie recalled that he "had an awful time thinking up a subject," and Moore came to the rescue when he recommended "the Billy Graham of the twenties."[7] Beeson noted that as he and Elmslie worked on *The Sweet Bye and Bye* and as Moore and Latouche worked on *The Ballad of Baby Doe*, the two composer-librettist teams "passed ideas and rhymes back and forth" and Beeson and Moore "played out [their] latest passages for one another."[8] Beeson and Elmslie completed *The Sweet Bye and Bye* in 1956, the same year that Moore and Latouche completed *The Ballad of Baby Doe*.[9] In 1961, when Plant became too ill to complete the libretto for *Lizzie Borden*, Beeson brought the opera to Elmslie. The NYCO premiered Beeson, Plant, and Elmslie's *Lizzie Borden* on March 25, 1965 with mezzo-soprano Brenda Lewis (1921–2017) in the title role.[10] One year

---

5   Lizzie ultimately adheres to Susan McClary's notion of operatic madwomen "first and foremost" as "male fantasies of transgression dressed up as women." See *Feminine Endings*, 110.
6   Beeson, *How Operas Are Created by Composers and Librettists*, 256.
7   See "Winston Leyland Interviews Kenward Elmslie" in Leyland, *Gay Sunshine Interviews*, vol. 2, 98.
8   Beeson, *How Operas Are Created by Composers and Librettists*, 257.
9   Juilliard Opera Theater premiered *The Sweet Bye and Bye* in 1957. In 1974, the Kansas City Lyric Theater orchestra, soloists, and chorus made the first recording of this opera. *The Sweet Bye and Bye* was Elmslie's first opera, but it was Beeson's third. Prior to *The Sweet Bye and Bye*, Beeson had written *Jonah* (1950) and *Hello Out There!* (1954), adapting his own librettos. After collaborating on *Lizzie Borden*, Beeson and Elmslie largely parted ways. Elmslie wrote the libretto for Ned Rorem's *Miss Julie* (1965), as well as for Thomas Pasatieri's *The Seagull* (1974) and *Washington Square* (1976).
10 The opera was also produced for television, and it was first telecast in January of 1967. The telecast is now available on DVD. See Beeson, Elmslie, and

later, Moore's final opera—about a different hatchet-wielding woman, temperance leader Carry A. Nation (1846–1911)—received its premiere at the University of Kansas, highlighting yet again Beeson's and Moore's shared interest in bringing notorious women of the past back to life—often for punishment—on the mid-twentieth-century American opera stage.[11] In the previous chapter, however, I noted that Moore grew somewhat ambivalent about punishing Baby Doe, and I showed how Beverly Sills capitalized on his ambivalence, as well as on her own convictions about the role, to paint a more sympathetic portrait of Elizabeth "Baby Doe" Tabor. Beeson, Plant, and Elmslie ultimately embraced wholesale the idea of punishing Lizzie Borden, leaving little room for Brenda Lewis—or anyone else—to resist or rewrite the role in any way.

There is yet another historical narrative embedded in *Lizzie Borden*, one that has less to do with the gradual resurgence of the feminist movement and more with the lasting trauma of World War II. Richard Plant, Beeson's initial librettist, was obsessed with Lizzie Borden. A gay German Jewish émigré who escaped Germany before the Holocaust, Plant struggled throughout his life with the fact that he had survived, while others, including his own father and stepmother, had died. During the 1940s, he grew increasingly attached to Lizzie Borden and to his belief in her guilt, seemingly because it mirrored his own.[12] Interestingly, it was Plant who approached Beeson with the idea of writing an opera about Lizzie Borden in the first place.

I begin this chapter by acknowledging the tumultuous convergence of past and present anxieties that informs *Lizzie Borden*. My examination of Beeson's, Elmslie's, and Plant's personal papers reveals just how much of the libretto Elmslie inherited from Plant and just how much Plant's experience informed that libretto. Plant's contributions and perspectives clearly set *Lizzie Borden* on her initial course, and they illuminate the opera's unlikely connection to the testimonies of and reckonings with the Holocaust that

---

    Plant, *Lizzie Borden*, directed by Kirk Browning.

11   On *Carry Nation*, see Hershberger, "Fifty Years Later."

12   Included in Plant's Papers in the New York Public Library is a shadow box, a strange shrine dedicated to two Lizzies: Lizzie Borden, the woman, and *Lizzie Borden*, the opera. Across the top of the box blares a headline from an article in the *New York Times*, dated March 21, 1965, four days before the NYCO premiere. The headline reads: "The Lizzie Borden Case." Lizzie's surname, however, is obscured by the head of a small plastic skeleton, its body splayed across the rest of the display, pelvis draping over a small hatchet dripping with fake blood. See Lizzie Borden Shadowbox, Richard Plant Papers (Box 38), Manuscripts and Archives Division, New York Public Library, Astor, Lenox, and Tilden Foundations.

began to appear in the US during the 1950s and 1960s.[13] Yet when Elmslie replaced Plant as librettist in 1961, *Lizzie Borden* became more about the anxieties that accompanied the burgeoning of the modern feminist movement. Thus as a text, the opera is indebted to two struggles in time, one rooted in the aftermath of World War II and the other looking ahead to women's liberation.[14] *Lizzie Borden* lays this latter struggle bare on stage, revealing deep-seated anxieties about women and gender in the US in the mid-twentieth century.

Richard Plant's Lizzie Borden

Richard Plant (1910–1998) discovered Lizzie Borden in 1945, at which point he had been living in the US for seven years. Born in Frankfurt, Germany, Plant fled to Switzerland in 1933 at his father's urging and enrolled as a graduate student at the University of Basel. He earned his PhD in history and German literature in 1937 and moved to New York City. Meanwhile, his parents (his father and stepmother) killed themselves to avoid persecution by the Nazis. During World War II, Plant worked with the US Office of War Information to produce anti-Nazi programs for radio broadcasting behind German lines. In 1947, he began teaching German language and literature at the City College of New York, and in 1948, he published *The Dragon in the Forest*, a fictionalized account of his childhood in Frankfurt and its coincidence with Hitler's rise to power.

According to a City College press release, dated February 21, 1965, Plant had become interested in the story of Lizzie Borden by sheer chance: "Back in 1945, before coming to the college, Dr. Plant was browsing in a library during a lunch hour and came upon a version of the Massachusetts murders in a book. 'I couldn't stop reading about the Borden family,' Dr. Plant

---

13 For examples, see Levi, *Survival in Auschwitz* and Wiesel, *Night*. First published in Italy in 1947, Levi's *Se questo è un uomo* (If This Is a Man) was published in the US as *Survival in Auschwitz* in 1959. Published in France in 1958, *Night* was first published in the US in 1960, the first of a trilogy chronicling Wiesel's path to recovery after surviving the Holocaust. *Dawn* was published in 1961, and *Day* was published in 1962.

14 In this chapter, I gravitate toward the term "women's liberation" rather than "second-wave feminism." Although the two terms are sometimes used interchangeably in reference to the resurgence of feminist activism during the 1960s and 1970s, "women's liberation" represented an earlier (1960s) and more radical faction(s) within what was eventually coined as the "second-wave" movement more broadly.

explains."¹⁵ City College then offered a brief portrait of Plant's life and career, noting that Plant's love for opera had been nurtured during his childhood by "his physician father, who treated many singers from the local opera house" and who "took him to a performance of *Hansel and Gretel* at the age of seven."¹⁶ When Plant approached Beeson with his idea for an opera about Lizzie in 1954, "the composer was fascinated," City College wrote, and the two men struck up their partnership; *Lizzie Borden* faltered in 1959, "when Dr. Plant was hospitalized for a slipped disc."¹⁷ It was shortly after this point that Kenward Elmslie stepped in to finish the libretto.

The story that City College advertised in February of 1965 was somewhat sanitized. Plant was hospitalized in 1959, and then again in 1961, but not for a slipped disc. As Beeson wrote in a 1986 article for *The Opera Quarterly*, Plant struggled with depression, and in the spring of 1959, he was hospitalized because of it.¹⁸ Beeson saw Plant's depression as being related to his heartbreaking family history:

> During the six years we had lived with the Borden family of Fall River, shaping facts to fit fantasies, Richard's European reticence occasionally permitted fleeting references to the *Plaut* family of Frankfurt am Main. The Catholic mother had died in 1932; Richard fled to Basel in 1933. No entreaties could induce the Jewish father to leave the still-flourishing medical practice and the *Heimatland*—but perhaps one could have been more forceful? By 1938 it was too late to emigrate, and in desperation Plaut took his own life and that of Richard's stepmother, with means easily available to a physician.¹⁹

Beeson explained how he "could see plainly the parallels" between the Plaut family and the Borden family, namely "the strong, obdurate fathers, the stepmothers, imagined patricide and matricide, and the guilt of survivors."²⁰ He wondered if Plant's "work on the libretto" was "a writing out and transferal of suffering" or if it was "actually contributing to his illness."²¹ In Beeson's mind, Plant was reading his family history into and through the Borden

---

15 Press release, The City College of New York, February 21, 1965, Richard Plant Papers (Box 7, Folder 5).
16 Ibid.
17 Ibid.
18 Beeson, "The Autobiography of *Lizzie Borden*," 22.
19 Ibid., 22–23. The Plaut Family finished compiling a family history in 1973. See "Descendants of Rabbi Rudolf Plaut," compiled by Susanne Herz, Evelyn Z. Plaut, and Thomas F. A. Plaut, 1973, Richard Plant Papers (Box 34, Folder 4).
20 Beeson, "The Autobiography of *Lizzie Borden*," 23.
21 Ibid.

family history, and in writing *Lizzie*'s libretto, Plant was working through his sense of responsibility for his parents' deaths.

On June 15, 1960, Plant wrote to Beeson, hinting that he might not be up to the task of finishing the libretto:

> In the event that I will not be able to work on our opera concerning the Lizzie Borden story in the fall—say, by October,—you must feel free to either hire another librettist, or write the text yourself, or provide me with a collaborator. In any case, you are then free to do with the material whatever you wish, and this includes the material which we have so far finished.[22]

By 1961, according to Beeson, things had worsened: "[Plant] was having recurrent nightmares: summoning Lizzie from the dead to force her once again to kill her parents was also summoning his parents. He was convinced that these dream spirits would be exorcised only when the opera should be finished, finally, and his surrogate, Lizzie, driven by motives in part of his own invention, should murder her father and stepmother before him and an audience."[23] Through Beeson's recollections, Plant emerges as a man utterly obsessed with Lizzie, who served as a figment of his life experience and subsequent imagination to free him from his past.

For his part, Plant wrote about his parents very briefly in his 1986 book *The Pink Triangle: The Nazi War against Homosexuals*, one of the first scholarly exposés on its subject. He began his study by recalling:

> I fled Frankfurt am Main on February 27, 1933, the day the Reichstag went up in flames. I was fortunate. My father ... insisted I leave Germany as quickly as possible for Basel, Switzerland, and enroll at the university there. After encountering many obstacles, I succeeded in obtaining a passport, an object that had suddenly acquired enormous value. I gathered a few belongings and some luggage, and rushed to the Frankfurt railroad station to take the earliest train to Switzerland. Only years later did I realize how lucky I had been.[24]

Plant remembered that in 1935, he "began bombarding" his father "with letters urging him to leave Germany, even if it meant abandoning his patients and his valuable library."[25] His father refused to listen to his pleas, and he and his wife died by suicide shortly after the *Kristallnacht*. Their desperate act marked a tragedy that continued to haunt Plant.

---

22 Letter, Plant to Beeson, June 15, 1960, Jack Beeson Papers (Box 12, Folder 1), University Archives, Rare Book & Manuscript Library, Columbia University Libraries.
23 Beeson, "The Autobiography of *Lizzie Borden*," 27.
24 Plant, *The Pink Triangle*, 1.
25 Ibid., 4.

Plant returned to Germany in the 1950s, at which time he was simultaneously conducting research relating to *Lizzie Borden* and to his study of homosexual persecution:

> As I sat down in the compartment of the Basel-Frankfurt express, it suddenly struck me that on the same track more than twenty years ago I had hurried away from Frankfurt to Basel. Now the train seemed to be welcoming me back as it clicked and clacked through southern Germany: "Lucky you. You came through. Lucky you ..." I had become an American, and nothing in a Frankfurt reborn or revisited could frighten me or shake me, I thought.
>
> I was wrong.[26]

It would seem that as Plant worked on *Lizzie* along with *The Pink Triangle*, he sought to come to terms with the trauma he continued to endure with the Holocaust persistently in his consciousness. As an American vessel through which to filter his European past and experience, moreover, Plant's *Lizzie* may be understood as a representation of Plant's struggle to "become an American" and to leave his past and his guilt behind.

Theories of survivor guilt began to proliferate in the US in the 1960s (around the time when Plant's mental health was deteriorating).[27] As historian Ruth Leys summarizes, Freudian psychologists at this time tended to gravitate toward two basic psychoanalytic assumptions: "that survivors suffered from guilt for outliving dead relatives, friends, and fellow prisoners, and that under extremity they tended to identify with their tormentors (which is why, according to the Freudian theory of the superego, they felt guilty)."[28] Such assumptions, however, were controversial. Many people objected on principle to the theory of survivor guilt because it shifted the blame from the real culprits onto victims themselves. According to Lawrence L. Langer, a scholar of Holocaust literature, Auschwitz survivor Primo Levi "noted an increasing interest in the conduct of the victims and a growing

---

26   Ibid., 197–198.

27   Survivor guilt was sometimes referred to as "concentration camp syndrome" during the 1960s, connecting the theory's emergence directly to the Holocaust and to efforts to come to terms with it. Survivor guilt has also been discussed in terms of the AIDS epidemic in the US. See Odets, *In the Shadow of the Epidemic*, 93–98. Since the early 2000s, the term "survivor guilt" has largely been considered under the umbrella of post-traumatic stress disorder (PTSD).

28   Leys, *From Guilt to Shame*, 61. Auschwitz survivor Primo Levi saw survivor guilt somewhat differently. As he put it, "privileged prisoners were a minority within the Lager population, nevertheless they represent a potent majority among survivors," for survival often "required a privilege—large or small, granted or conquered, astute or violent, licit or illicit—whatever it took to lift oneself above the norm." See *The Drowned and the Saved*, 40–41.

indifference to the behavior of the killers" as the years passed after World War II.[29] Langer theorized that Levi decided to write his collection of essays *The Drowned and the Saved* in 1986, a full "forty years after the collapse of Auschwitz," because "some of the gloomiest moments" in *Survival in Auschwitz* "might be misread as an effort to blame the victims."[30] In addition, as Leys points out, some people "objected that the notion of survivor guilt was simply a projection onto the survivor of American psychoanalysts' own feelings of guilt for having lived through the war in the safety of the United States."[31] While Leys notes that "this seems much too simplistic," this formulation of survivor guilt speaks closest to Plant's experience.[32] Strictly speaking, Plant *escaped* Nazi persecution, living in relative safety and comfort, first in Basel and later in New York. Plant may have struggled so acutely with the legacy of the Holocaust because he felt guilty for not having been forced to survive it, and he made it his life's work to illuminate more fully the atrocities committed by the Third Reich, as evinced by *The Dragon in the Forest* and *The Pink Triangle*.

Plant himself never wrote explicitly about any connection between his past and *Lizzie Borden*, but he apparently did not object to Beeson's writing about it. When Beeson sent a copy of his 1986 article for *The Opera Quarterly* to Plant, seeking the writer's feedback prior to publication, Plant's primary suggestion was that Beeson not downplay his role as the original librettist.[33] He voiced no objection to Beeson's discussion of his family's history and its relevance to *Lizzie Borden*.

Jack Beeson and Kenward Elmslie's Lizzie Borden

The relationship between Plant's lived experience and his attachment to Lizzie Borden is difficult to locate within the opera's music, libretto, staging, or reception, and for the remainder of this chapter, I examine the more visible gender and familial politics at play. Beeson (1921–2010) and Elmslie (1929–2022) amplified these politics. Both men were initially skeptical about the idea of writing an opera about Lizzie Borden, but eventually, each gravitated toward a particular gendered stereotype, Beeson toward the

---

29 Langer, *Preempting the Holocaust*, 34.
30 Ibid., 33–34.
31 Leys, *From Guilt to Shame*, 24.
32 Ibid.
33 Letter, Plant to Beeson, April 9, 1968, Richard Plant Papers (Box 1, Folder 22).

sexually frustrated spinster and Elmslie toward the evil stepmother.[34] Beeson admitted that he was enticed by Plant's description of "the Borden family in its Fall River setting as a distillation of the main currents of New England history," featuring Mr. Borden as "the latter-day version of the hanging judge of Salem" and Lizzie as "the passionate, repressed, upper-class unemployable Victorian spinster."[35] Beeson grew intent on the idea of writing "a psychologically oriented opera of characterization," for as he admitted, he sought not to write "an opera about murders, but about why a woman (largely of our making) would kill."[36]

By 1954, the year Plant approached Beeson, Beeson was well acquainted with some of the new possibilities for opera in the US. Born and raised in Muncie, Indiana, he had attended the Eastman School of Music in Rochester, New York, where he studied composition with Bernard Rogers and Howard Hanson.[37] During his childhood, Beeson had been fascinated with opera, mainly, as he recalled in a 1994 interview with Leonard Lehrman, by listening to the Met's weekly radio broadcasts.[38] But at Eastman, he did not feel encouraged to pursue opera. As he recalled in his 2008 memoir, Hanson was "terribly upset" by the "cool reception" his opera *Merry Mount* received at its 1934 premiere at the Met and "turned against the medium in his school."[39]

When Beeson moved to New York City in 1944, Douglas Moore took him under his wing, and Beeson became reacquainted with opera by way of Moore and Columbia University. In 1945, he served as a vocal coach and assistant conductor for Columbia's premiere of Normand Lockwood's opera *The Scarecrow*.[40] That same year he began teaching courses at the

---

34   Beeson, "The Autobiography of *Lizzie Borden*," 15.
35   Ibid. Plant did indeed emphasize Lizzie Borden's status as a spinster. In 1965, he told Theodore Strongin of the *New York Times* that one of the reasons he turned Lizzie into the older sister was to bring "closer the specter of spinsterhood." See Strongin, "The Lizzie Borden Case."
36   Beeson, "The Autobiography of *Lizzie Borden*," 16, 19.
37   Beeson earned his BM in 1942 and MM in 1943 at Eastman.
38   See Lehrman, "An Interview with Jack Beeson," 17.
39   Beeson, *How Operas Are Created by Composers and Librettists*, 53. Howard Hanson was director of the Eastman School of Music from 1924 until 1964. As Beeson recalled, during the 1920s and 1930s, Hanson had a keen interest in American opera, both at Eastman and beyond, yet his experience with *Merry Mount* dampened his enthusiasm. The Met premiered *Merry Mount* on February 10, 1934. Music critics were hard on the opera, and after the 1934 season, the Met dropped *Merry Mount* from its repertory.
40   See program, *The Scarecrow*, May 9–12, 1945, Columbia Theater Associates, 1893–1958 (Box 1), University Archives, Rare Book & Manuscript Library,

university.[41] In 1947, he served as assistant conductor, coach, and rehearsal pianist for Columbia's premiere of Virgil Thomson and Gertrude Stein's *The Mother of Us All*, and in 1950, he completed his first opera, *Jonah*.[42]

As Beeson recalled in 1986, Elmslie initially found Lizzie to be "something of a drip," but he loved Lizzie's stepmother Abbie.[43] Elmslie had a stepmother himself, and he delighted in amplifying Abbie's cruelty, turning her into something of a caricature of the evil stepmother.[44] In fact, Beeson and Elmslie molded both Lizzie's father and stepmother into despicable people, *almost* deserving of their ends and certainly deserving of the subtitle, "A Family Portrait in Three Acts," that they chose for the opera.

By 1965, the year of *Lizzie Borden*'s NYCO premiere, eleven years had passed since Plant and Beeson had begun the project, and more than seventy years had passed since the date of the Borden murders. Over the course of those years, perspectives on Lizzie Borden had changed. Lizzie's status as a "spinster" is a crucial case in point. Born and raised into a wealthy family in Fall River, Massachusetts, Lizzie was the second daughter of Andrew Jackson Borden and Sarah Anthony (Morse) Borden. In 1863, Sarah Borden died, and three years later, Andrew married Abby Durfee Gray. In 1892, both Lizzie and her older sister Emma (1851–1927) were still unmarried and continued to live in their father's house on 92 Second Street. The sisters were considered spinsters, and during Lizzie's trial, they were often described as such, yet at the time, the term "spinster" did not necessarily

---

Columbia University Libraries.

41   Beeson was appointed MacDowell Professor of Music at Columbia in 1967, five years after Moore's retirement from the position and two years after *Lizzie Borden*'s premiere.

42   See program, *The Mother of Us All*, May 12–15, 1947, Columbia Theater Associates, 1893–1958 (Box 1). *Jonah* is an adaptation of Paul Goodman's 1945 play by the same title. On *The Mother of Us All*, see Hershberger, "Feminist Revisions."

43   Beeson, "The Autobiography of *Lizzie Borden*," 28.

44   The grandson of Joseph Pulitzer, Kenward Elmslie earned his BA in literature from Harvard University in 1950. Upon graduation, he spent two years in Cleveland before moving to New York City and into the apartment of John Latouche. As Elmslie later recalled to Winston Leyland, in the early 1950s, he was primarily interested in writing a musical for Broadway. He greatly admired Latouche's work as a lyricist, describing Latouche as his "culture hero." See "Winston Leyland Interviews Kenward Elmslie" in Leyland, *Gay Sunshine Interviews*, vol. 2, 98–100. Latouche quickly became more than a mentor to Elmslie. The men engaged in a relationship until Latouche's sudden death in 1956. Latouche died of a heart attack at age forty-one. On Latouche's life, work, and legacy, see Pollack, *The Ballad of John Latouche*.

carry a negative connotation. As historian Carroll Smith-Rosenberg explains, the late nineteenth century marked the dawn of "the single, highly educated, economically autonomous New Woman."[45] Zsuzsa Berend writes similarly that New England spinsters could be regarded "as champions of uncompromising morality."[46] Indeed, prior to August 1892, Lizzie was a respected and engaged citizen of Fall River. Beeson's attraction to her in the 1950s as a "repressed, upper-class unemployable Victorian spinster" was heavily influenced by the contemporary culture surrounding marriage.[47]

Yet for all her apparent success and status as a single woman, Lizzie may have been profoundly unhappy in the 1890s. Numerous accounts suggest that life inside the Borden household was unpleasant. For example, when the family's maid testified at Lizzie's trial, she suggested that Lizzie and Emma scarcely spoke to their parents, explaining that Lizzie and Emma often ate their meals separately.[48] During Lizzie's inquest testimony, Lizzie's supposed animosity toward her stepmother revealed itself when she refused to refer to Abby Borden as her "mother."[49] Many people thus concluded that a deep-seated resentment caused Lizzie to snap on that sweltering morning in August, resulting in her murdering her stepmother and then, by necessity, her father.[50] This is certainly the explanation advanced by "Lizzie Borden Took an Axe," the popular schoolyard rhyme that Beeson, Plant, and Elmslie invoked at the conclusion of their opera.

Several scholars have theorized that Lizzie Borden was acquitted only because the evidence against her was circumstantial and because no one wanted to admit that a woman of her race and class could do such a thing. As historian Joseph A. Conforti argued, "a jury composed of traditional

---

45 Smith-Rosenberg, *Disorderly Conduct*, 245. See also Matthews, *The Rise of the New Woman*.

46 Berend, "'The Best or None!,'" 936.

47 Beeson, "The Autobiography of *Lizzie Borden*," 15.

48 See Bridget Sullivan's testimony in Pearson, *Trial of Lizzie Borden*, 139–140.

49 See "Inquest Testimony of Miss Lizzie Borden" in ibid., 397.

50 Other commentators believe that the murders were premeditated, suggesting, for example, that Lizzie may have been after her father's money and the role that money would play in furthering her social standing. Andrew Borden was a successful businessman. He owned stock in Fall River's mills and banks, as well as several rental properties and farms. Yet despite having amassed a small fortune, he was known to be quite stingy. The Borden house had none of the modern conveniences of its day and was located near the mill district. Whereas other prosperous White Anglo-Saxon Protestant families lived up on the hill, away from the mills and away from the primarily Portuguese and Irish immigrants who toiled in them, the Borden family, because of Andrew Borden's miserly insistence, lived among them.

Yankee men, who clung to the pities of virtuous, delicate womanhood, were not likely to convict Lizzie."[51] Similarly, after completing the ballet *Fall River Legend* (1948), an important precursor to *Lizzie Borden*, the dancer and choreographer Agnes de Mille explained how the jurors "couldn't bring themselves to think of this lady, 'the equal of your wife and mine,' as an agent of that wild and brutal butchery." "Had Lizzie been of another class or race, and penniless," de Mille continued, "I believe she must have hanged."[52] Historian Lisa Duggan asserts that while Lizzie's trial represented a "setback for the reputation of the white home and its daughters," highlighting "the contested place and possibly dangerous desires of unmarried white women," it "resolved itself in favor of bourgeois domesticity."[53] When Lizzie returned to Fall River following her acquittal, however, she was largely ostracized by the town's White Anglo-Saxon Protestant community. Lizzie's peers, despite refusing to disrupt the status quo by convicting a member of their class, truly believed her guilty, leaving those who came later to grapple with the question of why she did it.[54]

51 Conforti, *Lizzie Borden on Trial*, 118.
52 De Mille, *Lizzie Borden*, 76.
53 Duggan, *Sapphic Slashers*, 123.
54 Since 1892, a variety of people have returned to the Borden murders, hoping to solve the crimes once and for all, either by explaining Lizzie's motivation or by proposing a different killer. In 1939, the English novelist Marie Belloc Lowndes proposed that Lizzie had killed her parents after her stepmother discovered that she was having an illicit affair with a man she had met in Europe. See *Lizzie Borden: A Study in Conjecture*. As she explained in her preface, Lowndes simply did not believe that dissatisfied spinster daughters were likely to kill their fathers. Thus she suggested that passion must have "played a predominant part in the tragedy," and she set out to offer "a credible solution" or explanation for the "incredible" crime (p. vii). Somewhat similarly, in 1984, the American crime novelist Evan Hunter imagined that Lizzie was a lesbian who killed her parents after her stepmother discovered her relationship with the family maid. See *Lizzie*. Hunter asserted that although *Lizzie* was "a work of fiction, much of it is rooted firmly in fact" (p. 427). He wavered in discussing his approach to Lizzie's sexuality: "While not an entirely unsupported conjecture, Lizzie Borden's lesbianism should also be taken as part of the fiction" (p. 428). In 1961, Edward Radin argued that the maid and not Lizzie had committed the murders. See *Lizzie Borden: The Untold Story*. Six years later, Victoria Lincoln posited that Lizzie killed her parents in an epileptic fit. See *A Private Disgrace*.

Reconstructing *Lizzie Borden*

Lizzie Borden begins in the living room of Andrew Borden's "dark, imposing Victorian house" in Fall River.[55] Lizzie appears rehearsing a small children's choir. The Reverend Harrington arrives and thanks Lizzie for her devotion to the children and to the church. As the children and the Reverend leave, Andrew enters, and he and Lizzie argue when Lizzie asks him for money to buy a dress. Lizzie complains that her stepmother Abbie "wears a new gown made by the best dressmaker in the town."[56] Andrew ignores this comment and launches into his "credo," extolling the merits of all his hard work. In the second scene, Lizzie and her younger sister Margret lament their imprisonment in their father's house. Then Lizzie tells Margret that her suitor, a sea captain named Jason MacFarlane, is coming that evening to ask Andrew for Margret's hand in marriage.

Act II also begins in the living room, but this time, Abbie is the center of attention. She sits at a harmonium, accompanying herself as she sings a parlor song. Abbie then convinces Andrew that he should buy her a grand piano in honor of their upcoming wedding anniversary. When she complains about the reminders of Andrew's first wife, Evangeline—including Evangeline's children, Lizzie and Margret, and her furnishings—Andrew concedes that he will remove Evangeline's portrait from the living room and that together, they will purchase "new pictures to embellish the walls."[57]

Lizzie and Margret join their parents in the living room, and Abbie boasts about the changes she and Andrew are planning. Lizzie becomes visibly angry and lashes out at Abbie, but their quarrel is interrupted by the ringing of the doorbell. It is the Reverend Harrington, accompanied by Captain MacFarlane, who has come to ask for Margret's hand in marriage. Andrew wickedly responds that he will give the captain his consent to marry not Margret, but Lizzie. He then turns on Lizzie, mocking her for her age and lack of a suitor. "You should have been born a man: then you could *take* what you want," he snarls.[58] The captain leaves, and Lizzie and her father enact what appears to be a well-established ritual in which Andrew berates Lizzie physically and verbally, and she absorbs and internalizes his abuse. Act II concludes with an extended scene for Lizzie alone in the darkened living room. Beeson and Plant referred to this scene, in which Lizzie first begins to lose her ability to cope with her situation, as Lizzie's "mad scene."

---

55   See stage directions in Beeson, Elmslie, and Plant, *Lizzie Borden*, 4. According to the score, the setting is "Fall River, Massachusetts in the Eighties."
56   Ibid., 35–36.
57   Ibid., 92.
58   Ibid., 150–151. Italics in score.

In Act III, Captain MacFarlane returns to the Borden house to rescue Margret. As Lizzie faces the fact that she will be left alone with her father and stepmother, she slips into fantasy. She puts on her mother's wedding dress, intended for Margret, and imagines herself as a bride. She begins fantasizing about Captain MacFarlane and, as we are led to believe through the stage directions, masturbating.[59] Abbie catches Lizzie in the act and mocks her mercilessly. To make matters worse, she threatens to tell Andrew. Abbie goes up the stairs for her afternoon nap, and minutes later, Lizzie charges up after her, grabbing the scimitar (Beeson, Elmslie, and Plant's version of the hatchet) from the wall.[60] When Andrew comes home and calls for Abbie, he looks up the stairs and sees Lizzie, still in Evangeline's wedding dress. He rushes up the stairs and into the bedroom to find his wife; Lizzie follows him.

The opera concludes in the living room, several years after Lizzie's acquittal, with a scene that is strikingly similar to the opera's opening. Lizzie has taken her father's place in her father's house. She lives alone, hoarding her money, just like her father before her. As she counts her assets, a children's choir (composed of the same voices that she had dutifully conducted in Act I) jeers from off stage, singing the popular schoolyard rhyme:

> Lizzie Borden took an axe
> And gave her mother forty whacks.
> When she saw what she had done
> She gave her father forty-one.[61]

According to Beeson, Plant had "read all the extensive Lizzie Borden literature, as well as the trial testimony, newspaper accounts, and even a book on the Fall River Steamship Line."[62] In fact, Plant's personal papers reveal the lengths to which he had gone to engage in his research. A folder entitled "Lizzie Borden—Research Notes" contains Plant's drafts of aria texts and

---

59 Beeson later described "Lizzie's love scene aria" as "actually a kind of masturbatory scene." See "The Autobiography of *Lizzie Borden*," 33.
60 The scimitar, a short sword with a curved blade associated with Eastern countries, hangs on the wall of Abbie's "Turkish corner." During the 1880s and 1890s, Turkish corners were all the rage in the US. These were placed in nooks of Victorian homes, including stairwells, and included "exotic" furniture, pillows, textiles, knick-knacks, or weaponry like the scimitar, inspired by ideas about the "East." See Hinchman, *The Fairchild Books Dictionary of Interior Design*, 195.
61 Chaney, *New England Remembers Lizzie Borden*, 70–71. Chaney writes that "around the turn of the twentieth century, children started reciting an anonymous jingle that was popular even with President Teddy Roosevelt."
62 Beeson, "The Autobiography of *Lizzie Borden*," 18.

ideas for scenes, as well as musings on the relevance of Lizzie's membership in the Women's Christian Temperance Union, the history of Calvinism, Puritanism, Fall River and its shipping lines, and possible parallels between the Bordens' story and Greek tragedy. Plant took notes on Lizzie's trial, relying on Edmund Pearson's 1937 *Trial of Lizzie Borden*. He also had a copy of the uncorrected proofs of Edward D. Radin's 1961 book, *Lizzie Borden: The Untold Story*.[63] Plant was unconvinced, however, by Radin's theory that Bridget Sullivan, the Borden family maid, had committed the murders.[64]

Both Plant's and Beeson's personal papers include numerous drafts of the libretto for the opening scene of Act I, such that it is possible to partially reconstruct the evolution of the script. Plant's "first draft" of the libretto is undated and bears the title "The Prison," pointing quite explicitly to Lizzie's domestic captivity.[65] In this draft, Lizzie goes by the name Liza Barton and Margret by Maggie, and the Reverend Harrington refers to his church as St. James, rather than Old Harbor. The dramatic framework for the opera's opening scene, however, conforms completely to the final version. The scene begins with Liza conducting the children's choir. Then the Reverend Harrington arrives; he speaks to Liza about the sorry state of his church and thanks her for her efforts. When the children and the Reverend leave, Andrew enters. He and Liza argue about a new dress, and the scene concludes with Andrew's celebration of his Protestant work ethic, which Plant referred to as Andrew's "credo."

One of the most obvious differences between the opening scene in this draft and the opening scene in the final version of the opera concerns the opening hymn. In Plant's first draft, the children sing an exoticist hymn text of Plant's invention:

> Remember all the people
> Who live in far off lands
> In strange and lonely cities
> Or roam the desert sands
> Or farm the mountain pastures
> Or till the endless plains

---

63 Plant's copy of the uncorrected proofs of Radin's book may be found in the Richard Plant Papers (Box 16, Folder 1).

64 Plant mentioned *The Untold Story* to Haskel Frankel of the *Saturday Review*, and he described the criticism he received from Lizzie Borden buffs for omitting the housemaid Bridget from the opera's libretto. See Frankel, "Teaching in Triplicate." Radin wrote to Plant two days later, challenging him on his assertion that Radin had offered no motive for Bridget. See letter, Edward D. Radin to Professor Richard Plant, April 12, 1965, Jack Beeson Papers (Box 13, Folder 1).

65 See "The Prison, first draft," Richard Plant Papers (Box 7, Folder 1).

Where children wade through rice fields
And watch the camel trains[66]

Beeson later found an actual hymn text that he preferred for the opera's opening. In 1986, he recalled how he had "leafed through shelves of hymnbooks," searching for "the right text … free of copyright, characteristically a children's hymn, and shaped in such a manner that my musical setting would also fit the traditional doggerel ['Lizzie Borden took an axe'] with which we wished to *end* the opera."[67] Beeson finally found what he wanted to express the "'work for the night is coming' aspect of the Calvinist ethic" in the hymn "Toiling Early":

Toiling early in the morning,
Catching moments through the day,
Nothing small or lowly scorning,
While we work, and watch, and pray.[68]

Plant's papers include another undated copy of the opening scene. This one is titled "House of Darkness: The Prison, revised & shortened ed. 2."[69] By this point, Plant had changed Liza to Lizzie, Maggie to Margret, and St. James to Old Harbor Church. He had not, however, updated the opening hymn. That change occurred in "The Prison, revised & shortened, ed. 3," hand-dated 1959.[70] Thus together, Beeson and Plant completed the first half of the first act of *Lizzie Borden*. Both Plant's and Elmslie's papers include a bound copy of the piano-vocal score for the first act, as well as the beginning of the second act.[71] In the final, published version of the piano-vocal score, Beeson and Plant's second act became Scene 2 of Act I. Plant's copy of the partial score is inscribed by Beeson: "for Richard, from Jack:

---

66 Ibid.
67 Beeson, "The Autobiography of *Lizzie Borden*," 21.
68 See MacKellar and Converse, "Toiling Early (Christian Endeavor Hymn)." See also Beeson, "The Autobiography of *Lizzie Borden*," 21. A copy of the text for "Toiling Early in the Morning" appears in Plant's papers, its discovery attributed to the composer. See Richard Plant Papers (Box 7, Folder 1).
69 See "House of Darkness: The Prison, revised & shortened ed. 2," Richard Plant Papers (Box 7, Folder 1).
70 See "The Prison, revised & shortened, ed. 3," Richard Plant Papers (Box 7, Folder 1).
71 1961 piano-vocal score, Copy 3, Richard Plant Papers (Box 8). The 1961 piano-vocal score (Copy 5) also exists in Elmslie's papers. See the Kenward Elmslie Papers, Oversize Box FB-328-03, Special Collections, University of California, San Diego.

Twelfth Night, 1961," its date (January 6, 1961) indicating that Beeson and Plant completed this work prior to Elmslie's addition to the project.[72]

A comparison between this copy of the score and the published edition reveals that very little changed between these two versions of Act I, Scene 1.[73] At the same time, even the slightest changes to the libretto, many of which made the text more idiomatic and singable, tended to have the effect of reifying the characters, particularly Andrew.[74] For example, near the end of his credo, Andrew boasts about all his hard work and the wealth it has accumulated. In Plant and Beeson's 1961 score, Andrew sings: "The weak deceiver to failure doomed."[75] His line eventually became: "The weak shall never inherit the earth," adapting a well-known verse from Matthew's Gospel and turning it on its head.[76] This seemingly insignificant change, which required Beeson to make no adaptation to the music, presented Andrew in a decidedly negative light. Here was a man who did not simply mimic Biblical rhetoric; he actively intervened on the Bible, twisting its meaning. Beeson and Elmslie went on to make more extensive changes as well, often to condense the libretto. For example, in the 1961 piano-vocal score, Andrew interrupts himself in the middle of his credo, briefly recalling how his first wife gave all her money away to Reverend Harrington as she lay dying:

> When Evangeline was failing he cajoled and flattered,
> He beguiled her sick mind,
> Her put her against me
> She gave the church all she owned.[77]

When Beeson and Elmslie revised the libretto, they omitted Andrew's recollection, skipping ahead to the next phrase in his tirade:

> He deludes my daughters.
> He defrauds their minds.
> They waste my money.[78]

---

72 Plant's personal papers also include a copy of a 1962 letter to Plant, from Plant's lawyer Nathaniel L. Rock, explaining that Plant is to be credited with the scenario for the entire opera, as well as the libretto for Act I. See letter, Nathaniel L. Rock to Plant, October 19, 1962, Richard Plant Papers (Box 1, Folder 22). Beeson and Elmslie were sent copies of this letter.

73 There are occasional changes to notes, stage directions, and text, but generally, such changes are small.

74 In 1965, Plant stated that Elmslie "sharpened my characters and made the opera more American." See press release, The City College of New York, February 21, 1965, Richard Plant Papers (Box 7, Folder 5).

75 1961 piano-vocal score, 46.

76 Beeson, Elmslie, and Plant, *Lizzie Borden*, 42.

77 1961 piano-vocal score, 44–45.

78 Beeson, Elmslie, and Plant, *Lizzie Borden*, 41–42.

By cutting Andrew's recollection, which served to explain Andrew's anger with Reverend Harrington and the church, Beeson and Elmslie helped to ensure that from the opera's outset, Andrew would never elicit a sympathetic response from the audience.

In addition to the complete first scene of the opera, Elmslie inherited a few bits of material for later scenes. Plant, for example, had already begun to work on the second scene of Act I (Margret and Lizzie's "garden" duet), part of which was included in Beeson and Plant's 1961 piano-vocal score. Plant had also started drafting Abbie's parlor song, which ultimately served as the opening to Act II, as well as Lizzie's mad scene for the end of Act II. It was Abbie's song that apparently convinced Elmslie it was worth becoming involved in the *Lizzie Borden* project. Beeson noted that when he passed this material on to Elmslie, the poet was inspired:

> [Ken] says that at first he was disinclined to get involved ... But he says that R.'s idea of a "Bird Song" has won him over; he's begun filling it in—"like a magpie" he'll be able to use some of the leftovers from R.'s nest—and now he's hooked. He's falling in love with Abbie, he says. (Coincidence, *he* has a stepmother, too, his mother—a Joseph Pulitzer daughter—having died when he was quite young.)[79]

Elmslie and Beeson ultimately molded Abbie into a caricature of both the evil stepmother and the amateur soprano.

In the published piano-vocal score, as the prelude to Act II subsides, a gentle, arpeggiated accompaniment takes over (Ex. 3.1). Abbie appears seated in the living room, accompanying herself at the harmonium as she sings Beeson's imitation of a nineteenth-century parlor song. Unlike the "Willow Song" in *The Ballad of Baby Doe*, the "Bird Song" in *Lizzie Borden* is decidedly insincere. Its purpose is to make a mockery of Abbie's musical ambition and highlight Abbie's scheming nature.

The "Bird Song" begins innocently enough as Abbie sings the first binary-form verse without ornamentation. The A section opens in a lyrical A major, its melody unfolding mainly in intervals of seconds and thirds and concluding with a series of rising notes on a slight diminuendo and ritardando, above a $C\sharp^7$ chord. The B section begins in a more animated F-sharp major, characterized by an acceleration in tempo and a less conjunct melodic line. At the end of the B section, the key of A major returns, and following a series of rising notes on a diminuendo and ritardando (an allusion to the figure at the end of the A section), Abbie concludes:

> O I'd wing to you swiftly
> My springtime love.[80]

---

79   Beeson, "The Autobiography of *Lizzie Borden*," 28.
80   Beeson, Elmslie, and Plant, *Lizzie Borden*, 79.

Example 3.1. Beeson, Plant, and Elmslie, *Lizzie Borden*, mm. 798–819.

—(*continued*)

Example 3.1—*concluded*

As Abbie finishes the first verse, Andrew comes down the stairs, and although according to the stage directions, "Abbie pretends not to notice him," she launches enthusiastically into the song's second verse, now singing about a nightingale rather than a swallow and beginning to put on a bit of a show.[81] Beeson, for example, adds an octave leap at the beginning of the third phrase, thus allowing Abbie to highlight her imagined vocal prowess (Ex. 3.2). When Abbie reaches the end of the second verse, however, she finds that she cannot finish it. As she sings the final phrase, she omits the final word ("love"), because, as indicated in the stage directions, "the keys [on the harmonium] will not sound."[82] She tries to make the notes sound again. Finally, she becomes "quite irritated and punches out the faulty keys," exclaiming:

I can't go on!
This key doesn't work,
And this key, and this key![83]

Abbie and Andrew then argue about the harmonium, about Evangeline, and about Lizzie and Margret. When Abbie threatens to retreat to the servant's quarters and withhold sex, Andrew relents. He agrees to buy Abbie a piano, as well as new furnishings for the house. Satisfied, Abbie returns to her song. She sings the second verse again, a little faster now, and going wild with embellishments, she adds running sixteenth notes and a chromatic descent spanning more than an octave (Ex. 3.3).

As Lizzie and Margret enter the living room, Abbie begins her third and final verse, adding still more embellishments. In the production of the opera that was telecast in 1967, Brenda Lewis steps into the frame, a stony-faced Lizzie, and Margret, played by soprano Anne Elgar, joins her, looking weary and exasperated.[84] Before Abbie finishes her song, she turns to Andrew, Lizzie, and Margret, and as indicated in the stage directions, "She pantomimes: the diva, bowing elegantly; then the audience; then the diva accepting adulation; then the audience again. Her daughters ignore her."[85] Margret buries her head in her book, and Lizzie, her animosity toward her stepmother palpable, busies herself with an embroidery project. Only Andrew (Herbert Beattie) claps enthusiastically. Played by soprano Ellen Faull, Abbie styles herself an obnoxious amateur diva, her supposed talent having completely gone to her head.

---

81 Ibid.
82 Ibid., 82.
83 Ibid.
84 See Beeson, Elmslie, and Plant, *Lizzie Borden*, directed by Kirk Browning.
85 Beeson, Elmslie, and Plant, *Lizzie Borden*, 98.

Example 3.2. Beeson, Plant, and Elmslie, *Lizzie Borden*, mm. 822–831.

Example 3.3. Beeson, Plant, and Elmslie, *Lizzie Borden*, mm. 1031–1042.

Later in Act II, Beeson and Elmslie established more fully the antagonism between Lizzie and Andrew. Most notably, Andrew abuses Lizzie in front of Captain MacFarlane, berating her and shaking her like a ragdoll. After the captain leaves, Andrew continues to bully his eldest daughter. According to the stage directions: "[Andrew's] glance falls on Lizzie, collapsed near the door to her room. He draws strength from her weakness...strides toward her, commandingly and she cringes, kneeling, head bowed...almost as though repeating yet again a well-remembered ritual."[86] Lizzie asks: "What am I forbidden now?"[87] Andrew answers: "To see the preacher."[88] As the scene progresses, Andrew forbids Lizzie from any contact with the outside world. When he goes up the stairs to join Abbie (who has gone to bed), Lizzie continues the abusive "ritual" she has just endured in her head, and her imprisonment—both physical and psychological—becomes increasingly apparent. The scene concludes with Lizzie essentially giving up her sense of self. In the 1967 telecast, Lewis wrapped herself up in the rug from the living-room floor, covering herself almost entirely, as she made her final switch from the first-person to the third-person perspective:

I'll breathe water, swallow earth.
Lizzie has a body.
Lizzie has a head.
Lizzie's cut to pieces.
Lizzie must be dead.[89]

Mezzo-soprano Phyllis Pancella (b. 1963) characterized this tour de force mad scene as "very rangy," replete with coloratura passages that require the singer to switch back and forth between head and chest voice.[90] By the end of the scene, the audience should pity Lizzie. Indeed, John W. Freeman contextualized the Glimmerglass Opera's 1996 revival of *Lizzie Borden* (which featured

---

86   Ibid., 155.
87   Ibid.
88   Ibid.
89   Ibid., 178. See also Beeson, Elmslie, and Plant, *Lizzie Borden*, directed by Kirk Browning.
90   Phyllis Pancella, in conversation with Beverly Sills, Rhoda Levine, and Lauren Flanigan, broadcast during the intermission of the NYCO's performance of *Lizzie Borden* on March 24, 1999. Pancella played the role of Lizzie in this performance. In an informal conversation with me in Tallahassee, Florida, on May 22, 2015, Pancella noted that another of the difficulties of Lizzie's mad scene is that it is so lonely. Pancella recalled that when she played Lizzie in the 1990s, she did so on a stark, minimalist set and that it was challenging to pull off the mad scene without anyone else or anything on stage.

Pancella in the title role) by pointing to the opera's connection to "the timely subject of domestic abuse," emphasized most acutely in this scene.[91]

Ultimately, however, it is not Andrew's abuse but Abbie's plot to throw Lizzie out of the house that causes Lizzie to resort to violence. In Act III, Abbie catches Lizzie masturbating, clothed in her mother's wedding dress and imagining Captain MacFarlane's hands "mov[ing] like warm clouds" on her body.[92] As Brenda Lewis pointed out during an interview with me, Abbie's threat was significant, for Abbie had caught Lizzie doing the unmentionable, certainly in terms of the year 1892, and something that was daring even in the year of the opera's premiere.[93] If Abbie were to tell Andrew what she had seen Lizzie doing, Lizzie would no longer be welcome in his house. In this way, Beeson and Elmslie argued that Lizzie was not merely giving Abbie what she deserved but rather, if Lizzie wanted to remain in her father's house—and if she wanted to claim that house as her own—she had no choice but to murder Abbie.

On October 23, 1962, Plant wrote a letter to Elmslie, congratulating him for making "the characters more vivid."[94] He described Abbie as "a real fat bitch, with more brain than I had given her—which is all the better: my original plan was to have the audience identify with Lizzie's loathing."[95] Plant's description of Abbie is both telling and troubling. While the Act III scene between Lizzie and Abbie (which Beeson, Plant, and Elmslie referred to as the "Bitch Scene"), coupled with the "forbidden" ritual between Lizzie and Andrew in Act II, helps to shape Lizzie as a victim of domestic violence and patriarchal oppression, Plant's employment of a gender slur in reference to Abbie also implicates him in a contemporary system of patriarchal oppression.[96]

---

91   Freeman, *The Metropolitan Opera*, 21.
92   Beeson, Elmslie, and Plant, *Lizzie Borden*, 213. According to the stage directions, "when [Abbie] catches a glimpse of Lizzie, she moves more decisively toward the open door into the girls' room; when she sees and hears clearly what Lizzie is doing, she stops short, on the threshold …" (p. 215). In the 1967 telecast of the opera, Lizzie makes her way over to the bed as she sings.
93   Brenda Lewis, interview with the author, Westport, CT, March 7, 2016.
94   Letter, Plant to Elmslie, October 23, 1962, Jack Beeson Papers (Box 13, Folder 1).
95   Ibid.
96   Plant was not alone in using the term "bitch," even if his employment of it was the most offensive. It seems that collectively, Beeson, Plant, and Elmslie referred to Lizzie and Abbie's scene in Act III, Scene 1 as the "bitch scene." See Beeson, "The Autobiography of *Lizzie Borden*," 33.

Revealing Anxieties about Women and Gender

In 1968, three years after *Lizzie*'s premiere, feminist attorney Jo Freeman penned "The BITCH Manifesto," seeking to reclaim that slur. According to Freeman:

> A Bitch takes shit from no one. You may not like her, but you cannot ignore her ... [Bitches] have loud voices and often use them ... Bitches seek their identity strictly thru themselves and what they do. They are subjects, not objects ... Often they do dominate other people when roles are not available to them which more creatively sublimate their energies and utilize their capabilities. More often they are accused of domineering when doing what would be considered natural by a man.[97]

Whereas Plant used the term "bitch" to refer to Abbie, Freeman's reclamation of the term maps onto Lizzie, who eventually "takes shit from no one" and "dominate[s] other people when roles are not available to [her]." In a publicity performance and event prior to the NYCO's 1999 production of *Lizzie Borden*, director Rhoda Levine explained that this opera was "about what happens in a world where people cannot listen to the needs of others," noting that Lizzie in particular "is left in a world" where no one hears her needs, acknowledges them, or offers help.[98] Levine suggested that "if one is not listened to ... you often commit violence, because it's the only way you can in fact express yourself."[99] Lizzie ultimately expresses herself, perhaps not only by committing violence, but by being a "bitch" in the terms Freeman would later outline. I was initially tempted to read the opera as a process of her transformation to this identity; as I realized, however, Beeson, Plant, and Elmslie take Lizzie's transformation a step too far.

Lizzie Borden contains occasional references—musical and textual—to Lizzie's gender and its limitations. Earlier I noted that in Act II, Andrew tells Lizzie: "You should have been born a man: then you could *take* what

---

97   Freeman, "The BITCH Manifesto." As Freeman explains on her website, "this paper was first published in *Notes from the Second Year*, ed. Shulamith Firestone and Anne Koedt, 1970. It was later reprinted as a pamphlet by KNOW, Inc., and reprinted in several books."
98   Rhoda Levine, speaking to moderator during a "Works & Process" performance series devoted to the NYCO's 1999 production of *Lizzie Borden*. This event took place at the Solomon R. Guggenheim Museum, New York, New York, on February 21, 1999. See *Lizzie Borden: New Visions, Works & Process at the Guggenheim*, produced by Mary Sharp Cronson, DVD, Performing Arts Research Collections—Dance, New York Public Library, New York, NY.
99   Ibid.

you want."[100] Musically, Lizzie seems to struggle with this predicament, particularly in the moments when she sings her father's music and performs the "wrong" gender. During the argument between Lizzie and Andrew in Act I, Scene 1 (over Lizzie's desire to purchase a store-bought dress), Andrew bursts out:

> Make it do,
> Wear it out;
> Use it up or do without![101]

This becomes rather like a musical and verbal mantra, and Andrew repeats the injunction a few moments later, beginning a half step higher than before. Within the scene, Andrew's mantra is isolated both melodically and textually. The first measure is characterized by a descending half step, followed by a descending octave, a distinct melodic motion that catches the ear (Exx. 3.4 and 3.5).

The melodic distinction of Andrew's mantra is important because when Lizzie sings a bit of Andrew's melody in the following scene, it is almost immediately recognizable. As Margret worries about what will happen when Captain MacFarlane approaches her father, she explains:

> I'm afraid;
> Father will mock him, and hurt him:
> He will *not* listen to him![102]

Lizzie tries to reassure her younger sister, who remains unconvinced, responding:

> What if they quarrel and fight.
> Jason will leave.[103]

At this, Lizzie bursts out:

> Let them quarrel!
> Let them fight![104]

Melodically, her injunction recalls the first two lines of Andrew's mantra. At Beeson's indication of "pushing forward," Lizzie begins by descending by half step and then by major seventh (thus an octave away from her opening

---

100 Beeson, Elmslie, and Plant, *Lizzie Borden*, 150–151. Italics in score.
101 Ibid., 34–35.
102 Ibid., 58. Italics in score.
103 Ibid., 59.
104 Ibid. Later, in Act II, Andrew sings a similar line to exactly the same melody: "Let them listen! Let them wait!" See Beeson, Elmslie, and Plant, *Lizzie Borden*, 107.

Example 3.4. Beeson, Plant, and Elmslie, *Lizzie Borden*, mm. 309–312.

Example 3.5. Beeson, Plant, and Elmslie, *Lizzie Borden*, mm. 333–336.

pitch). Lizzie's second phrase—ascending by half step and then by a minor seventh—is identical to her father's second phrase (Ex. 3.6). Margret begs Lizzie to back off, and Lizzie begins to lecture Margret, returning to her (father's) mantra. This time, as in Andrew's first iteration, the mantra is set off from the preceding music by Beeson's indications of *più pesante* and *fortissimo* (Ex. 3.7). Thus Lizzie begins her transformation, taking over her father's music. As soprano Lauren Flanigan (b. 1958) noted in 1999, the audience knows that Lizzie is changing because "we hear it in her voice."[105]

Another significant transformation for Lizzie occurs through the word "forbidden." After the Act II ritual between Andrew and Lizzie, during which Andrew forbids Lizzie from seeing the preacher, the children's choir, and Captain MacFarlane, Lizzie continues the ritual in her head. Andrew heads up the stairs to join Abbie in their bedroom, and Lizzie continues to ask:

> What am I forbidden?
> What else am I forbidden?
> What else, what else, what else?[106]

The forbidden ritual comes back to haunt Lizzie and her parents later in the opera. When Abbie catches Lizzie masturbating in Act III, Lizzie is incredulous:

> Forbidden
> You have no right…
> Our room is forbidden to you.[107]

Abbie's response is extremely telling:

> Forbidden this, forbidden that!
> Point A, Point B!
> Can't ever tell your voices apart
> When you and Andrew have a set to.
> God should have made *you* the banker.[108]

Thus Abbie realizes the extent to which Andrew and Lizzie have come to resemble each other.

A little later in Act III, Lizzie charges up the stairs to murder Abbie. When Andrew comes home and calls up the stairs for his wife, Lizzie appears

---

105 Lauren Flanigan, in conversation with Beverly Sills, Rhoda Levine, and Phyllis Pancella, broadcast during the intermission of the NYCO's performance of *Lizzie Borden* on March 24, 1999. Flanigan played the role of Abbie in this performance.
106 Beeson, Elmslie, and Plant, *Lizzie Borden*, 159.
107 Ibid., 216–217.
108 Ibid., 217–218. Italics in score.

Example 3.6. Beeson, Plant, and Elmslie, *Lizzie Borden*, mm. 561–562.

Example 3.7. Beeson, Plant, and Elmslie, *Lizzie Borden*, mm. 576–580.

instead. Seeing the blood on Lizzie's dress, Andrew begins to cry out Abbie's name. Lizzie responds ferociously:

> Abbie is forbidden!
> Must not see her ever again![109]

Here, Lizzie's melody recalls the very melody her father sang to her during their Act II ritual. This time, however, Lizzie does the forbidding; Andrew is no longer the one in charge, musically or physically (Exx. 3.8 and 3.9).

The enormity of Lizzie's transformation becomes clear in the final scene of the opera. This scene opens with Lizzie singing in a detached, emotionless recitative as she counts "up the columns and add[s] up the numbers," just like her father in Act I (Exx. 3.10 and 3.11).[110] As Beeson noted in 1999,

---

109 Ibid., 271.
110 Ibid., 276–277.

Example 3.8. Beeson, Plant, and Elmslie, *Lizzie Borden*, mm. 1731–1733.

Example 3.9. Beeson, Plant, and Elmslie, *Lizzie Borden*, mm. 1541–1542, mm. 1546–1547.

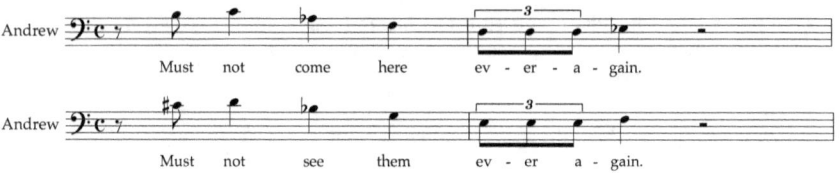

Example 3.10. Beeson, Plant, and Elmslie, *Lizzie Borden*, mm. 265–268.

Example 3.11. Beeson, Plant, and Elmslie, *Lizzie Borden*, mm. 1817–1819.

Lizzie is now the "spitting image" of her father.[111] At first glance, *Lizzie Borden* looks like a progressive opera. It is a work that seemingly encourages its heroine to smash the patriarchy once and for all, to be a "bitch" and be proud of it. Yet after her Act II mad scene, Lizzie simply remolds herself in the shape of her authoritarian father. At its core, *Lizzie Borden* may be a work that recasts and then imprisons its heroine.

---

111 Beeson, speaking at the "Works & Process" performance series devoted to the NYCO's production of *Lizzie*. See *Lizzie Borden: New Visions*.

The *Lizzie Borden* Mystique

By the 1960s, the men behind *Lizzie Borden* were thoroughly fascinated with the question of why a woman might commit murder. It is likely no coincidence that they concerned themselves with this question at the very moment when many women in the US were entertaining the question of feminine discontent from another angle. Just two years before *Lizzie Borden*'s premiere, Betty Friedan published her landmark manifesto *The Feminine Mystique*. Friedan's primary purpose was to uncover and explicate the deeply rooted "problem that has no name" that plagued so many American women who wanted more than the very circumscribed roles of wife and mother.[112] Lizzie Borden, both as a real woman and as a fictional heroine, may have suffered from a version of the "problem that has no name" as well. She was supposed to be content inside the home; instead, she felt imprisoned.

With *The Feminine Mystique*, Friedan also challenged much of the supposedly psychological analysis of women that became popular in the US after World War II, yet to a certain extent, this was precisely the kind of analysis in which Beeson, Plant, and Elmslie engaged as they sought to create a woman struggling with domestic discontent, along with a psychosexual complex that would finally drive her over the edge.[113] Ultimately, Beeson, Plant, and Elmslie's Lizzie appears almost as a reincarnation of psychiatrist Richard Freiherr von Krafft-Ebing's "Mannish Lesbian," first coined during the 1880s.[114] As Carroll Smith-Rosenberg writes, "Krafft-Ebing's lesbians seemed to desire male privileges and power as ardently as, perhaps more ardently than, they sexually desired women"; to put it another way, the "Mannish Lesbian" was a "male soul trapped in a female body."[115]

Rather than turn Lizzie into a positive symbol of "women's lib," Beeson, Plant, and Elmslie contributed to the culture fueling the modern feminist movement. Indeed, a more liberating conclusion to the opera might have

---

112 See Friedan, "The Problem That Has No Name" in *The Feminine Mystique*, 15–32.

113 Friedan, "The Sexual Solipsism of Sigmund Freud" in ibid., 103–125. In the booklet that accompanies the 1967 telecast of *Lizzie Borden*, re-mastered to DVD, the final scene involving Lizzie and Andrew is titled "Seduction Scene," as if to suggest Lizzie's attraction to her father.

114 According to Carroll Smith-Rosenberg, Krafft-Ebing was "the leading spokesman for sexology in nineteenth-century Europe." She notes that he defined sexology "as the study of 'abnormal' and 'perverse' sexual practices, which did not involve a primary interest in reproductive intercourse … Predominantly among these perversions, Krafft-Ebing listed homosexuality." See *Disorderly Conduct*, 268.

115 Smith-Rosenberg, *Disorderly Conduct*, 271, 287.

been one that was more historically accurate. Immediately after her acquittal in real life, Lizzie and her sister Emma left their father's house, carving out a new space for their lives. In 1999, when asked to describe Lizzie Borden, soprano Phyllis Pancella offered this portrait:

> Repressed ... very frustrated, very stuck. She's a woman in her early thirties without a husband in a very unpleasant household, and there is nothing a woman in her early thirties in the 1890s without a husband could do but stay in said household, no matter what the conditions were ... And so she stayed, and that's where she was gonna have to stay ... The first thing she did after she was acquitted was get out of that house."[116]

Once again, the concept of the spinster is refracted through contemporary culture, but Pancella's final point is intriguing. Transitioning seamlessly from the operatic Lizzie back to the historical Lizzie, Pancella reveals the fault lines of Beeson, Elmslie, and Plant's creation. The real Lizzie Borden did not become her father. She did not become the "man" of the house. As an upper-middle-class white woman, she had some power to remake herself—to pursue her own activities and interests. She gave time and money, for example, to the Animal Rescue League of Fall River, and she threw lavish parties at her new Fall River home, a sprawling mansion called Maplecroft, entertaining guests from New York City in a fashion that would have been impossible in her previous life.[117] Perhaps the real Lizzie Borden escaped, only to be re-imprisoned by Beeson, Plant, and Elmslie in 1965.

To a limited extent, Beeson, Plant, and Elmslie's Lizzie Borden recalls Grace Metalious's Selena Cross. Just as Beeson, Plant, and Elmslie modeled their Lizzie Borden after a real woman from Massachusetts, Metalious modeled Selena Cross after Barbara Roberts, the New Hampshire woman who confessed to killing her father in 1947. In their respective fictions, novel and opera, both New England women end up in a kind of solitary confinement. Selena finds herself alone in *Peyton Place*, abandoned by her boyfriend, presumably because Metalious did not believe that anyone was likely to associate with a working-class woman in Selena's situation. Metalious also seemed determined that Selena should not run away from *Peyton Place*. Selena's friend Allison struggles with Selena's decision to remain in town, grumbling that "all the fine friends who didn't want to see her hang for murder are hanging her themselves with their vicious talk."[118] In this way,

---

116 Pancella, speaking at the 1999 "Works & Process" performance series devoted to *Lizzie Borden*. See *Lizzie Borden: New Visions*.

117 In fact, the Animal Rescue League in Fall River continues to benefit from the money Lizzie Borden left in her will. See Hageman, "Lizzie Borden, Animal Lover."

118 Metalious, *Peyton Place*, 351.

Metalious revealed some of the oppressive structures at play in the US, as though implicitly asking her readers to consider what it would take to dismantle such structures. The operatic Lizzie, on the other hand, finds herself alone in Fall River because her creators chose to rewrite history. The opera's epilogue ultimately punishes Lizzie Borden for trespassing the bounds of proper womanhood, locking her up inside her father's house and turning her into a "mannish lesbian" because she refused to act like the upper-middle-class "lady" that she was supposed to be. Thus there is no possibility for liberation in *Lizzie Borden*. The title heroine's transformation, written so completely into the opera's libretto and score that resistance through performance seems impossible, is decidedly anti-feminist. When the NYCO revived *Lizzie Borden* in 1999, Lauren Flanigan and Phyllis Pancella spoke to this reality. Like me, Flanigan initially tried to regard the axe murders as a kind of "macabre act of freedom" for Lizzie, but Pancella quickly noted Lizzie's "lack of options," explaining how the opera sets "a very tight trap by the end."[119] Even Beverly Sills, who had the ability to resist some of the sexist stereotypes embedded in Baby Doe's character, reinforced this trap when she introduced *Lizzie Borden*. Acting in her role as host of the NYCO's 1999 *Live from Lincoln Center* broadcast, Sills suggested that "what makes opera grand is violence, villainy, and wickedness. Now there's a cue for Lizzie Borden if I ever heard one."[120] Her words, unfortunately, left no room for resistance.

---

119 Flanigan and Pancella, in conversation with Beverly Sills and Rhoda Levine, broadcast during the intermission of the NYCO's performance of *Lizzie Borden* on March 24, 1999.
120 Sills, introducing *Lizzie Borden* at the beginning of the NYCO's performance of *Lizzie Borden* on March 24, 1999.

Chapter Four

A Chaste White Woman: Laurie Moss

In contrast to *The Ballad of Baby Doe* and *Lizzie Borden*, both of which conclude with older women paying for their sins against the family, Aaron Copland and Erik Johns's *The Tender Land* (1954, rev. 1955) concludes with a still-young woman named Laurie Moss striking out on her own, leaving her family and their farm behind her. Laurie's mother cannot understand why her daughter must leave, and she begs her not to go. Finally, she resigns herself, turning her attention to the younger daughter still in her care. She will begin anew with her. She will seek to protect her and ensure that she makes it to her high school graduation, unsullied by the outside world.

Laurie Moss is a key figure in American operas of the 1950s, for her assertion of self prefigures that of Susannah Polk, the tragic heroine of Carlisle Floyd's *Susannah* (1955) and the subject of the next chapter. Laurie and Susannah are both young, fiercely independent, and fatherless women. Both are the victims of patriarchal cultures that rely on sexual violence, threatened or realized, to keep women in a position of subservience. When Susannah, for example, supposedly "acts out," she is slut-shamed and then raped. Her older brother finds out and seeks to avenge her (but also his) honor. Similarly, Laurie's mother and grandfather are so intent on protecting Laurie's virginity, and so worried that Laurie *could* be raped or seduced, that they seek to control her every move. Yet musicologists have glossed over the sexual violence on display in *The Tender Land* and *Susannah*, preferring to read the operas as coded critiques of the McCarthy era.[1] These readings are incomplete, for they do not account for the gendered and racialized violence that informs *The Tender Land* and *Susannah*.

In this chapter, I scrutinize the sexual and gender politics emphasized in *The Tender Land* by analyzing several of the texts that informed the opera

---

1   For example, see Wierzbicki, *Music in the Age of Anxiety*, 115–121; Crist, "Mutual Responses in the Midst of an Era," 485–527; Gross, "McCarthyism and American Opera," 164–187.

and revealing how the threat of sexual violence underscores the entire story. Musicologists have long acknowledged James Agee and Walker Evans's *Let Us Now Praise Famous Men* (1941) as Copland and Johns's primary source material, but I show how Erskine Caldwell's 1944 novel *Tragic Ground* served as an additional source of inspiration. In the 1940s, Copland began adapting *Tragic Ground* into a musical for Broadway; even after he abandoned the idea, Caldwell's novel lingered with him. Some of the music from Copland's *Tragic Ground* sketches made it into *The Tender Land*, as did some of Caldwell's obsession with the dangers of female sexuality. Whereas musicologists have previously passed over the relevance of *Tragic Ground* to *The Tender Land*, I emphasize *Tragic Ground*'s importance, asserting that this novel helps to illuminate *The Tender Land* as an opera that turns on the threat of sexual violence against young, unmarried women.[2]

Timing, of course, is everything. Americans in the 1950s were deeply anxious about sex. In 1987, writer Vivian Gornick recalled her mother's apprehension during her teenage years: "Safeguarding my virginity was a major preoccupation. Every boy I brought into the house made my mother anxious. She could not but leap ahead in her thoughts to the inevitable moment when he must threaten her vital interest."[3] Similarly, Esther Greenwood, the protagonist of Sylvia Plath's novel *The Bell Jar*, sees "pureness" as "the great issue" of the 1950s.[4] As she explains: "Instead of the world being divided up into Catholics and Protestants or Republicans and Democrats or white men and black men or even men and women, I saw the world divided into people who had slept with somebody and people who hadn't, and this seemed the only really significant difference between one person and another."[5] Sociologist Wini Breines describes "the obsession with female virginity until marriage" as "one version of sexual anxiety" during the 1950s, while historian Elaine Tyler May goes so far as to describe the decade as an era of "sexual paranoia."[6] She asserts that "the media focused attention on 'sexual psychopaths,' who, like communists and homosexuals, might be lurking anywhere," and as a result, "the hysteria whipped up by the publicity

---

[2] Ryan Patrick Jones and Howard Pollack acknowledge Copland's recycling of musical material from *Tragic Ground* but they do not pursue further the connections between *Tragic Ground* and *The Tender Land*. See Jones, "*The Tender Land*," 36–37 and Pollack, *Aaron Copland*, 419–21.

[3] Gornick, *Fierce Attachments*, 110.

[4] Plath, *The Bell Jar*, 82. *The Bell Jar* opens in 1953, in "the summer they electrocuted the Rosenbergs" (p. 1).

[5] Ibid., 82.

[6] Breines, *Young, White, and Miserable*, 8; May, *Homeward Bound*, 92.

surrounding an alleged wave of sex crimes reached grotesque proportions in the postwar years."[7]

As historian Estelle B. Freedman points out, throughout most of US history, rape has "been defined either in law or through practice as a crime committed largely by African American men against chaste white women."[8] This was the framework at play in the 1950s, when "nice girls" (i.e., white girls) like Laurie Moss were thought to require protection from dangerous (i.e., often non-white) outsiders. This script, of course, could also be flipped. "Bad girls" like Susannah were often vilified—oversexualized and coded as racial outsiders. "Nice boys" needed protection from them. It was nothing more than the age-old paradigm of the virgin or the whore, now infused with American racism.

Somewhat remarkably, *The Tender Land* begins within the constricting virgin/whore binary but concludes by gesturing beyond it, as Copland and Johns ultimately wanted to imagine Laurie as a woman with the power to make her own decisions and live her life on her own terms. Yet *The Tender Land* is still decidedly ambivalent. The opera's gestures toward Laurie's promise all result in more questions than answers. I conclude this chapter by reflecting on the lives of three of the women who sang the role of Laurie in the 1950s. None of these women clearly broke through the constraints of the 1950s and early 1960s in their professional lives. Indeed, none of these women became opera "stars." Two left opera altogether. This is not to say that they did not live full and rich lives. Often, they did. Yet like Laurie, they had to maneuver through a world that was not made for their autonomy. The trajectories of these women's lives—and the challenges to interpreting them—demonstrate how difficult it could be for women to claim the autonomy that *The Tender Land* seemed to want to suggest.

Situating *The Tender Land*

The Tender Land premiered on stage on April 1, 1954, but Copland (1900–1990) and his librettist conceived the work somewhat differently. In 1952, Copland was awarded a $1,000 commission from the League of Composers (funded by Richard Rodgers and Oscar Hammerstein II) to write an opera for television. Copland was delivering the Charles Eliot Norton Lectures at Harvard University, and he eagerly accepted the commission, employing Erik Johns (1927–2001), with whom he had been romantically involved

---

7   May, *Homeward Bound*, 92–93.
8   Freedman, *Redefining Rape*, 288.

during the late 1940s, to do the libretto.[9] Johns was known primarily as a dancer and painter, and he wrote the libretto for *The Tender Land* under the pseudonym Horace Everett.[10]

When Copland and Johns presented *The Tender Land* to Peter Herman Adler, who ran the NBC Opera Theatre, Adler turned the opera down. Copland and Johns then showed the libretto to Copland's longtime close friend Harold Clurman, a theater director and drama critic, who encouraged them to keep working and find a producer.[11] Under the direction of Joseph Rosenstock, the NYCO ultimately agreed to present *The Tender Land* alongside Gian-Carlo Menotti's *Amahl and the Night Visitors*, another opera conceived for television (one that had enjoyed a successful television premiere in 1951).[12] Yet unlike *Amahl*, which moved rather seamlessly from screen to stage, *The Tender Land* stumbled. New York's music critics were so harsh in their initial reviews that Copland later confessed he "was not sorry to have a legitimate reason to leave town soon after the premiere."[13] Johns has suggested that the main problem was that his and Copland's "intimate" approach to the opera, while ideal for television, did not translate to the stage.[14] In the dismal aftermath of the premiere, Copland and Johns revised *The Tender Land*, seeking, as Johns described, to make it "more explicit" by explaining the "things that we had in our heads but that weren't shown on the stage."[15] A new version of *The Tender Land* was presented at Tanglewood in August 1954, and in May 1955, the Oberlin College Opera Workshop gave the final revised version. In 1986, Copland granted conductor Murry Sidlin permission to reorchestrate the score in a thirteen-instrument arrangement for a revival at the Long Wharf Theatre in New Haven, Connecticut. Copland wrote happily that this production "worked

---

9   Pollack, *Aaron Copland*, 245–248.
10 As Johns later explained, he "did not want to confuse" his dancing and painting career with his burgeoning writing career. See Johns, quoted in Copland and Perlis, *Copland since 1943*, 216.
11 Clurman and Copland had shared an apartment in Paris in the 1920s.
12 Jennifer Barnes discusses *Amahl and the Night Visitors* at length in *Television Opera*, 15–41.
13 Copland, quoted in Copland and Perlis, *Copland since 1943*, 223.
14 Johns, quoted in ibid., 219. Drawing on Johns's perspective, Christopher W. Patton argued that "*The Tender Land*'s small, intimate scale, meditative, introspective libretto and strong but finely wrought emotional content were lost somewhere in the vast reaches of City Center." See "Discovering *The Tender Land*," 318.
15 Johns, quoted in Copland and Perlis, *Copland since 1943*, 220.

like a charm!"[16] Yet for the most part, *The Tender Land* has remained in the college and university opera circuit in its 1955 form.[17]

The Tender Land's path to production somewhat recalls that of Kurt Weill and Arnold Sundgaard's one-act folk opera *Down in the Valley*. Whereas Copland and Johns initially envisioned *The Tender Land* as a television opera, Weill and Sundgaard conceived *Down in the Valley* as a radio opera. According to musicologist Naomi Graber, the composer and librettist "intended the piece as the first in a series of folk song-based operas for radio."[18] The series did not work out, but as Graber explains, Hans Heinsheimer of Schirmer Publishing "contacted Weill in 1947 to request a 'school opera.'"[19] Weill and Sundgaard quickly set about revising *Down in the Valley* for its 1948 stage premiere at Indiana University.[20] Musicologist Stephen Hinton notes that within a year of the premiere, *Down in the Valley* had been produced eighty times.[21] In 1949, Weill proudly commented on the accessibility of his opera, explaining that it could "be performed wherever a chorus, a few singers and a few actors are available."[22] Over the next decade, *Down in the Valley*'s accessibility proved fruitful.[23] As Hinton writes, "within nine years, more than 1,500 productions with some 6,000 performances, most of them at U.S. colleges, universities, and conservatories, had been staged."[24]

When Copland recalled *The Tender Land* in 1989, he wrote of his opera in terms of accessibility similar to those touted by Weill. Copland argued that with *The Tender Land*, he "was trying to give young American singers material that they do not often get in the opera house; that is, material that

---

16   Copland, quoted in ibid., 225.
17   In the last five years, for example, productions of *The Tender Land* have taken place on college campuses such as Kent State University (Ohio), Luther College (Iowa), Northwestern University (Illinois), the University of Nebraska, and Valdosta State University (Georgia).
18   Graber, *Kurt Weill's America*, 116. Graber notes that the planned radio series was "instigated by Charles MacArthur and *New York Times* music critic Olin Downes." See also Hinton, *Weill's Musical Theater*, 388.
19   Graber, *Kurt Weill's America*, 116.
20   Graber summarizes the differences between the radio performance and stage production in ibid., 122.
21   Hinton, *Weill's Musical Theater*, 394.
22   Kurt Weill, quoted in Heinsheimer, "Right Kind of Opera Has Market in America."
23   On January 22, 1950, *Down in the Valley* appeared on television, marking the first opera production by NBC Opera Theatre. See Barnes, *Television Opera*, 18.
24   Hinton, *Weill's Musical Theater*, 394.

would be natural for them to sing and perform."[25] He suggested that he "deliberately tried to combine the use of traditional operatic set pieces—arias, duets, choruses, etc.—with a natural language that would not be too complex for young singers at opera workshops throughout the country."[26] Thus both Weill and Copland reframed their apparent failures in the short-lived movements for opera on radio and television as successful contributions to the growing body of opera for young singers.[27]

The Tender Land connects to *Down in the Valley* in other ways as well. Weill and Sundgaard's opera tells the story of the ill-fated romance between Brack Weaver and Jennie Parsons through preexisting American folk songs.[28] As musicologist John Graziano argues, "the folk song idiom so infuses" *Down in the Valley* "that Weill's newly composed song for Jennie, 'Brack Weaver, My True Love,' approaches the 'folk authenticity' of the preexistent tunes."[29] *The Tender Land* also features a number of preexisting folk songs. Copland incorporated "Zion's Walls," "Cottage by the Sea," and "If you want to go a courtin'" into his score, and as Hinton argues, Copland, like Weill, used these songs to imbue his entire opera with a decidedly folk-like quality.[30]

Of the four operas spotlighted in this book, *The Tender Land* has received the most scholarly attention. The explanation is rather simple: Copland has long been regarded as the "Dean of U.S. Music."[31] Copland's popularity and fame grew during the 1940s, and as Howard Pollack explains, "by the early 1950s, the concert-going public widely considered him the time's foremost serious American composer."[32] Yet the 1950s were difficult for Copland, who famously found himself a target of Senator Joseph R.

---

25   Copland, quoted in Copland and Perlis, *Copland since 1943*, 220.
26   Ibid., 220.
27   Here it is worth mentioning that Copland's only other operatic venture was also designed with young singers in mind. In the 1930s, Copland worked with Edwin Denby on *The Second Hurricane* (1937), a short opera for high school students with roots in the *Lehrstücke* (learning plays) of Bertolt Brecht, Weill's longtime collaborator. For a discussion of Brecht's *Lehrstücke*, see Calico, "Lehrstück, Opera, and the New Audience Contract of the Epic Theater" in *Brecht at the Opera*, 16–42.
28   The opera's title, for example, refers to "Down in the Valley." This folk song appears in George Lyman Kittredge's 1917 collection of ballad and song texts, published in the *Journal of American Folklore*. See "Ballads and Songs," 346–347.
29   Graziano, "Musical Dialects in *Down in the Valley*," 300.
30   Hinton, "Down in the Valley," *Grove Music Online*.
31   See Smith, "Aaron Copland, Dean of U.S. Music, Dies at 90."
32   Pollack, *Aaron Copland*, 550.

McCarthy's anti-communist crusade.³³ Musicologist Emily Abrams Ansari has demonstrated how Copland worked to rebuild his stylistic brand after his run-in with McCarthy.³⁴ Noting his success, she asserts that "Copland has for many decades been thought of by the concertgoing public as the quintessential American Everyman: a down-to-earth, hard-working, nonpolitical yet somehow also highly patriotic composer—an example of the best of his nation."³⁵

Musicologists have often struggled to reconcile *The Tender Land*, Copland's only full-length opera and a critical failure, with Copland's status as "the best of his nation." It was not until 2005, fifteen years after Copland's death, that Ryan Patrick Jones completed the first extensive study of *The Tender Land*, outlining the history of the opera's composition and working to contextualize what he described as its "overrated weaknesses" and "underrated strengths."³⁶ Around this same time, other scholars sought to locate value in *The Tender Land* by decoding its underlying messages. In 2002, Daniel E. Mathers argued that *The Tender Land* reflected "something of [Copland and Johns's] shared outlooks, interest, and lives as gay men in mid-twentieth-century America."³⁷ He read the opera's conclusion as an allegorical "coming out," emphasizing Laurie's decision to leave "the confines of the picket fence, itself a type of social, cultural closet."³⁸ Mathers suggested that Laurie "goes out in early homophile, fifties style, with a quiet, secret knowledge of who she is," having "uncover[ed] through a transgressive desire a new, formerly repressed, authentic self."³⁹ In 2006, Elizabeth B. Crist asserted that *The Tender Land* offered a commentary "on anticommunist red-baiting and the Cold War culture of fear."⁴⁰ She maintained that the opera was "suffused by a 'mood of suspicion, ill-will, and dread,' as Copland himself described the Cold War climate."⁴¹ The underlying messages that

---

33 Copland was called to testify before the Senate Permanent Subcommittee in 1953.
34 Ansari, *The Sound of a Superpower*, 151.
35 Ibid., 151–152.
36 Jones, "*The Tender Land*," xxiv.
37 Mathers, "Expanding Horizons," 118.
38 Ibid., 133.
39 Ibid.
40 Crist, "Mutual Responses in the Midst of an Era," 486.
41 Ibid., 501–502. When Copland began working on *The Tender Land* in 1952, McCarthyism was indeed in full swing. In her reading of *The Tender Land*, Crist disagreed with musicologist and oral historian Vivian Perlis, who had previously asserted that "except for one moment in the plot [of *The Tender Land*], there is no trace of bitter taste left from the McCarthy hearing and its aftermath," See Copland and Perlis, *Copland since 1943*, 202–203.

Mathers and Crist propose are certainly plausible, but their narrow lenses (and resulting silences) ultimately erase the sexual violence of the opera.

Anxiety and *The Tender Land*

At the beginning of his synopsis of *The Tender Land*, Johns explained that in this opera, "the isolated world of a rural family turns around the graduation of its elder daughter. Yet she is unsure of her place in that world. It is invaded by a threat and then an actuality of two outsiders who excite in the girl dreams of a larger life."[42] *The Tender Land* is set on a farm in the Midwest in the 1930s. There, eighteen-year-old Laurie Moss lives with her mother, grandfather, and younger sister Beth. The opera opens on Ma, who is contemplating her parental responsibilities as she watches Beth playing in the yard. When the postman arrives to deliver Laurie's graduation dress, he also brings news of a rash of sexual assaults committed by unknown men drifting through the community. The postman leaves, and Laurie appears, daydreaming about life beyond the family farm. Laurie complains to her mother about her controlling grandfather; her mother assures her that she will be able to have her own life but that she must obey her grandfather until after her graduation. Suddenly, two itinerant workers named Top and Martin arrive, looking for work. Grandpa reluctantly hires the men to help with the harvest, and Laurie invites them to her graduation party.

Act II takes place later that night, as friends and neighbors gather at the Moss farm to celebrate Laurie's graduation. Ma worries that Top and Martin could be the men the postman warned her about and sends him to fetch the local sheriff. Meanwhile, Laurie and Martin dance together. When Grandpa discovers them kissing, he is outraged. Ma chimes in, accusing both Top and Martin of sexually assaulting her neighbor's daughter Jessie Kane. The postman returns and reports that the two men who assaulted Jessie were caught earlier in the afternoon, thus clearing Top and Martin. Grandpa, however, is not moved and asserts that "they're guilty all the same."[43]

---

42 See the synopsis at the beginning of Copland and Everett, *The Tender Land*.

43 Copland and Everett, *The Tender Land*, 149. Musicologists have made much of this line, which as Crist writes, Johns added to the libretto "only after the premiere, apparently as a conscious reference to McCarthy." Crist suggests that it was safe for Copland and Johns to add this "obvious indictment" only in the late spring and summer of 1954, by which time McCarthy's public stock was "falling fast." See "Mutual Responses in the Midst of an Era," 504. See also Wierzbicki, *Music in the Age of Anxiety*, 116. The widely publicized Army–McCarthy hearings that eventually led to the tide turning against McCarthy

In Act III, Martin and Laurie meet just before dawn. They make plans to elope, and Laurie returns to her house to pack her things. Top then convinces Martin to reconsider, pointing out that Grandpa Moss will hunt them down if he and Laurie elope. Top argues, moreover, that Laurie is not suited to life on the run. Martin sneaks away with Top regretfully. Laurie returns, discovers that Martin has abandoned her, and resolves to set off on her own anyway. The opera concludes with Beth and Ma alone on stage. As though forgetting Laurie, Ma sings of "graduation days still out of sight."[44] Ma's final word—and the final word of the entire opera—is the word "beginning."[45] Thus Ma suggests that she will start anew with Beth.

In 1999, Howard Pollack likened *The Tender Land*'s "distinctive ambience" to "the calm of a sunbaked cornfield."[46] Beneath this ambience, however, there lurks a deep-seated anxiety. Earlier I noted Elizabeth B. Crist's assertion that *The Tender Land* is "suffused by a 'mood of suspicion, ill-will, and dread.'"[47] I agree, although I am not entirely convinced by Crist's interpretation of the sense of foreboding that runs throughout the opera. Crist argues that "the very first scene finds Ma singing about the 'cold, cold weather,' a sure reference to the temperature of American domestic and international politics at the time."[48] The "cold, cold weather" might be read as a coded reference to the temperature of the time, but it is a "sure reference" to Ma's anxiety about her ability to protect her daughters' innocence and bodily autonomy.

The Tender Land begins with a short prelude that Copland repurposed from his sketches for the abandoned *Tragic Ground* musical. Featuring a transparent texture and diatonic melody carried by the flute, the prelude is typical of the folkloric idiom that Copland cultivated during the 1930s and 1940s.[49] As Julia Smith noted in 1955, "the simple aura of simple folk, remindful of the quality of the music from *Our Town*, pervades the atmosphere."[50] When the curtain rises, Beth appears in her front yard, dancing with a doll she calls Daniel, while Ma sits in a rocker on the porch, sewing in hand. Daydreaming, Beth ponders her future, speaking excitedly over Copland's optimistic and homespun-sounding music:

---

  concluded in June 1954. On December 2, 1954, the Senate voted 67–22 to censure the Wisconsin senator. See Fried, *Nightmare in Red*, 171.
44 Copland and Everett, *The Tender Land*, 202.
45 Ibid.
46 Pollack, *Aaron Copland*, 476.
47 Crist, "Mutual Responses in the Midst of an Era," 502.
48 Ibid.
49 On this topic, see Levy, *Frontier Figures*, 293–368.
50 Smith, *Aaron Copland*, 218.

> When I grow up will you take me to live in a big house?
> With a big lawn?
> I'd like a fountain and a pool.
> A pool with lots of carrot-fish.
> I'd like that, Daniel.[51]

With childlike innocence, Beth imagines the man who will eventually take care of her. But when Ma begins her first aria a few moments later, Johns's text and Copland's music begin to lose their ease and optimism:

> Two little bits of metal,
> My needle and my thimble,
> A woman has to sew her family's clothes
> Against the cold, cold weather.[52]

As Ma sings the final line, the tempo slows, and on the word "weather," Ma lingers on a minor v7 chord, clearly indicating her anxiety about something in her family's future (Ex. 4.1). Ma makes the same ominous shift on the word "weather" in the second verse of her aria:

> Two larger bits of metal,
> My wood stove and my kettle,
> A woman has to stew her family's food
> Against the cold, cold weather.[53]

Eventually, the precise reason for Ma's anxiety begins to emerge:

> For as two girls are growing,
> Are feeling and are knowing,
> One cannot always bear a daughter's cares
> For when the child grows older,
> And when the wind blows colder,
> A woman sometimes knows that doors won't close
> Against the cold, cold weather.[54]

Ma finally makes it clear that she is thinking about her eventual inability to protect her daughters from the dangers of the world. While Ma sings, Beth continues to dance and play, oblivious to her mother's concerns. Within the first few moments of the opera, Copland and Johns create a subtle juxtaposition between the optimism of childhood and the anxiety that often comes with adulthood.

As the story continues, optimism and anxiety vie for the listener's attention. When the postman Mr. Splinters arrives, he engages Ma in easy small

---

51   Copland and Everett, *The Tender Land*, 1–2.
52   Ibid., 2–3.
53   Ibid., 3–4.
54   Ibid., 6–7.

Example 4.1. Copland and Everett, *The Tender Land*, mm. 43–54.

talk for a few moments. The two converse in a folkloric arioso style, punctuated by allusions to the sound of fiddling. Yet once again, the tone of the conversation—and the music—gradually shifts as Mr. Splinters gets up to leave. Addressing Ma in a terse recitative, Mr. Splinters asks if she has heard "the news" about Missus Gray's girl:

> Seems she met with a feller in the fields.
> A strange feller here about's they say.
> Poor girl's shook up for a spell.
> She got an awful fright.[55]

---

55 Ibid., 13–14.

Mr. Splinters concludes that he "wouldn't be surprised if they turned out to be the one's [*sic*] that set on Jessie Kane two month ago," explaining that Jessie is "gonna have a young 'un," and finally leaving no ambiguity as to what he and Ma are talking about: Jessie was raped.[56] Ma shudders as she considers "if that ever happened to Laurie."[57] She notes that if "Grandpa Moss found out, it's terrible to think what he'd do."[58] Thus Copland and Johns established Ma's and Grandpa's mission—to protect their eldest daughter and granddaughter from the dangerous men who wander through their community preying on young women. Notably, this framework was part of *The Tender Land* from the very beginning; the script that Copland and Johns submitted to NBC—when they thought their opera was going to be premiered on television—features Ma and Mr. Splinters's dialogue almost exactly as it appears in the final published version of the opera.[59] Johns also prefaced this version of the script with a synopsis in which he explicitly stated that Grandpa Moss had "ruled" Laurie and Beth "with a stern discipline both to keep them within the family fold and 'protected' from men."[60]

Yet Laurie resists her grandfather's attempts to rule her. As Daniel E. Mathers writes, "from her first entrance, Laurie is marked as special and different, with secret yearnings."[61] When Laurie arrives home from school, Ma and Beth have left to prepare for the evening's party and Laurie lingers in the yard, reflecting on her sudden desire to see the world beyond her family's farm. She sings an aria, popularly known outside the opera as "Laurie's Song." The opening is characterized by a circular-sounding melody anchored by a return to the E above middle C (Ex. 4.2). As the aria unfolds, and as Laurie expresses her amazement that she has indeed grown, despite the "time [that] dragged heavy and slow," this E loses its status as an anchor.[62] Laurie finally admits that she feels "strange inside," concluding with a leap of a minor seventh as she marvels that "the time has grown so short; the world so wide" (Ex. 4.3).[63]

After this entrance, Laurie becomes increasingly frustrated when her mother and grandfather ignore her attempts to express her feelings and

---

56 Ibid., 15.
57 Ibid., 16.
58 Ibid.
59 See Aaron Copland and Horace Everett, *The Tender Land: A Musical Drama*, 3–4, Folder 18, Box 419, Aaron Copland Collection, Music Division, Library of Congress, Washington, DC.
60 Ibid., p. B.
61 Mathers, "Expanding Horizons," 132.
62 Copland and Everett, *The Tender Land*, 26.
63 Ibid., 29–30.

Example 4.2. Copland and Everett, *The Tender Land*, mm. 403–405.

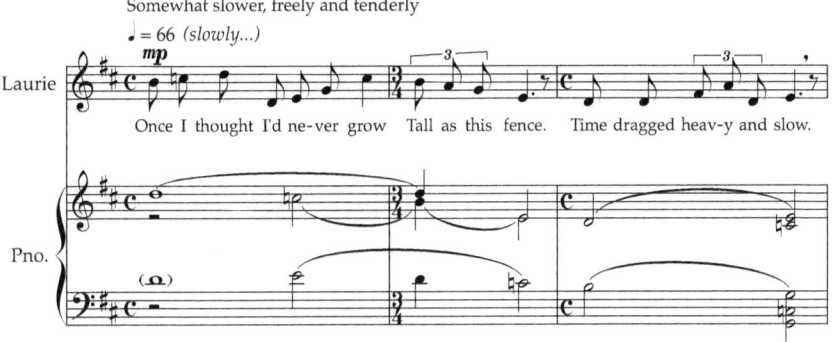

Example 4.3. Copland and Everett, *The Tender Land*, mm. 441–445.

desires for her own life. At the beginning of Act II, for example, Grandpa makes a toast in honor of Laurie. He likens her to the harvest, explaining that some harvests "are good; others not so good," just as some girls "are good; others not so good."[64] He notes that he is thankful that Laurie is "a good one ... nice as spring and clean as winter," a barely veiled reference to her virginity.[65] Grandpa concludes by boasting that Laurie is "the first of our whole family that's ever graduated."[66] Laurie, however, resists the certainty of her grandfather's words. She responds to Grandpa's toast with a toast of her own. Picking up on some of the feelings she articulated in her aria, she thanks the guests at her party but describes the moment as "queer," explaining:

> The closer I feel to our land,
> The more I wonder what those other lands are like.
> The more I want to wear this dress,
> The more it doesn't seem to be a part of me.[67]

Suddenly flustered, Laurie backtracks:

> Maybe I say it all wrong.
> I'm not sure what I say.[68]

Rather than listen, Grandpa laughs off Laurie's desire to express herself. He quickly glosses over the content of her toast and focuses on her good looks:

> Ah Laurie you are a puzzle,
> But such a pretty puzzle to your old grandpa.[69]

At the end of Act II, Laurie finds her voice, and she forces her grandfather to engage with her. When Grandpa discovers Laurie and Martin kissing, he shouts at Laurie to "get inside" and mutters in disgust:

> Giving yourself to the first guy that comes along.
> How could you do it Laurie?[70]

Laurie responds with the conviction she lacked at the beginning of the act, singing in an emotive arioso style that stands in stark contrast to her grandfather's brusque recitative:

---

64 Ibid., 93–94.
65 Ibid., 94.
66 Ibid., 95.
67 Ibid., 97–100. Laurie's references to feeling "strange inside" and "queer" may lend support to Mathers's argument about *The Tender Land*'s gay subtext.
68 Ibid., 100.
69 Ibid., 101.
70 Ibid., 150.

No one can stop the way I feel!
No one can ever tell me I can't love.
And Grandpa listen, listen, I love him.[71]

Ma insists that Laurie doesn't know what she is saying, and Grandpa angerly asserts that the family is "disgraced," finally threatening to "curse" the day Laurie was born.[72] Here, Laurie responds with measured maturity, telling her mother: "I feel so sorry for him."[73] In the end, Laurie and Grandpa do not reconcile. When Laurie decides to leave the farm, she does so not because she wants to follow Martin but because she wants to become her own person.

After Johns saw the NYCO's second performance of *The Tender Land* in 1954, he wrote to Copland, outlining his ideas for revisions.[74] Many of his plans concerned the strengthening and clarifying of Laurie's character. Johns commented, for example, on Laurie's "revolt," noting that it had to be built into the story from the beginning of Act I. That way, by the time Top and Martin entered the picture, Laurie would have already voiced frustration at the "real constrictions" in her life. According to Johns, Laurie would find in Martin not the love of her life but an "extension of her own dreams" and her "need to escape."

The Texts behind *The Tender Land*

Copland and Johns drew on several texts as they worked on *The Tender Land*. While they were most vocal about their reliance on James Agee and Walker Evans's *Let Us Now Praise Famous Men* (1941), Copland was also influenced by Erskine Caldwell's work from the 1930s and 1940s, mostly notably by *Tobacco Road* (1932), *You Have Seen Their Faces* (1937), and *Tragic Ground* (1944). It was Copland who initially charted the direction of the libretto, urging Johns to read *Famous Men*, a notoriously difficult book-length essay about three tenant farmers and their families in Alabama. Agee wrote the text, and Evans took the photographs that precede it. According to Johns, Copland "greatly admired" *Famous Men*.[75] Presumably, Copland had read the book carefully. Johns, however, claimed that he never read Agee's words. Instead, he explained, he was inspired by the notion of Agee

---

71 Ibid.
72 Ibid., 151–152.
73 Ibid., 152.
74 See letter, Erik Johns to Aaron Copland, April 24, 1954, Folder 37, Box 256, Aaron Copland Collection. All quotations in this paragraph are from this letter.
75 Johns, quoted in Copland and Perlis, *Copland since 1943*, 216.

and Evans as outsiders "'invading' the inside world of a provincial family."[76] Johns also maintained that he gravitated toward two of Evans's photographs, a sharecropper mother and daughter, as the inspiration for Ma and Laurie Moss (Figs. 4.1 and 4.2).[77]

Johns may have gravitated toward Evans's photographs, rather than Agee's text, because of the challenging nature of Agee's writing. As Agee explained in the preface to *Famous Men*, he and Evans traveled to Alabama in 1936 to spend approximately four weeks living with three different families in Hale and Greene counties. They had been assigned by *Fortune* magazine to write and photograph "an article on cotton tenantry in the United States, in the form of a photographic and verbal record of the daily living and environment of an average white family of tenant farmers."[78] But *Fortune* never published Agee and Evans's article. According to journalist Lawrence Downes, Agee's text, "brilliant yet bloated with guilt and literary grandeur ... was rejected by the magazine, which had been expecting something readable."[79]

Left to their own devices, Agee and Evans ultimately published their findings in 1941 as the book that Copland so admired. At this point, they felt compelled to set *Famous Men* apart from another Depression-era publication, writer Erskine Caldwell and photographer Margaret Bourke-White's *You Have Seen Their Faces* (1937). Caldwell and Bourke-White's book had also highlighted the plights of tenant farmers—black and white—in the Deep South, and it had been so popular among readers that the publication plans for *Famous Men* were temporarily shelved in the late 1930s. Agee and Evans clearly resented this. They made several jabs at Caldwell and Bourke-White's book in *Famous Men*, revealing not only their jealousy but also their fundamentally different journalistic stance.

At the beginning of *Famous Men*, Agee warned his reader not to expect another *You Have Seen Their Faces*, asserting that *Famous Men* was "intended, among other things, as a swindle, an insult, and a corrective" and advising the reader "to bear the nominal subject [the North American cotton tenantry], and his expectation of its proper treatment, steadily in mind."[80] Agee

---

76 Ibid.
77 To protect the anonymity of their subjects, Agee and Evans used pseudonyms for the families they described in *Famous Men*. Evans, however, used real names in his photographs when they appeared outside *Famous Men*. The result is somewhat confusing as Maggie Louise Gudger, the apparent inspiration for Laurie Moss, is actually Lucille Burroughs. Similarly, Annie Mae Gudger, the apparent inspiration for Ma Moss, is actually Allie Mae Burroughs.
78 Agee and Evans, *Let Us Now Praise Famous Men*, ix.
79 Downes, "Of Poor Farmers and 'Famous Men.'"
80 Agee and Evans, *Let Us Now Praise Famous Men*, xi.

Figure 4.1. *Alabama Tenant Farmer Wife*. With respect to Walker Evans (American, St. Louis, Missouri 1903–1975 New Haven, Connecticut), *Alabama Tenant Farmer Wife*, 1936, Gelatin silver print, 20.9 × 14.4 cm (8 1/4 × 5 11/16 in.), The Metropolitan Museum of Art, Purchase, 2000 Benefit Fund, 2001 (2001.415): © Walker Evans Archive, The Metropolitan Museum of Art.

Figure 4.2. *Lucille Burroughs, Daughter of a Cotton Sharecropper, Hale County, Alabama*. With respect to Walker Evans (American, St. Louis, Missouri 1903–1975 New Haven, Connecticut), *Lucille Burroughs, Daughter of a Cotton Sharecropper, Hale County, Alabama* [1936 summer]: © Walker Evans Archive, The Metropolitan Museum of Art.

also argued that Evans's photographs were "not illustrative."[81] Instead, he explained, "they, and the text, are coequal, mutually independent, and fully collaborative."[82] Of his text, he recommended that it be read aloud and "continuously, as music is listened to or a film watched, with brief pauses only where they are self-evident."[83] He concluded his preface with the following: "This is a *book* only by necessity. More seriously, it is an effort in human actuality, in which the reader is no less centrally involved than the authors and those of whom they tell."[84] After the preface, Agee inserted two quotations, the first from Act III of Shakespeare's *King Lear*, the second a political rallying cry, drawn from *The Communist Manifesto*:

> Poor naked wretches, wheresoe'er you are,
> That bide the pelting of this pitiless storm,
> How shall your houseless heads and unfed sides,
> Your loop'd and window'd raggedness, defend you
> From seasons such as these? Oh! I have ta'en
> Too little care of this! Take physick, pomp;
> Expose thyself to feel what wretches feel,
> That thou may'st shake the superflux to them,
> And show the heavens more just.
>
> Workers of the world, unite and fight. You have nothing to lose but your chains, and a world to win.

In a footnote, Agee wrote out a winding explanation of his employment of these words:

> These words are quoted here to mislead those who will be misled by them. They mean, not what the reader may care to think they mean, but what they say. They are not dealt with directly in this volume; but it is essential that they be used here, for in the pattern of the work as a whole, they are, in the sonata form, the second theme; the poetry facing them is the first. In view of the average reader's tendency to label, and of topical dangers to which any man, whether honest, or intelligent, or subtle, is at present liable, it may be well to make the explicit statement that neither these words nor the authors are the property of any political party, faith, or faction.[85]

This footnote is characteristic of Agee's approach throughout *Famous Men*, for the writer rarely makes a statement without also offering a detailed explanation or a list of caveats. In 2009, cultural historian Morris Dickstein aptly

---

81 Ibid.
82 Ibid.
83 Ibid.
84 Ibid.
85 Ibid., no page number.

described the book as a collection of "471 dizzying pages" of text, each page characterized by Agee's desire to "take[s] full account—too full, some would say—of the relation of the observer to the thing observed."[86] Two years later, when Lawrence Downes recalled *Famous Men* in the *New York Times*, he noted how it revealed Agee's "tortured questions about poverty, dignity and 'honest journalism.'"[87]

In contrast to Agee and Evans, Caldwell and Bourke-White had been far less concerned with their relationship to their subjects. Caldwell considered himself a cultural insider familiar with the plight of Southern tenant farmers. He wrote the text for *You Have Seen Their Faces* in a straightforward manner; he never indulged in the soul-searching reflexive meditations that characterize and complicate Agee's text. Additionally, whereas Agee and Evans left Evans's photographs uncaptioned, Caldwell and Bourke-White made up the captions that accompany each of Bourke-White's photographs, freely imagining what their subjects might have said and making heavy use of dialect. According to Bourke-White's biographer Vicki Goldberg, "Evans reportedly felt that Caldwell and Bourke-White's book exploited people who were already exploited."[88] Photographer Dorothea Lange and her husband Paul Schuster Taylor criticized *You Have Seen Their Faces* on similar terms. When Lange and Taylor published their book *An American Exodus: A Record of Human Erosion* in 1939, two years after the publication of *You Have Seen Their Faces*, they noted pointedly that their quotations "report what the persons photographed said, not what we think might be their unspoken thoughts."[89]

Since the 1940s, *You Have Seen Their Faces* has been largely forgotten, and when it is mentioned, it tends to be relegated to the status of "poverty porn."[90] *Famous Men*, on the other hand, is taken more seriously. For example, novelist and travel writer Paul Theroux contemplated *Famous Men* in his 2015 travelogue *Deep South: Four Seasons on Back Roads*, and

---

86   Dickstein, *Dancing in the Dark*, 98, 105.
87   Downes, "Of Poor Farmers and 'Famous Men.'"
88   Goldberg, *Margaret Bourke-White*, 192–193. Indeed, Evans claimed that in *Famous Men*, "you notice that Agee is saying ad nauseum almost throughout the book: 'For God's sake, we must *not* exploit these people, and how awful it is if we are.'" See Evans, quoted in Stott, *Documentary Expression and Thirties America*, 223.
89   Lange and Taylor, *An American Exodus*, 15. As Goldberg points out, Lange and Taylor were taking "a quiet swipe" at Caldwell and Bourke-White in this statement. See *Margaret Bourke-White*, 191.
90   Dickstein writes that *You Have Seen Their Faces* "point[s] an accusing finger at the spectator, who must now rise to the moral challenge of those faces he has seen." See *Dancing in the Dark*, 100.

he recalled reading *Famous Men* as a college student in the 1960s, when the book "found many more readers and admirers" than in the 1940s.[91] According to Theroux, readers in the 1960s valued Agee's text "for its density, obliqueness, and poetic descriptions—whole chapters on old clothes, for example; pages of leaky roofs; lofty renderings of the textures of planks and shingles, of patches and slop buckets."[92] *Famous Men* surfaced again at the end of the century, when writer Dale Maharidge and photographer Michael Williamson won the 1990 Pulitzer Prize for General Nonfiction for their book *And Their Children after Them* (1989), a follow-up on the land and families featured in *Famous Men*.

Yet even if Copland—and eventually Johns—gravitated more toward *Famous Men* than toward *You Have Seen Their Faces*, *The Tender Land* owes a certain debt to Caldwell's writing. In the 1930s and 1940s, Caldwell was one of the most popular writers in the US, and Copland was among his many fans. The son of a Presbyterian minister, Caldwell was born in Coweta County, Georgia. He grew up in a number of small farming communities throughout the South, observing his father attend to the physical and spiritual needs of impoverished tenant farmers. Caldwell established his reputation for writing about rural Southern poverty through his 1932 novel *Tobacco Road*. As Caldwell's biographer Dan B. Miller points out, Caldwell largely based this story on an actual family that his father had attempted to rehabilitate and integrate back into the community of Wrens, Georgia.[93]

Tobacco Road centers on the Lester family. Jeeter Lester has lived on the same plot of land since his birth, and even though sharecrop farming has proven an impossible means to make a living, he cannot stomach the idea of moving to the city to work in the cotton mill. Caldwell describes the Lester's struggle in prose that is at times humorous and at times painfully biting and grotesque. He spills a great deal of ink, for example, describing the sexual depravity of Jeeter's eighteen-year-old daughter Ellie Mae, who was born with a cleft lip. Much of the action of the story involves Jeeter's sixteen-year-old son Dude, whom Jeeter marries off to a thirty-nine-year-old preacher named Bessie with a facial deformity. As a book, *Tobacco Road* was only mildly successful initially, but when Jack Kirkland adapted the novel into a play, Caldwell and the fictional Lester family became famous. Kirkland's *Tobacco Road* opened at the Theatre Masque (now the John Golden Theatre) on Broadway on December 4, 1933.[94] After a slow start, the play captured audiences' imaginations, running until May 31, 1941, and totaling

---

91 Theroux, *Deep South*, 79.
92 Ibid.
93 Miller, *Erskine Caldwell*, 129.
94 See *Tobacco Road*, Internet Broadway Database.

3,182 performances.[95] In February 1941, as *Tobacco Road* continued its Broadway run, 20th Century Fox released a film adaptation of the story. Yet *Tobacco Road* became a national phenomenon, not necessarily because of its social commentary, but because of Caldwell's lurid depictions of sex. Miller explains that "most of the play's notoriety sprang from what came to be known as 'the scene'—the segment in the first act when Ellie Mae masturbates against the ground and eventually seduces her brother-in-law in the Lesters' dirt yard."[96] *Tobacco Road*'s popularity foreshadowed readers' later obsession with and perhaps also misunderstanding of Grace Metalious's *Peyton Place*. When a reporter for the *Boston Post* characterized *Peyton Place* as "a lusty *Tobacco Road* type of book about New England small town life," their words demonstrated how many readers focused on the salacious content of both books, rather than on the critical commentaries embedded within them.[97]

Caldwell followed *Tobacco Road* with another successful, albeit controversial, novel entitled *God's Little Acre* (1933). The book was banned in several cities, and the New York Society for the Suppression of Vice unsuccessfully sued Caldwell and Viking Press for the dissemination of pornography. Soon, as Miller points out, Caldwell was a household name, and as a result, he became "widely and enthusiastically despised" in the South.[98] Yet Caldwell seems to have regarded himself as something of a champion of the South's underclass.[99] When he returned to the South, first on his own in 1934 to work on a series of articles for the *New York Post*, and later with Bourke-White to commence work on *You Have Seen Their Faces*, he sought, according to Miller, "to answer criticism that his fictional portrayals were too brutal to be true."[100]

In the 1940s, Copland became interested in the idea of writing a musical based on *Tobacco Road*.[101] When he could not secure the rights, he turned to Caldwell's 1944 novel *Tragic Ground*. Copland's collaborators for

---

95 *Tobacco Road* was revived on Broadway in 1942, 1943, and 1950.
96 Miller, *Erskine Caldwell*, 200.
97 See Toth, *Inside Peyton Place*, 128. Toth points out that people in Gilmanton, New Hampshire "were more than miffed when they realized reporters actually considered Gilmanton a northern Tobacco Road." (p. 125).
98 Miller, *Erskine Caldwell*, 208.
99 As his son points out, some of Caldwell's novels were initially admired in socialist circles, yet Caldwell described himself as apolitical. By the mid-1930s, Caldwell was a wealthy celebrity, putting himself somewhat at odds with other artists and thinkers associated with the Popular Front. See Jay E. Caldwell, *Erskine Caldwell, Margaret Bourke-White, and the Popular Front*, 15.
100 Miller, *Erskine Caldwell*, 217.
101 Pollack, *Aaron Copland*, 419.

this project included producer Schuyler Watts, set designer Oliver Smith, choreographer Agnes de Mille, and playwright Lynn Riggs.[102] As Copland noted, he and Riggs "did several songs together, among them 'I bought me a cat' (an arrangement of an Arkansas folk song) and an original ballad, 'Alone at night.'"[103] Producer after producer, however, turned down the script for *Tragic Ground*, until finally, in November 1946, de Mille concluded: "There is not enough humor in the story. We are at a deadlock. The project is abandoned."[104] Copland, however, never quite let go of *Tragic Ground*.

When Copland and Johns began writing *The Tender Land*, Copland looked for ways to recycle at least some of the music he had written for the abandoned musical.[105] As he explained in a letter to Victor Kraft, dated July 1952, "part of the attraction" of writing an opera at this point in his life was that "some of the *Tragic Ground* material c[ould] be utilized," making the opera "seem easier to do."[106] Copland had in fact already repurposed parts of *Tragic Ground*, importing some of the music into his 1949 film score *The Red Pony* and his 1950 collection *Old American Songs*.[107] Copland played excerpts from *Tragic Ground* for Johns when they met to discuss their new opera, but after they had worked together for several months, Johns claimed that he and Copland decided the music did not suit *The Tender Land*.[108] According to Johns, the *Tragic Ground* music "was gradually dropped out of the opera" because "it was too popular in style, perhaps too folksy."[109] As Ryan Patrick Jones has shown, however, Copland did not drop all of the music from *Tragic Ground*, for the prelude to Act I, the Act I finale ("The promise of living"), and the Act II square dance ("Stop your foot") can all be traced back to music that Copland had sketched for *Tragic Ground*.[110] Thus, the music and, as I argue below, elements of the story from *Tragic Ground* lurk behind *The Tender Land*.

---

102 Ibid.
103 Copland, quoted in Copland and Perlis, *Copland since 1943*, 76.
104 Letter, Agnes de Mille to "Fellow Grounders," November 22, 1946, quoted in ibid.
105 Dobrin, *Aaron Copland*, 180.
106 Letter, Aaron Copland to Victor Kraft, July 20, 1952, quoted in Copland and Perlis, *Copland since 1943*, 179.
107 On *Old American Songs*, see Hartford, "A Common Man for the Cold War." On Copland's work as a film composer, see Bick, "*Of Mice and Men*."
108 Dobrin, *Aaron Copland*, 180.
109 Johns, quoted in Copland and Perlis, *Copland since 1943*, 219.
110 Jones, "*The Tender Land*," 36–39.

A terse story centering on Spence Douthit, who lives with his ailing wife Maud in a rundown house, *Tragic Ground* is set in Poor Boy, a shanty town located on the outskirts of a sprawling port city on the Gulf. Spence arrived in Poor Boy in the middle of a wartime boom to work in a gunpowder plant. Now the plant is closed, and Spence is out of work. He longs to return to his home in Beaseley County, Georgia, but he does not have the money for the bus fare. He spends his days wondering how he will ever catch up on the rent he owes.

Spence also wonders occasionally about his two daughters. As it turns out, thirteen-year-old Mavis has not been home for several days. According to the social workers who pay Spence a visit, Mavis is in trouble: she has turned to prostitution. Spence is not entirely surprised. Before the social workers arrived at his house, Spence had gotten into an argument with his neighbor Chet Mitchell, who Spence had learned had raped Mavis. According to Chet, Mavis was "ripe" and somehow asking to be raped: "You know good and well everybody in this part of town had his eyes on her. If there was one, there was a dozen just itching for the chance. Even a blind man could tell she was wanting to be jumped."[111] Spence tries to explain to the social workers that after Chet "adapted her just like—well, just like you'd adapt any young girl who'd give you the chance," Mavis was a lost cause.[112]

Through *Tragic Ground*, Caldwell argues that people are the products of their environments, or, as James E. Devlin put it, that "depressed surroundings produce scarred people."[113] When the social workers try to help Spence, arranging for the payment of his debts and giving him the bus fare for the trip back to Beaseley County, Spence gambles and drinks the money away. Spence has accepted his poverty and lot in life, and he has no reason to believe his actions will ever change his future.[114] But *Tragic Ground* has an underlying (and interlocking) thesis as well. According to Devlin, "the most vulnerable victims of life in Poor Boy are its young girls ... all children sexually exploited by adults."[115] Unfortunately, Caldwell ultimately blames these victims. As Devlin so bluntly states, Caldwell in *Tragic Ground* is "obsess[ed]" with "the concept of woman as 'flowing bitch.'"[116] Caldwell

---

111 Caldwell, *Tragic Ground*, 29.
112 Ibid., 64.
113 Devlin, *Erskine Caldwell*, 105.
114 Howard Pollack suggests that *Tragic Ground* "bespeaks Caldwell's communist affiliations in its suggestions that the degrading conditions of modern life create misfits like Spence," yet Pollack also correctly notes that Caldwell was regarded less as "a social critic" and more as "a fanciful storyteller." See *Aaron Copland*, 420.
115 Devlin, *Erskine Caldwell*, 109.
116 Ibid.

argues that young women must be protected, not only from men but also from themselves. They must be controlled because they do not have the capacity to control themselves or as Devlin writes, their "offensive female biology."[117]

The notion that young women must be protected and controlled also runs through much of *The Tender Land*, but because of the way Johns attended to the issue of class and the depiction of violence, it does so more subtly. The subjects of both *Tragic Ground* and *Famous Men* are families who belong to the white working poor. The outsiders who intrude—the social workers in *Tragic Ground* and the writer and photographer in *Famous Men*—are members of the white middle class. *The Tender Land*, however, centers on a respectable, presumably white, farm family, whereas the outsiders, Martin and Top, are members of the working poor. They are the ones who are vilified as they drift from town to town, looking for work.[118] In 1989, Johns recalled that he and Copland had "considered including a murder or rape scene to add dramatic impact" to *The Tender Land*.[119] They ultimately decided that such a scene would have been "at odds with the modest pastoral quality" that they sought, yet it is clear that they relied on the power—and anxiety—of suggestion.[120] What if a young white woman found herself in a situation where she *could* be raped or seduced? What would her grandfather do?

Interestingly, in Johns's first draft of the libretto, Grandpa Moss was originally Pa Moss. It was Copland who advocated that Pa become Grandpa to emphasize, as he explained in an annotation to the second draft of the libretto, the "mother-daughter relationship" and to put Ellie (whose name became Laurie; the name Ellie was possibly a holdover from when Copland was planning to adapt *Tobacco Road*) "in greater danger in Act I."[121] Thus, Copland constructed Laurie as a young fatherless woman, someone who would seem to require her grandfather to step up and protect her, not only

---

117 Ibid.
118 In 2014, the Lyric Opera of Melbourne played up this angle in its production of *The Tender Land*. In a program note, director John Kachoyan noted that Australia sometimes felt "increasingly small, afraid of newcomers and desperate to preserve a way of life (real or imagined) that seems to be slipping away," and as reporter Barney Zwartz argued, the decision to cast two people of color, Henry Choo and Raphael Wong, in the roles of Martin and Top "seem[ed] quite pointed." See "Review: Lyric Opera Produces Compelling Performance in The Tender Land."
119 Johns, quoted in Copland and Perlis, *Copland since 1943*, 219.
120 Ibid.
121 Copland, annotation to *Graduation Harvest* libretto, typescript draft, 1952, Aaron Copland Collection, cited in Jones, "*The Tender Land*," 78.

from the unsavory men who wandered through the community but also from herself.

The setting and plot of *The Tender Land* are strikingly similar to those in yet another literary source from the 1950s. William Inge's play *Picnic* (1953) centers on eighteen-year-old Madge Owens, who lives with her mother and younger sister in a small town in Kansas.[122] It is Labor Day weekend, and everyone in town is preparing for the neighborhood picnic. Madge is dating one of the most eligible men in town, Alan Seymour, and it seems as though the two are destined to marry. Her mother is excited about the match, given that it will help Madge to move up the social ladder. But Madge and Alan's relationship falls apart when a drifter named Hal Carter arrives in town. Madge eventually falls for Hal and spends the night with him. Alan runs Hal out of town, but right before he leaves, Hal tells Madge he loves her. Hal is already on the train to Tulsa by the time Madge realizes that she loves him as well. The play ends with Madge packing up her things and heading off to Tulsa to find Alan, against her mother's wishes.

When music critic Olin Downes reviewed *The Tender Land* in the *New York Times* on April 2, 1954, he commented on the opera's similarities to *Picnic*. Yet for Downes, *The Tender Land* did not come close to measuring up to Inge's play. He explained that "anyone who has seen 'Picnic' with its play of passions and powerful dénouement, and compared it with last night's affair, will immediately have realized the difference between the thing that is real and the thing that is theoretical and artificial."[123] Born and raised in Independence, Kansas, Inge tended to set his plays in places like Kansas, Missouri, and Oklahoma, relying on his insider knowledge of the culture of the Midwest and south central US. Whereas Copland and Johns, who considered themselves outsiders like Agee and Evans, were inclined to hang back, observe, and suggest, Inge, like Caldwell, sought to engage. Inge also relied on the explicit (although he was never quite as explicit as Caldwell). When Madge spends the night with Hal, there is no question as to what has transpired, although Madge and Hal's sexual encounter is not staged. At the end of Act II, Madge "suddenly and impulsively, takes [Hal's] face in her hands and kisses him."[124] Hal responds, his voice "deep and firm," as he carries Madge off stage and utters the line: "We're not goin' on no goddamn

---

122 William Inge (1913–1973) was one of the most successful playwrights of the 1950s. He enjoyed an unbroken string of Broadway successes during the decade, including *Come Back Little Sheba* (1950), *Picnic* (1953), *Bus Stop* (1955), and *The Dark at the Top of the Stairs* (1957). Privately, however, Inge was quite miserable. He died by suicide in 1973. On Inge's life and career, see Voss, *A Life of William Inge*.
123 Downes, "Music: Premiere of One-Act Opera."
124 Inge, "*Picnic*," 127.

picnic."[125] In Act III, a local boy named Bomber taunts Madge, shouting, "let me be next."[126] His words demonstrate that Madge no longer has the reputation of a respectable woman who is "saving herself" for marriage.

Picnic opened at the Music Box Theatre on Broadway on February 19, 1953, running for 477 performances and earning the New York Drama Critics' Circle Award for Best Play.[127] It also earned Inge the 1953 Pulitzer Prize for Drama. According to Pollack, Copland and Johns saw *Picnic* on Broadway in early 1953, well after Johns had completed his libretto for *The Tender Land*.[128] Thus, I maintain that the similarities between texts like *Tragic Ground*, *Picnic*, and *The Tender Land* speak directly to Elaine Tyler May's characterization of the 1950s as an era of sexual "paranoia," primed during the years of World War II.[129] On this point, Richard Rodgers and Oscar Hammerstein II's *Oklahoma!* (1943) also deserves mention. The musical revolves around the romance between a farm girl named Laurey Williams and a rancher named Curly McLain living in the Oklahoma Territory in 1906. A sinister farmhand named Jud Fry threatens Laurey and Curly's relationship. Near the end of the musical, Curly and Jud fight, and Jud falls and dies on his own knife. Thus Curly "saves" Laurey from Jud, and the two go on (presumably) to live happily ever after. As historian Andrea Most has argued, Jud is coded as a dangerous racial outsider.[130] He lives alone in a dirty smokehouse, the walls of which he has adorned with pornography. Most explains that "Laurey fears the racial 'other' ... that threatens to invade the white woman's private space and steal her virginity."[131] Laurey Williams's fears in *Oklahoma!* parallel the fears of Laurie Moss's mother and grandfather in *The Tender Land*. One of the things, however, that sets *The Tender Land* apart from *Picnic* and *Oklahoma!* is that unlike Madge Owens

---

125 Ibid.
126 Ibid., 136.
127 See *Picnic*, Internet Broadway Database.
128 Pollack, *Aaron Copland*, 473.
129 May, *Homeward Bound*, 92.
130 Most, *Making Americans*, 108.
131 Ibid., 108–110. According to Kara Anne Gardner, it was Agnes de Mille, rather than Rodgers or Hammerstein, who was particularly "intrigued by the love triangle between Laurey, Curley and the predatory farmhand Jud." Gardner explains that "de Mille believed Laurey was secretly drawn to Jud because he represented something dangerous and forbidden." She argues that in the famous dream ballet that rounds out the first act of *Oklahoma!*, de Mille "delved into aspects of Laurey's character that, based on letters and draft librettos, never occurred to Rodgers and Hammerstein." See *Agnes de Mille*, 24–25.

and Laurey Williams, Laurie Moss does not really fall in love with anyone.¹³² She thinks initially that she has fallen in love with Martin, but really, she has fallen in love with her newfound autonomy and independence. When she sets out at the opera's conclusion, she suggests that she will become her own woman, not necessarily someone's wife.

Searching for Laurie Moss

Throughout this book, I have considered both the real and the fictional, examining the real women who portrayed these male-authored, operatic heroines, as well as the real women who often inspired them. It is along these lines that I have often wondered about the sopranos who portrayed Laurie Moss in the 1950s. Did Laurie's story resonate with them? How did they interpret her struggle for autonomy and independence? Rosemary Carlos (1925–2005), who made her NYCO debut as Laurie in 1954, was not impressed. Born and raised in Kansas, Carlos recalled in an interview with Ryan Patrick Jones that when she revealed this information to Copland at her audition, he "just hollered" and said, "'young lady, we just wrote an opera for you!'"¹³³ Yet as Carlos admitted, she ultimately did not find anything about *The Tender Land* particularly compelling. No matter how much Copland may have wanted to think that Carlos—who had set out from Kansas in her early twenties, moving to New York City to embark on a career in opera—was destined to sing and perhaps identify with the role of Laurie, Carlos had other ideas. In August 1954, a writer for the *Boston Globe* commented on the Tanglewood production of *The Tender Land*, explaining that Carlos had "created the part of Laurie."¹³⁴ Carlos would likely not have agreed with this characterization, despite its being a common way to describe a performer who has originated a particular role. As she recalled to Jones, from the very beginning, she questioned the authenticity of *The Tender Land*: "Frankly, when I first encountered the libretto I did not particularly care for it because it was a little too folksy. I didn't think the librettist was terribly interested [in his subject matter]. For some reason, it didn't seem to have any snap to it, or any real zest. [It] didn't seem to me that he'd ever been to Kansas."¹³⁵ Carlos also felt that Johns's libretto was poorly written, and she explained that she "blamed [the opera's poor reception] all

---

132 Pollack makes this point as well, writing that *The Tender Land* "contained a liberating message different from *Picnic*'s." See *Aaron Copland*, 474.
133 Rosemary Carlos, quoted in Jones, "*The Tender Land*," 108.
134 "'The Tender Land,' Aaron Copland Opera, Heard at Tanglewood."
135 Carlos, quoted in Jones, "*The Tender Land*," 126.

on the book."[136] She noted that she "would like to have told [Erik Johns] that if he had written a better story, we'd have had a better opera."[137] For Carlos, Johns's story was "too shallow" and "too namby-pamby."[138]

Carlos's perspective echoes some of Olin Downes's assessment of *The Tender Land*. Downes argued that Johns's libretto failed to "convince, or present much that is of character, or motivation, or consequence."[139] Downes gave Copland some credit for his music, but overall, he characterized it as "a very one-sided affair," explaining that "of the women, their natures and feelings, Mr. Copland's music tells us very little."[140] Ultimately, Downes found the women "sexless and negligible," whereas the men at least had "outline and contour."[141] Downes seemed to feel that the performers got somewhat stuck in this shortcoming, stating that the men were "excellent," the women, "uninteresting and insipid."[142] But "what could [the women] do?" he asked.[143]

Carlos is a difficult figure to track because unlike Patricia Neway, Beverly Sills, or Phyllis Curtin (who figures prominently in the next chapter), she did not bolster her career by performing in an American opera. In fact, Carlos's singing career fizzled shortly after her performances in *The Tender Land*. From what I could uncover, she was born in Walnut, a small town in Crawford County, Kansas. Her father, Edward Bernard Carlos (1887–1978), worked for the Missouri–Kansas–Texas Railway.[144] He married her mother, Eulah Rose Mudd (1893–1977), in Walnut in 1912.[145] The couple had eight children, six girls and two boys, and throughout their lives, they were active members of St. Patrick's Catholic Church in Walnut.[146]

Rosemary grew up singing. Local newspapers carried regular reports of her various performances during the 1940s. In 1943, for example, the Wichita-based *Catholic Advance* reported on Carlos's performance in *An Old Kentucky Garden*, a 1936 operetta based on music by Stephen Foster, at the

---

136 Ibid.
137 Ibid.
138 Ibid. Given that "namby-pamby" is sometimes derogatorily employed to refer to a man's sexuality, Carlos's use of the word may lend further support to Mathers's argument about *The Tender Land*'s gay subtext.
139 Downes, "Music: Premiere of One-Act Opera."
140 Ibid.
141 Ibid.
142 Ibid.
143 Ibid.
144 See "Edward Bernard Carlos"; "Carlos."
145 See "Eulah Rose Carlos."
146 See "Walnut Couple Celebrates 63rd Wedding Anniversary."

College of Paola.[147] An article in the *News-Journal* (Mansfield, Ohio) shows that in 1946, Carlos was studying with Emelie Severson, a voice teacher at Saint Mary College (now the University of Saint Mary) in Leavenworth, Kansas.[148] In May of 1947, the *Kansas City Times* reported that Carlos had appeared in a concert before an audience of 1,000 at Saint Mary College, receiving "a long ovation after she sang 'Pace, pace, mio dio'" from Verdi's *La forza del destino*.[149]

By the fall of 1948, Carlos was in New York City, studying at the Juilliard School of Music under Florence Page Kimball, best known for teaching Leontyne Price (b. 1927).[150] In May of 1950, the *Walnut Eagle* reported that Carlos had appeared as Violetta in the Juilliard Opera Theatre's recent production of *La Traviata*.[151] Two years later, Carlos and Price appeared together in the Juilliard Opera Theatre's production of *Falstaff*. Writing in the *New York Daily News*, Douglas Watt credited Carlos, "a lyric soprano who played Anne," with "the most beautiful singing of the evening."[152] He also noted that "Mary Leontyne Price, as Mistress Ford, revealed the makings of an impressive dramatic soprano and gave a good acting performance."[153] When Watt reviewed Carlos's performance in *The Tender Land* in April of 1954, he wrote only that she sang her part "acceptably."[154]

After Carlos sang the role of Laurie in the August 1, 1954, performance of *The Tender Land* at Tanglewood, she returned to Walnut to visit her parents. *The Parsons Sun* reported that she spent "considerable time fishing, relaxing and making ice cream," explaining that "this is all by way of relief from the strenuous life of an opera singer."[155] Yet beyond this report, it is difficult to locate evidence of Carlos's "life of an opera singer." The mid-1950s were challenging for the NYCO, and it is possible that Carlos got lost in what Heidi Waleson termed the "cloud" that "hung over" Joseph

---

147 "Rosemary Carlos Has Paola Operetta Lead." Theodosia Paynter wrote the libretto for *An Old Kentucky Garden*, and G. A. Grant-Schaefer adapted and arranged Foster's music.
148 See Gresmer, "It's Purely Personal."
149 "A Concert Draws 1,000." In April of 1948, the *Kansas City Times* reported that Carlos had appeared in the Saint Mary College Spring Festival, singing selections by Bizet and Mascagni. See "Music and Musicians."
150 See Hughes, "Florence Kimball, Teacher, Dies at 87."
151 "Rosemary Carlos Stars in Opera."
152 Watt, "'Falstaff' Gets a Fine Revival."
153 Ibid.
154 Watt, "Copland Opera Has Premiere at City Center."
155 "Rosemary Carlos."

Rosenstock's years as the company's general director.[156] It is also possible, of course, that Carlos did not ultimately have what it took to be a professional opera singer in the US during the 1950s, or that she simply turned her attention to other pursuits. In March of 1955, the *Boston Globe* reported that Carlos and other members of the American Opera Society had appeared with the Zimbler Sinfonietta in Boston, but after this notice, references to Carlos's name drop out of the East Coast press.[157]

In 1956, Carlos married Victor Trucco (1913–1964), a conductor and vocal coach who spent most of his career at the Met.[158] Carlos changed her name and according to Jones, by the end of the 1950s, she had stopped singing professionally.[159] Thus, she disappeared from the world of opera and, at least momentarily, from the small-town world of southeast Kansas. I could not locate a wedding announcement, or even a single mention of Carlos and Trucco together, in the *Walnut Eagle* or *Parsons Sun*. On May 19, 1964, newspapers on the East Coast reported that Trucco had died from a heart attack while on tour with the Met in Atlanta.[160] As reports in local Kansas papers indicate, Carlos, now widowed, made several trips home to Kansas with her two children in the late 1960s. At some point, Carlos moved back to Kansas permanently. She died in Pittsburg, the largest city in Crawford County, in 2005 and was buried in the cemetery in Walnut alongside her parents.

Despite the challenges to tracking Carlos's life and career, during the 1940s and early 1950s, the singer's life and career appear to have been quite

---

156 Waleson, *Mad Scenes and Exit Arias*, 15. In her autobiography, Beverly Sills recalled that when she joined the NYCO in 1955, she did not realize that the company "had been losing business for several seasons." See *Beverly*, 90. Waleson offers some context, explaining that lots of people in New York, including members of the New York press, were upset when the NYCO board fired Laszlo Halasz, the company's first general director, in 1951. After Joseph Rosenstock's dismal four years as general director, Erich Leinsdorf took over, but he lasted only a year before the NYCO board called upon Julius Rudel to finally right the ship.

157 See "Zimbler Sinfonietta Closes Sixth Season."

158 Interestingly, Victor Trucco was the conductor who helped to prepare contralto Marian Anderson for her debut at the Met in 1955. According to Anderson, "Mr. Trucco made sure that I knew not only the tempi and phrasing as the Metropolitan would want them but also the meaning of the words I was to sing. He encouraged me to interline my score with the English translation of the Italian text." See Anderson, *My Lord, What a Morning*, 300.

159 Jones, "*The Tender Land*," 108.

160 "Conductor of Met Dies." See also "Rites Are Set in New York for Met's Trucco"; "Victor Trucco, 51, Conductor at Met."

full. It is true that Carlos grew up in a tiny farm town, but as the *Walnut Sun* indicates, Walnut was not exactly a cultural backwater. The town was served by the Missouri–Kansas–Texas Railway, as well as the Atchison, Topeka & Santa Fe Railway, and Carlos spent considerable time in cities such as Kansas City and St. Louis. In 1950, for example, the *Walnut Eagle* reported that Carlos would be spending her summer with the St. Louis Municipal Opera Company.[161] Perhaps Carlos did not feel she needed to "escape" from her life in the Midwest. Until her marriage to Trucco, she went back and forth between Walnut and New York City with apparent ease, and after her husband's death, she resumed this pattern before returning "home" for good. When Carlos sang the role of Laurie in 1954, she had the full support of her parents, who were proudly submitting reports of her operatic accomplishments to local papers. Thus, she may not have identified with the tension between Laurie and her mother and grandfather. Perhaps like writer Susan Allen Toth, she would have regarded her girlhood in the Midwest in "mostly … happy" terms, rather than in deep-seated anxiety over her sexual and political autonomy.[162]

If the role of Laurie did not resonate with Carlos, did it resonate with other sopranos? I continued to look for Laurie through these women, researching Alice (van Ausdal) Hotopp (b. 1932) and MaVynee Betsch (1935–2005), the sopranos who alternated in the role of Laurie when Oberlin College presented *The Tender Land* in 1955. Born in Richmond, Indiana, Alice van Ausdal graduated from Richmond High School in 1950. She earned her Bachelor of Music degree from Oberlin in 1954, staying on for an additional year on a graduate assistantship. She then toured professionally, most notably with the popular bandleader and radio and television personality Fred Waring (1900–1984); she traveled across the upper Midwest and down the California coast, and ultimately spent three weeks in Las Vegas.[163] In 1956, she returned to Ohio to marry Thomas Hotopp, also a graduate of Richmond High School. The couple spent their life in Dayton, Ohio, about an hour's drive from their hometown in Indiana. Alice Hotopp quickly built her reputation as a teacher in Dayton, establishing a private voice studio and teaching on the faculties at the University of Dayton

---

161 See "Rosemary Carlos Stars in Opera."
162 Toth, *Blooming*, 5. Toth was born and raised in Ames, Iowa. She studied at Smith College, the University of California at Berkeley, and the University of Minnesota before joining the English faculty at Macalester College in St. Paul, Minnesota, in 1969.
163 In a 2022 email exchange with me, Hotopp recalled that at one point, she performed on a nationwide television Christmas show where she had a solo in "The Twelve Days of Christmas." Alice Hotopp, email correspondence with the author, July 22, 2022.

and Antioch College. She also continued to sing, appearing occasionally as a soloist with the Cincinnati Symphony Orchestra, Dayton Philharmonic Orchestra, and Richmond Symphony Orchestra, and as a member of the choirs of First Baptist Church and Temple Israel in Dayton. In 1976, Hotopp was one of four singers selected from Ohio to sing in a 200-voice bicentennial chorus at Interlochen Arts Camp. Betty Dietz Krebs, reporting on the honor in the *Dayton Daily News*, described Hotopp as "one of Dayton's busiest singers."[164] A smaller local paper, the *Daily Advocate*, marveled that Hotopp, a mother of three, had "manage[d] to combine an active professional career with a home and family."[165]

In 2021, Hotopp recalled in an interview with me that although she did not have that many distinct memories of the opera itself, she thought that *The Tender Land* "went over very well" at Oberlin.[166] She also stated that she "loved" singing "Laurie's Song," musing that there was "so much" to the text. She could remember "standing behind this fence" on stage and singing the aria rather simply, without any extraneous physical movement. The biggest challenge, she explained, was "to sing that last note softly." After the performance, she recalled that Copland came backstage to congratulate her. He was apparently so impressed with her singing that he sought to arrange for a scholarship for her so that she could attend Tanglewood that summer. Hotopp already had plans for the summer, but admitted it was thrilling for her, at the outset of her career, to have the confidence of one of the country's preeminent composers.

MaVynee Betsch, the other soprano who sang the role of Laurie at Oberlin, was born and raised in Jacksonville, Florida. In 1998, journalist Russ Rymer documented much of Betsch's life, noting that the granddaughter of Abraham Lincoln Lewis (1865–1947), the founder of the Afro-American Life Insurance Company and Florida's first African American millionaire, grew up in a house with two pianos, "an upright in the upstairs den and a baby grand in the glassed-in downstairs porch."[167] Betsch and her two younger siblings, Rymer explained, "started their music and dance lessons before they started school."[168] It was apparently on the advice of baritone Todd Duncan that Betsch decided to apply to Oberlin College to

---

164 Krebs, "Alice Hotopp Selected for Ohio Quartet."
165 "Alice Hotopp Is Chosen to Sing with Bicentennial Group."
166 Alice Hotopp, telephone interview with the author, June 15, 2021. All quotations in this paragraph are from this interview.
167 Rymer, *American Beach*, 150.
168 Ibid. Betsch's sister, Johnnetta Betsch Cole (b. 1936) is an anthropologist and educator. In 1987, she became the first African American woman to serve as president of Spelman College. From 2009 to 2017, she was director of the Smithsonian's National Museum of African Art. John Betsch (b. 1945) is a

study piano. Once, when Duncan came through Jacksonville, he stayed at the Betsch house; he heard MaVynee at the piano and made his recommendation. At Oberlin, Rymer wrote, Betsch quickly "found her campus, but not yet her calling."[169] Then, during her sophomore year, she saw a production of *Aida* in Cleveland. She recalled that when she heard soprano Zinka Milanov "hit that ending with the high A, you could have heard a pin drop, and she held it for a minute and a half, pianissimo, and—oh, chile!—every hair on you stood up."[170] It was an experience she never forgot, and it prompted her to double major in piano and voice.

Betsch earned her Bachelor of Music degree in 1955, the same year she alternated with Hotopp in the role of Laurie. After her college graduation, Betsch moved to Paris, where she continued to take voice lessons. In 1959, she made her operatic debut as Salome at the Staatstheater Braunschweig. From there, she had a successful career singing in cities and opera houses throughout Germany. Yet according to Johnnetta B. Cole, "something happened to my sister in Europe."[171] As Cole explains, when Betsch returned to Jacksonville in 1965 to care for their ailing mother, "she began to display very erratic behavior, but her behavior was not so erratic that she could not talk about what it meant to be an African American woman living in Germany."[172] Cole writes that Betsch recalled "occasions when members of the audience came backstage and exclaimed: '*Ach!* Now it is clear why the Black one can sing Wagner. The name is Betsch!'"[173] What her sister's experience showed Cole, a highly accomplished anthropologist, educator, and administrator, was "that African Americans are victimized by the myth of White superiority at home *and* abroad, and that there are many ways to call us 'N*****.'"[174] Back home in Florida, Betsch never returned to opera. Instead, she became an environmental activist, dedicating the rest of her life—and a substantial amount of her inheritance—to the preservation of American Beach, one of the largest and most popular Blacks-only beaches in Florida. According to Rymer, Betsch left opera "partly in the inchoate comprehension that she must do so to defend her community."[175]

---

  jazz drummer. He has performed with musicians such as Abdullah Ibrahim, Archie Shepp, and Steve Lacy.

169 Rymer, *American Beach*, 150.
170 MaVynee Betsch, quoted in ibid., 132.
171 Cole, *Conversations*, 14.
172 Ibid.
173 Ibid. Kira Thurman examines the history of Black musicians in German-speaking Europe in *Singing Like Germans*.
174 Cole, *Conversations*, 14.
175 Rymer, *American Beach*, 337.

Located on Amelia Island, just north of Jacksonville, American Beach was founded in 1935—the year of Betsch's birth—by Betsch's grandfather. In 1964, Florida's beaches were desegregated, and American Beach fell into a period of decline. As one American Beach resident put it, "first we had segregation, and then integration. Then disintegration."[176] In the 1980s, white developers began buying up the land, but Betsch fought back, reinventing herself as the "beach lady" and seeking to preserve the beach's history and land. In 1999, Mike Williams, a staff writer for the *Atlanta Journal-Constitution*, called Betsch the community's "colorful, exuberant, unofficial mayor."[177] He described her appearance in detail: "Now 63, Betsch's skin is as smooth as a 20-year-old's. Her eyes are clear and piercing. She dresses in felt wraps or wool Mexican serapes over sweatpants, one arm dangling stacked bracelets, fingers festooned with seashell rings. The other hand sports 18-inch fingernails, which she usually keeps clutched to her middle for protection."[178] Williams continued:

> And then there is her hair—gloriously gray-black, nearly 8 feet of it, teased into what [Russ] Rymer called a "cock's comb" over her head, then tucked under the collar of her serape and bundled at her side.
> She usually wears a black lace headband, and a tiny dot of a silver earring pierces one nostril, with four or five more lining her ear lobes.
> Matching her appearance are her voice, rich and radiant, and her words, erudite but earthy and radical to the core. Her feminism and eco-warrior outlook must leave her piney woods neighbors in Nassau County—the ones driving the beat-up pickups and building the condos for the rich folks—scratching their heads in puzzlement.[179]

In 2003, the *Palm Beach Post* reported on the fruits of Betsch's labors and activism, noting that American Beach had become the first location on the Florida Black Heritage Trail and that it had been added to the National Register of Historic Places.[180]

Given that Betsch was a Black woman and given that Copland and Johns clearly coded Laurie as a white woman, it is somewhat ironic that it is the trajectory of Betsch's life that best maps onto the future that Johns

---

176 Anonymous American Beach resident, quoted in ibid. 220. As Rymer explains, "integration represented the greatest opening of a domestic American market in the nation's history, but the windfall only worked one way. Black customers flocked to the stores and hotels and restaurants—and beaches—where they had formerly been prohibited ...Whites did not storm across the same open border to spend money in black establishments." *American Beach*, 219–220.
177 Williams, "The Once and Future American Beach."
178 Ibid.
179 Ibid.
180 Salome, "The Queen of the Beach."

imagined for Laurie Moss. In 1994, Johns mused that Laurie "might have gone on to become a 'flower child,' a war protestor, or a worker in a civil rights campaign."[181] In other words, Laurie might have joined the countercultural movement(s) of the 1960s. She might even have become a feminist like Betsch, who described herself as a "terra-ist" and a "black, radical eco-feminist"[182] In 1993, Cole recalled that when she and her sister were growing up, neither "could have predicted where the other would end up in life."[183] Yet Cole noted that while in high school in the 1950s, she and her sister "agreed that the cooking classes that taught us to make cinnamon toast and hot chocolate were not the best preparation for whatever life held in store for us."[184] Like Laurie, Betsch and Cole looked forward to exploring "the world so wide." Still, Betsch's life demonstrates that a clear victory is never a given. When Betsch moved onto American Beach, many people thought she had lost her mind.[185] Close friends of the family wondered why she had changed her life so drastically. Some speculated that she had been betrayed by the man she loved. Others pointed to health problems and the anti-Black racism she encountered in Germany. Betsch herself claimed that back on American Beach, she had never felt more free.

Testing the Limits of *The Tender Land*

Scholars like Wini Breines have emphasized that many of the women who tested the constraints of the 1950s "pioneered the social movements of the 1960s."[186] They were the ones who became "the civil rights workers, campus activists, and youthful founders of the women's liberation movement of the late 1960s."[187] It is interesting to me how similar Breines's language is to the language Johns used to imagine Laurie Moss's future. While I am not convinced it is possible to read *The Tender Land* as a feminist text per se, Johns's words help to illuminate some of the nascent feminist themes in the story of the opera and its evolution, as well as in the stories of the women who portrayed Laurie Moss. As Copland and Johns wrote *The*

---

181 Johns, quoted in Pollack, *Aaron Copland*, 474.
182 Betsch is quoted as calling herself a "terra-ist" in Rymer, *American Beach*, 101. Betsch is referred to as "a professed black, radical eco-feminist" in Dahlburg, "'Beach Lady' Triumphed over Tide of Development."
183 Cole, *Conversations*, 15.
184 Ibid.
185 Rymer, *American Beach*, 108.
186 Breines, *Young, White, and Miserable*, 129.
187 Ibid.

Tender Land, drawing on elements from *Tragic Ground* and *Famous Men*, they made a woman their central character, and they granted that woman a certain amount of agency. Laurie rebels against her grandfather's authority, and when he will not allow her to be who she wants to be, she leaves, determined to find her way. Thus *The Tender Land* finally departs from its literary ancestors. *Tragic Ground* and *Famous Men* treat women like objects, whereas *The Tender Land* centers Laurie as a free-thinking subject.

Still, I find myself pondering the fault line between Laurie and the real woman who Copland and Johns claimed inspired her. On March 28, 1954, just a few days before the NYCO premiered *The Tender Land*, Copland described the origins of his new opera to *New York Times* music critic Howard Taubman. Referring to the two photographs that served as the inspiration for Laurie and Ma, he explained that "there was something so full of living and understanding in the face of the older woman, and something so open and eager in the face of the younger one. ..."[188] I must confess, however, that Copland's optimistic words do not seem to me to map onto the people in Evans's photographs. I see defeat in the face of the twenty-seven-year-old mother. As Jane Robbins Mize writes, "Her gaze has a certain resignation, and her mouth doesn't quite smile." "This is the face of a woman old before her time, who has known not only hard work but the realization that her children have gone to bed hungry," Mize concludes.[189] From my perspective, the daughter also appears trapped. Her eyes grip the viewer, and she—unlike the generally optimistic Laurie—seems already hardened by the harsh realities of her young life.

The daughter was Maggie Louise Gudger, one of Agee's favorite subjects from the summer of 1936.[190] In *Famous Men*, Agee described Maggie Louise as being "fond of school," noting that she got "unusually good 'marks.'"[191] He also explained how proud George and Annie Mae Gudger were of their daughter's intellectual potential: "Her father and much more particularly her mother is excited over her brightness and hopeful of it: they intend to make every conceivable effort by which she may continue not only through the grades but clear through high school. She wants to become a teacher, and quite possibly she will; or a trained nurse; and again quite

---

188 Aaron Copland, quoted in Taubman, "Copland's New Opera." Interestingly, in this article, Copland suggests that he, rather than Johns, was initially inspired by these two photographs.
189 Mize, "From the Outside In."
190 Here, I am continuing to use the name Gudger, the pseudonym for the Burroughs family, because I am referring to Agee's text.
191 Agee and Evans, *Let Us Now Praise Famous Men*, 266.

possibly she will."[192] According to Agee, George had finished the second grade and could "spell and read and write his own name" but "beyond that," he was "helpless."[193] Annie Mae could "read, write, spell, and handle simple arithmetic"; she was also "excited by such matters as the plainer facts of astronomy and geology."[194] Both of their educations strangled by the demands of their labors, George and Annie Mae clearly wanted more for their daughter. Their desires parallel the desires of Laurie's mother and grandfather in *The Tender Land*.

Yet if Agee recognized Maggie Louise's potential, he also expressed some doubts about her future: "She already has traces of a special sort of complacency which probably must, in time, destroy all in her nature that is magical, indefinable, and matchless: and this though she is one of the stronger persons I have ever known."[195] In the 1980s, writer Dale Maharidge and photographer Michael Williamson returned to Alabama to follow up with the three families featured in *Famous Men*, ultimately publishing their book *And Their Children after Them* in 1989, one year before Copland's death.[196] Copland, who suffered from Alzheimer's disease in his final years, and Johns, who never admitted to reading *Famous Men* in the first place, probably never read *And Their Children after Them*. But if they had, they would have been sobered to learn of Maggie Louise's fate. According to Maharidge:

> She never did become a nurse or a teacher ... Each passing year mocked the dreams she had dreamed with Agee, reducing her a little each year, so that at the end of each year the vacant spot inside her took up more and more of the space that defined her to herself. Maggie Louise finally discovered she could no longer aspire to anything, because the part of her that used to aspire was no longer there.[197]

Maharidge reported that in 1971, Maggie Louise drank a bottle of rat poison, killing herself. If Copland and Johns wanted to imagine that Maggie Louise-turned-Laurie was going to strike off on her own, heroically making her way in the world beyond the conclusion of their opera, the sequel to *Famous Men* demonstrates that a brighter, better future is never guaranteed, especially for the woman from an economically disadvantaged background.

The sequel to *Famous Men* also demonstrates, once again, the tension between the real and the fictional—between seeing what we want to see and

---

192 Ibid.
193 Ibid., 269.
194 Ibid.
195 Ibid., 275.
196 In *And Their Children after Them*, Maharidge and Williamson continued to use the pseudonyms used by Agee and Evans.
197 Maharidge and Williamson, *And Their Children after Them*, iii–iv.

engaging with what are often more painful and deeply complicated realities. Moreover, even though Johns eventually speculated positively on Laurie's countercultural future, he apparently cautioned Daniel Mathers against reading too much into Laurie's character and struggle. He told Mathers, for example, that "to limit the opera as being about womanhood or femininity is not to go far enough," and he argued that "it was not so much feminism I was after, but humanism [or humanitarianism]."[198] Mathers used Johns's words to advance his reading of Laurie's sexual awakening as a broader metaphor for "a gay person on the verge of self-acceptance."[199] As he pointed out, because of the time period, "any reference in the story to homosexuality" could "exist[s] only as subtext."[200] Mathers's reading is quite compelling. As film critic Molly Haskell argues, "the repressiveness of the fifties both enabled and forced the homosexual writer to disguise himself."[201] "For him," Haskell explains, "the frustrated woman who purported to express heterosexual desire was really a cover, an alter ego, a pretext and outlet for themes and feelings he was forced to hide."[202] Yet I continue to pause over the fact that Johns was so comfortable mapping all of this onto a young woman and, more specifically, onto an eighteen-year-old virgin. This is why it is difficult to read *The Tender Land* as an explicitly feminist text. Copland did not really "see" the women who initially inspired the opera, and Johns—even in the late 1990s—thought that centering women in *The Tender Land* would "limit the opera."

For me, however, *The Tender Land* reveals the limits that some women in the 1950s were trying to test. The basic architecture of the story is quite simple: a mother and grandfather, both of whom are at a clear disadvantage because they do not have the authority of a father, take great pains to protect their daughter and granddaughter. To a certain extent, they succeed. Laurie is never raped. Nevertheless, as Laurie sets off on her own at the opera's conclusion, her future appears somewhat uncertain, and as the lived experiences of real women such as Maggie Louise Gudger (whose name was actually Lucille Burroughs) show, it is possible that Laurie may never overcome the obstacles that stand in her way. This unsettling reality is more clearly visible in Carlisle Floyd's *Susannah*, the subject of the next chapter.

---

198 Johns, quoted in Mathers, "Expanding Horizons," 128.
199 Ibid., 132.
200 Ibid.
201 Haskell, *From Reverence to Rape*, 251.
202 Ibid. See also Locke, "What Are These Women Doing in Opera?," 74–75.

Chapter Five

A Dangerous Jezebel: Susannah Polk

In Act I, Scene 2 of Carlisle Floyd's *Susannah* (1955), the title heroine sings a hopeful and arresting entrance aria. Similar to Laurie Moss, who marveled in her entrance at "the world so wide," eighteen-year-old Susannah Polk imagines the world "beyond them mountains." Like Copland, Floyd relies on an ascending major-seventh motive, painting a picture of a young woman who has just reached the cusp of adulthood. The whole world, it seems, lies at Susannah's feet. Moments before the final curtain descends on the opera, Susannah sways in the yard outside her family's cabin, singing a very different kind of song. In a much lower voice, she pretends to seduce one of her former friends. When he finally reaches out to touch her, she slaps him across the face, sending him fleeing from her property.

At the end of *Susannah*, the title heroine reasserts her right to her body and voice, yet she is far from whole. She is clearly traumatized by the violence she has endured over the course of the opera. According to Floyd, she is an "inexorably lonely prisoner of a self-imposed exile."[1] One might say that Susannah resembles Baby Doe and Lizzie Borden, also imprisoned at the end of their operas. I think, however, that there is an important difference. Susannah's imprisonment brings no closure. As Susannah sings her final number, eerily reminiscent of the deadly conclusion to Richard Strauss's *Salome* (1905), she troubles her opera's conclusion, seemingly compelling her audience to consider uncomfortable questions about the nature of opera, rape, and survival. Thus *Susannah* has the potential to illuminate, rather than gloss over, the longstanding tradition of violence against women in opera.

Sopranos have perhaps known this all along, for many have identified something special in this opera and in the title role. In September 2014, the San Francisco Opera mounted a new production of *Susannah* starring soprano Patricia Racette (b. 1965). Prior to the production's opening, Racette recalled that she had first sung the title role while in college.

---

1 Floyd, *Susannah, Libretto*, 36.

"Susannah is the only role I've ever paid to sing," she declared dramatically in an interview for *Opera News*:

> I was a sophomore at the University of North Texas when I heard they were doing *Susannah* at a small college in Fort Worth—and I was in Denton, about an hour north. I wanted to do it, but I was told that in order to participate, I had to register at this other college—even though I was going to school full-time in Denton. So I paid to join a class so that I could sing Susannah.[2]

On an earlier occasion, Racette apparently told Floyd, "I'm in opera because I saw 'Susannah' when I was in college."[3] Racette's words offer a glimpse into the way in which this role has appealed to an impressive line of American sopranos since Phyllis Curtin (1921–2016), the very first Susannah. Along with Racette, sopranos such as Phyllis Treigle, Renée Fleming, Cheryl Studer, Patricia Craig, Maralin Niska, Karen Armstrong, Sharon Daniels, and Nancy Gustavson have taken custody of the defiant woman, falsely accused, abused, yet committed to her existence. More than any other opera spotlighted in this book, *Susannah* has garnered a following that extends into the present day and contributes, no doubt, to the piece's status as the most-performed American opera.[4]

Like *The Tender Land*, *Susannah* has often been understood as a folk opera and a commentary on the McCarthy era.[5] During the 1930s and 1940s, music critics and composers talked almost constantly about folk opera, and in the 1950s, many critics still sought to situate *Susannah*—with its Appalachian setting—in this context.[6] In the 1970s, critics turned their attention to the theme of false accusation in *Susannah* and began reading the opera as a work akin to Arthur Miller's *The Crucible* (1953). Yet I maintain that these interpretations of *Susannah* erase many of the issues that lie at the heart of the opera. In this chapter, I emphasize *Susannah*'s connections to European opera, testing the usefulness and accuracy of the folk opera

---

2   Racette, quoted in Driscoll, "All American," 22.
3   Floyd, quoting Racette in Campbell, "Prolific Composer Says Music 'Illuminates Our Emotional Lives.'"
4   See "North American Works Directory."
5   For examples of these approaches to *Susannah*, see Wierzbicki, *Music in the Age of Anxiety*, 118–121; Hutchins-Viroux, "Witch-Hunts, Theocracies and Hypocrisy"; Kirk, *American Opera*, 286–290. In 2012, Helen Smith took a different approach, analyzing Floyd's construction of community in *Susannah* by emphasizing the importance of the chorus. See "Faith and Love in New Hope Valley."
6   Much of the initial conversation around folk opera stemmed from the 1935 premiere of *Porgy and Bess*. See Allen, "An American Folk Opera?"

label. I also test the notion of *Susannah* as a commentary on McCarthyism. I assert that at its core, *Susannah* is a traditional opera with traditional arias dressed in a veneer of localized folksiness. I read the opera's title heroine, moreover, not so much as a victim of false accusation but as a young woman whose sexuality is regarded as a problem. Like Laurie Moss, Susannah Polk is beautiful and unmarried. Yet unlike Laurie, Susannah is vilified, rather than protected. She is presumed to be unchaste, perhaps because she is presumed not to be white. The people of Susannah's community regard her as a dangerous Jezebel, a sexually promiscuous woman who seeks to lead good men astray. For this, she is punished, first through rumors and ostracization and then through rape, that ultimate expression of patriarchal order.[7] As the final curtain descends on this opera, I find myself wondering if and how Susannah will find a way to move on from the trauma she has endured. Reading the end of *Susannah* against the end of *The Tender Land*, I find myself wondering what a patriarchal world will do to Laurie, particularly as she tries to make her way without the protections of her family. This is why I maintain that a feminist perspective—specifically one that acknowledges the power dynamics of gender, class, and race—matters deeply to any discussion and interpretation of *The Tender Land* and any discussion and interpretation of *Susannah*.

I begin this chapter by situating *Susannah*. I show how music critics approached *Susannah* first as a folk opera and later as a commentary on McCarthyism. I then turn to soprano Phyllis Curtin, who long asserted that she identified quite personally with the role of Susannah. In the spring of 1954, Curtin experienced a public shaming related to her sexuality, and she told Floyd about this experience the following summer, when he asked her to consider the title role in his new opera. I keep Curtin's perspective—and the perspectives of several other sopranos—at the forefront as I analyze Floyd's music and libretto, emphasizing its debts to European opera. Finally, I shift back to the US, offering a reading of Susannah as a woman suspected of having African American ancestry. I argue that if we read *Susannah* in this way, the opera might serve to highlight not only the long history of sexual violence against women in opera but also the long history of sexual violence against Black women in the US. I conclude this chapter by zooming back out, contemplating the various ways *Susannah* continues to resonate for American women in the twenty-first century and illuminating how the questions that *Susannah* poses continue to linger.

---

7   Key texts for interpretating rape and rape culture include Freedman, *Redefining Rape*; Buchwald, Fletcher, and Roth, eds., *Transforming a Rape Culture*; Cahill, *Rethinking Rape*; Brownmiller, *Against Our Will*.

Situating *Susannah*

Carlisle Floyd (1926–2021) began writing *Susannah* in the spring of 1953 at Florida State University (FSU).[8] He came up with the idea for the opera in a conversation with Nathan Samuel Blount.[9] A graduate student in English at FSU, Blount apparently asked Floyd if he knew the Apocryphal tale of Susanna and the Elders.[10] The tale goes as follows: The two elders of the people of Babylon have been lusting after and spying on Susanna, the beautiful and faithful wife of Joakim, a wealthy and respected member of the community.[11] The elders decide to approach her one day as she bathes in her husband's garden; they threaten to accuse her of adultery unless she agrees to have sex with them. Susanna refuses and is later arrested. She is about to be put to death but is saved when the prophet Daniel speaks on her behalf, insisting that her accusers be questioned before she is pronounced guilty. Daniel then interrogates the elders separately, and when discrepancies emerge in their stories, Susanna is acquitted and the elders are put to death.[12]

---

8   Born in Latta, South Carolina, Carlisle Floyd attended Converse College in Spartanburg, South Carolina, where he studied piano with Ernst Bacon. When Bacon left Converse for Syracuse University, Floyd followed him, earning his BM in 1946 and MM in 1949, both from Syracuse. In 1947, Floyd was appointed to the piano faculty at Florida State University, and until 1955, the year of *Susannah*'s FSU premiere, he identified primarily as a pianist.

9   Carlisle Floyd, interview with the author, Tallahassee, FL, May 19, 2015. See also Holliday, *Falling Up*, 117. Nathan Samuel Blount eventually earned his PhD in English at FSU. He later became an English professor at the University of Wisconsin.

10 In the Roman Catholic and Eastern Orthodox churches, "Susanna" appears as chapter 13 in the Book of Daniel. In Protestant churches (and this includes Floyd's background and tradition), "Susanna" is one of the additions to the Book of Daniel, considered Apocryphal. The son of a Methodist circuit minister, Floyd was familiar with the rough outlines of the story. See Holliday, *Falling Up*, 11.

11 See Hartman and Di Lella, *The Book of Daniel*, 19–20, 315–317. Since at least the sixteenth century, painters have depicted Susanna and the Elders. As art historian Mary D. Garrard points out, "the subject was taken up with relish by artists from the sixteenth through eighteenth centuries as an opportunity to display the female nude." See "Artemisia and Susanna," 149.

12 The story of Susanna and the elders has a long history of being set to music. In 1681, for example, Alessandro Stradella wrote the oratorio *La Susanna* for his employer Francesco II, Duke of Modena. In 1987, Susan McClary wrote *Susanna Does the Elders*, a music-theater piece in which she drew on Stradella's music and reputation for preying on the women to whom he gave

When I interviewed Floyd in 2015, he recalled, as he had in prior interviews with others, how in 1953 he immediately perceived the tale's "dramatic potential," explaining how "everything seemed to gel ... very quickly."[13] Yet in terms of collaboration, Floyd and Blount did not exactly "gel," and when Blount failed to produce a libretto in a timely manner, the composer took matters into his own hands, writing first the text and then the music. Floyd was no novice, however, when it came to libretto writing, as he had written both the music and the text for his first two operas, *Slow Dusk* (1949) and *The Fugitives* (1951, retracted).[14] Floyd was also aware of Gian-Carlo Menotti's success in supplying his own librettos, and he labeled *Susannah* a "musical drama" (the same term Menotti had used for *The Consul*).[15]

Floyd wrote the libretto for *Susannah* swiftly.[16] He envisioned his protagonist as eighteen-year-old Susannah Polk, who lives not with her husband but with her older brother Sam in an isolated Tennessee mountain

---

voice lessons. *Susanna Does the Elders* was commissioned and premiered at the Southern Theater in Minneapolis, Minnesota. McClary has described it as her "very first feminist venture." See McClary, "Lives in Musicology," 9. In 2018, McClary led students in the Historical Performance Program at Case Western Reserve University in a performance of Stradella's *La Susanna*. McClary's own *Susanna Does the Elders* was also revived at Case Western at this time.

13 Floyd, interview with the author.
14 Floyd composed *Slow Dusk* while working on his master's degree in piano performance at Syracuse University. He composed *The Fugitives* after joining the FSU piano faculty. Notably, Floyd also had a background in creative writing, having contributed several short stories and prose pieces to student publications while working toward his bachelor's degree in music. Some of these writings may be found in Floyd's papers, housed in the South Caroliniana Library at the University of South Carolina. For example, see Carlisle Floyd, "Which Shall Not Perish from the Earth" in *We, the Freshman* 4, no. 1 (Autumn 1943): 2–3; "Low-Country Town" in *We, the Freshman* 4, no. 2 (Winter 1944): 2–5; "'Tschaikowsky's Sixth' (A Sketch)" and "The 'Pounding'" in *The Concept* 43, no. 4 (May 1944): 21, 24–25, 37–38, in "Writings" Folder, Box 1, Carlisle Floyd Papers, South Caroliniana Library, University of South Carolina. This "Writings" folder includes several loose-leaf manuscripts as well.
15 Floyd, interview with the author. Floyd labeled his first opera, *Slow Dusk*, "a music play in one act." He has used the designation "musical drama" for most of his large-scale operas. These include *Susannah* (1955), *Wuthering Heights* (1958), *The Passion of Jonathan Wade* (1962, rev. 1990), and *Of Mice and Men* (1970). Both *Bilby's Doll* (1976) and *Willie Stark* (1981) are designated operas in three acts. *Cold Sassy Tree* (2000) is a "musical play in three acts" but is also commonly referred to as Floyd's first "comic opera."
16 According to Ronald Eyer, Floyd completed the libretto for *Susannah* "in the remarkably short period of ten days." See "Carlisle Floyd's 'Susannah,'" 7.

community, ironically called New Hope Valley. From the beginning of the opera, Susannah and Sam are something of outsiders; their parents are dead, and Sam is notorious for his drinking problem. Susannah's small world crumbles when the Valley Elders spy her bathing naked in the creek that they plan to use for baptisms. Embarrassed by their feelings of lust, the Elders pronounce Susannah wicked and plot to run her out of the valley.

The Elders spread vicious rumors and coerce other members of the community to testify against her. Susannah's friend Little Bat, for example, gets bullied into claiming that Susannah slept with him.[17] In Act I, Scene 5, Little Bat admits to Susannah that he told the Elders:

> I said you'd let me love you up.
> That's what they made me say.
> I said you'd let me love you up
> An' in the worse sort o' way.[18]

A traveling preacher, the Reverend Olin Blitch, takes it upon himself to try to save Susannah's soul. He exhorts her to confess her sin publicly. When she refuses, he seeks her out in private, visiting her at home while Sam is out hunting. Blitch tries yet again to get Susannah to confess. Still, she refuses, and Blitch rapes her. He begs for forgiveness the next morning, as he comes to terms with the fact that he has "defiled" a virgin, and he tries unsuccessfully to clear Susannah's name.[19] Importantly, he is willing only to tell the Elders that the Lord spoke to him of Susannah's innocence; he does not implicate himself or admit that he raped her. Later, Sam returns from his hunt. When Susannah tells him what has happened, he shoots and kills Blitch, who is in the midst of a baptizing session. In the opera's final scene, an angry mob storms the Polk property. Susannah laughs derisively in their

---

17 In his libretto, Floyd describes Little Bat as "a shifty-eyed youth, not too strong mentally," suggesting that Little Bat has some kind of developmental or cognitive disability. See Floyd, *Susannah, Libretto*, 7. Some productions of *Susannah* really play up this suggestion, whereas other productions simply portray Little Bat as cowardly. Musicologist Stephanie Jensen-Moulton has examined Floyd's depiction of disability in one of Floyd's later operas, *Of Mice and Men* (1970). Jensen-Moulton argues that Floyd "composes Lennie in terms of his polar extremes of sweetness and violence, solidifying pre-existing tropes of intellectual disability," noting that Floyd presents Lennie as "a virile (though unaware) sexual predator." Floyd's characterization of Little Bat prefigures this presentation. See "Intellectual Disability in Carlisle Floyd's *Of Mice and Men*," 132, 135.

18 Floyd, *Susannah, Libretto*, 15.

19 Ibid., 29. As Blitch begs God for forgiveness, he sings: "She was untouched before her young body was defiled by hands, defiled by my lust."

faces, chases them away from the property with a shotgun, and then pretends to seduce Little Bat.

After completing his libretto, Floyd continued to work on his own, turning his attention to the score and to casting decisions. By the summer of 1954, he had a full draft of the opera. Floyd then traveled to the Aspen Music Festival, where he approached up-and-coming soprano Phyllis Curtin to see if he could interest her in the title role.[20] Floyd outlined the opera's plot for Curtin, and he played through Susannah's two arias, "Ain't it a pretty night!" and "The trees on the mountains." According to Floyd, he offered to play through the entire score at the piano, but Curtin said that was unnecessary.[21] She was apparently already emotionally invested in the story and hooked by the two arias. On February 24, 1955, Curtin starred in FSU's premiere of the opera. In the fall of 1956, she sang Susannah at the NYCO, and she continued to sing the role well into the 1960s.

As Floyd has pointed out, Curtin's investment was key to *Susannah*'s success, yet acknowledgment of her investment is strangely lacking in many discussions of the opera. During the 1950s and 1960s, music critics and musicologists were quick to link *Susannah* to the American folk opera tradition. In 1955, Warren D. Allen, a music history professor at FSU, congratulated Floyd, saying that he "showed himself a man to be reckoned with in setting American grassroots traditions to effective words and music."[22] Allen also described Floyd's score, explaining how the composer-librettist had been inspired by "the Tennessee Mountain storehouse of square dance fiddle tunes, revivalist gospel-melodies, and modal folk-tunes."[23] He clarified that Floyd had not actually quoted any preexisting tunes but argued that he had nevertheless absorbed "the authentic spirit of mountaineer idioms."[24] In 1956, *New York Times* music critic Howard Taubman admitted that Floyd's music took "its inspiration" from a wide variety of sources "including the nineteenth-century Italian opera house," yet he too focused on what he called *Susannah*'s "grass roots."[25] He directed his readers' attention to what he regarded as "one of the finest scenes in the growing catalogue of American opera":

---

20 Floyd, interview with the author; Holliday, *Falling Up*, 123.
21 Floyd, interview with the author; Holliday, *Falling Up*, 123.
22 Dr. Warren D. Allen, "American Traditions Set to Music," *Tallahassee Democrat*, Friday, February 25, 1955, in Scrapbook, Oversize Box 14, Carlisle Floyd Papers.
23 Ibid.
24 Ibid.
25 Taubman, "The Opera: 'Susannah.'"

In the second scene of the second act, Mr. Floyd's opera achieves stunning cogency. The occasion is a revival meeting in the village church. As the congregation sings a hymn, the preacher works himself up into a state of religious ecstasy. At first, he speaks against the singing of the congregation; then his voice takes on a vibrato, and finally it bursts into song. The scene builds to a strong climax. As musical theatre, it is of the first order.[26]

Francis D. Perkins of the *New York Herald-Tribune* evaluated *Susannah* in similar language in 1956, also focusing on larger ensemble scenes like the "Revival Scene." He argued that in these moments, Floyd managed to achieve "local color with some suggestion, but not imitation, of folk tunes."[27]

These commentaries on Floyd's ability to absorb folk material somewhat prefigure John Graziano's analysis of "Brack Weaver, my true love" from Kurt Weill and Arnold Sundgaard's folk opera *Down in the Valley* (1948), noted in the previous chapter.[28] Indeed, in 2015, Floyd commented briefly on *Susannah*'s relationship to *Down in the Valley*, suggesting that *Down in the Valley* served as something of a model for him.[29] In particular, the rural setting of *Down in the Valley* may have given Floyd a precedent for transporting the tale of Susanna and the Elders to the mountains of Tennessee. It is noteworthy, however, that unlike *Down in the Valley* (and unlike *The Tender Land*), *Susannah* makes no use of preexisting folk tunes. Moreover, while *Susannah* premiered at a university, it was hardly composed for young singers or amateurs—the title roles were sung by professional opera singers. Conversely, when Weill revised *Down in the Valley* for Indiana University, his purpose was to create a new genre of opera, suitable for colleges, universities, and amateur groups. It is certainly useful to consider *Susannah* in proximity to the folk opera genre of the 1940s and 1950s, but ultimately, *Susannah* remains somewhat apart from it. During an onstage interview in St. Petersburg, Florida, in 2014, Floyd asserted that the folk element was only a "small part" of *Susannah*'s score, and he clarified his references to folk traditions such as the Appalachian ballad as a means for telling his story.[30]

By the 1970s, after the publication of an increasing number of scholarly examinations of the McCarthy era, music critics began approaching

---

26 Ibid.
27 Perkins, "City Opera Gives 'Susannah' Its First N.Y. Performance."
28 Graziano, "Musical Dialects in *Down in the Valley*," 300.
29 Floyd, interview with the author.
30 Carlisle Floyd, onstage interview with Michael Unger. See "Special Features" on Floyd, *Carlisle Floyd's Susannah*. This production by the St. Petersburg Opera in Florida was filmed at the Palladium Theater in St. Petersburg on January 31 and February 2 and 4, 2014.

Susannah's national significance from a new angle.[31] When the Cincinnati Opera produced *Susannah* in the summer of 1979, Nancy Malitz explained to readers of the *Cincinnati Enquirer* that this opera was "about intolerance, and the helpless victims of it."[32] It was "no accident," she asserted, "that it was completed 29 years ago, in 1955, during a terrifying period of political intolerance in America."[33] *Susannah*, she concluded, "spoke a special message to the America of the McCarthy Era."[34] Writing in 2013, Floyd's biographer Thomas Holliday also advanced the opera's connection to McCarthyism, explaining that Nathan Samuel Blount, who planted the seed for *Susannah* in 1953, "proposed updating the action to the present day" because he was "influenced by the recent McCarthy and Johns investigations."[35] As Holliday notes, Charley Eugene Johns (1905–1990) enacted Joseph R. McCarthy's national anti-communist campaign on a local level, spending his two years as the Governor of Florida (1953–1955) and eleven subsequent years in the Florida Senate campaigning against supposed communists, civil rights advocates, and homosexuals in the state.[36] He became infamous for his work as chair of the Florida Legislative Investigation Committee, established in 1956 and nicknamed the "Johns Committee." Through this committee, Johns ruined the lives of hundreds of teachers and students in Florida's state university system, including some known to Floyd.[37]

---

31 For an example of an early biography of McCarthy, see Griffith, *The Politics of Fear*. In 1976, playwright Lillian Hellman published her memoir of the McCarthy era (*Scoundrel Time*). In 1978, British novelist and historian David Caute published *The Great Fear*. During the 1980s and 1990s, even more scholarship on the McCarthy era began to appear. See Landis, *Joseph McCarthy*; Fried, *Nightmare in Red*; Schrecker, *The Age of McCarthyism*; Fariello, *Red Scare*.
32 Malitz, "'Susannah' Dares to Be Different." 1979.
33 Ibid.
34 Ibid.
35 Holliday, *Falling Up*, 118.
36 Ibid., 117. Charley Eugene Johns was elected to the Florida State Senate in 1947. He served as Acting Governor of Florida from 1953 to 1955, following the death of Governor Dan McCarty. He ran for re-election in 1955 but was defeated by Leroy Collins. He then returned to the Florida Senate, serving until 1966.
37 On Charley Eugene Johns and the Florida Legislative Investigation Committee, see Graves, *And They Were Wonderful Teachers*; Wright, "The Florida Legislative Investigation Committee and its Conflict with the Miami Chapter of the National Association for the Advancement of Colored People"; Schnur, "Cold Warriors in the Hot Sunshine"; Stark, "McCarthyism

Whether or not Blount truly sought to provide a commentary on McCarthyism through a recasting of the story of Susanna and the Elders remains unclear. Blount never spoke about his involvement during the early stages of *Susannah*'s development, and he died in 1989. Floyd has suggested, moreover, that he did not make the McCarthy connection until well into the 1970s. As he put it, he "began ultimately to think in the back of my head that [*Susannah*] was my *Crucible*, because certainly, the heart of the story is very much the same."[38] Floyd was referring, of course, to Arthur Miller's 1953 dramatization of the Salem Witch Trials, which at the time of its premiere was understood to be a commentary on McCarthyism. As Brooks Atkinson noted in the *New York Times* on January 23, 1953: "Neither Mr. Miller nor his audiences are unaware of certain similarities between the perversions of justice then and today."[39] *The Crucible*'s initial run on Broadway coincided with *Susannah*'s genesis, yet it is noteworthy that throughout the 1950s and 1960s, *Susannah* appears not to have been understood as a commentary on McCarthyism.[40] To my knowledge, music critics at the time never spoke of the opera in this way.

Since the 1970s, however, *Susannah*'s ability to shed light on the McCarthy era has proven especially compelling—for audiences, performers, opera companies, and even the composer himself. Over the years, Floyd embraced political readings of *Susannah*, and he spoke increasingly of his experience of Florida's version of McCarthyism and the man who fanned its flames. In 1979, Floyd told Nancy Malitz that the "general atmosphere of the witch hunt spilled over into everything."[41] Similarly, one year later, he told Robert Croan of the *Pittsburgh Post-Gazette* that for anyone who lived during the McCarthy era, it was "impossible not to have been touched by it."[42] In 2010, Raymond Gouin reported on a production of *Susannah* at Boston University, noting that Floyd, who advised the production and participated in a pre-performance question-and-answer session, "spent several minutes describing the reign of terror that descended upon Florida State University

---

in Florida." See also Julian E. Farris's historically informed novel *The Sin Warriors*.
38 Floyd, interview with the author.
39 Atkinson, "At the Theatre." See also Miller, "It Could Happen Here—and Did."
40 *The Crucible* opened at the Martin Beck Theatre on January 22, 1953, closing on July 11, 1953. See *The Crucible*, Internet Broadway Database. The NYCO commissioned an operatic adaptation of *The Crucible* in 1961. Robert Ward composed the music, and Bernard Stambler supplied the libretto.
41 Floyd, quoted in Malitz, "'Susannah' Dares to Be Different."
42 Floyd, quoted in Croan, "Composer Floyd Staging His Own 'Susannah' to Open Opera Season."

during this period, of the campus committees set up there and elsewhere to insure 'correctness,' and how even the slightest suspicion was enough to destroy a career."[43] Floyd spoke with audiences in St. Petersburg, Florida, in similar terms in 2014. He described the McCarthy era as "one of the darkest periods" of his life, recalling that at FSU, he was "aware of the fact that there was a kind of a witch hunt going on for two things: communists and homosexuals ... It was called the Johns Committee."[44] Yet it is difficult to take Floyd at his word here. Although he and his biographer infer connections between Floyd's (and Blount's) experiences of Florida McCarthyism and their work on *Susannah*, it is important to note that Floyd completed *Susannah* in 1954, two years before the formation of the Johns Committee. The precise relationship between *Susannah* and McCarthyism seems to be one brought out by reflection, and thus while a link between this opera and the domestic political landscape of the early Cold War remains, it is heavily colored by the benefit of historical hindsight and likely also indebted to a desire to fashion the composer as hero, resisting the repressive politics of his time.[45]

Phyllis Curtin's Investment in *Susannah*

If we must look for a hero in the story of how and why *Susannah* became the centerpiece in the American-opera canon, I maintain that we ought to look—as Floyd himself often did—to Phyllis Curtin. In 1956, Floyd acknowledged Curtin's "invaluable contribution," "unfailing belief in the opera," and "laudable creation of the title role" in the preface to *Susannah*'s piano-vocal score.[46] In 2007, he noted that "without Phyllis, *Susannah* might still be moldering on a shelf in my studio, unheard for these fifty-two years outside the city limits of Tallahassee."[47] Like Beverly Sills, who invested so much in *The Ballad of Baby Doe*, Curtin invested much in *Susannah*.[48] It was she

---

43 Gouin, "Floyd's Susannah in Boston."
44 Floyd, onstage interview with Unger.
45 It is interesting to note that audiences began reading *Susannah* as a critique of McCarthyism at approximately the same time as audiences began searching for resistance in the music of Dmitri Shostakovich. Following the 1979 publication of the composer's purported memoirs, many listeners sought to uncover anti-Soviet messages in Shostakovich's music. See Fay, "Shostakovich versus Volkov." Fay was responding to Volkov's *Testimony*.
46 See Floyd, *Susannah, Vocal Score*.
47 Floyd, "An Homage to Phyllis," quoted in Holliday, *Falling Up*, 402.
48 I discuss Beverly Sills's investment in Douglas Moore and John Latouche's *The Ballad of Baby Doe* in Chapter 2.

who telephoned Mack Harrell, also at the Aspen Music Festival in the summer of 1954, and encouraged him to consider the role of Olin Blitch.[49] After leading FSU's production of *Susannah*, Curtin and Harrell peddled the opera throughout New York City, speaking with Broadway producers such as Chandler Cowles and NYCO general director Joseph Rosenstock.[50] Finally, the pair convinced Erich Leinsdorf, who succeeded Rosenstock at the NYCO in 1956, to take a chance on *Susannah*. The NYCO presented the first New York performance of *Susannah* on September 27, 1956, with Curtin in the title role. Norman Treigle (1927–1975) sang the role of Blitch, taking over for Harrell, who had a schedule conflict.[51] As Elise K. Kirk points out, *Susannah* was "the major event" of the NYCO's 1956 season.[52] The opera quickly became a staple in the company's repertory, largely as a vehicle to feature Curtin and, to a lesser extent, Treigle.

Curtin identified strongly with *Susannah*'s Appalachian setting and characters. In 1997, she wrote that it was her "great fortune to be the very first Susannah," explaining that "this girl, this opera … are engraved on my heart."[53] Similarly, in a 2003 interview, she asserted that she "understood Susannah right to the ground."[54] Curtin took *Susannah* under her wing just as her career with the NYCO was gaining momentum. Born Phyllis Smith in Clarksburg, West Virginia, Curtin had attended Wellesley College, where she took voice lessons with soprano Olga Averino.[55] In 1946, three years after her graduation from Wellesley, she made her opera debut, singing the role of the First Niece in the American premiere of Benjamin Britten's *Peter*

---

49 In 2015, Floyd recalled how Curtin had immediately telephoned Harrell in his Aspen cabin. Holliday writes about this important chapter in *Susannah*'s history as well. See *Falling Up*, 123.

50 Chandler Cowles, who had produced Menotti's *The Medium* and *The Consul* on Broadway, apparently found *Susannah* too grim for Broadway by the mid-1950s. The NYCO's Joseph Rosenstock simply stated that he did not have the funds or support. See Holliday, *Falling Up*, 131.

51 Born in New Orleans, Norman Treigle made his debut with the NYCO in 1953. On Treigle's life and career, see Morgan, *Strange Child of Chaos*.

52 Kirk, *American Opera*, 286. As Kirk points out, *Susannah* was the "one bright spot" of Leinsdorf's single dismal year leading the company. In his memoir, Leinsdorf himself admitted that his year at the NYCO amounted to "a spectacular failure." See *Cadenza*, 159.

53 Curtin, "Phyllis Curtin: In Her Own Words."

54 Duffie, "Soprano Phyllis Curtin."

55 Curtin earned her bachelor's degree in political science from Wellesley College in 1943. She remained in Boston after college, pursuing graduate study in vocal performance at the New England Conservatory of Music.

Grimes (1945) at Tanglewood.⁵⁶ That same year, she met and married Philip D. Curtin, a historian who was also from West Virginia.⁵⁷ As he recalled in his 2005 memoir, Phyllis worked tirelessly to build her singing career in the late 1940s and early 1950s, but she was slow to earn "the recognition she hoped for or deserved."⁵⁸ Finally, she made her debut with the NYCO in 1953. The following year, she appeared in the title role of the NYCO's production of *Salome*. Her husband explained that "in addition to her vocal performance, her figure was trim enough, and she had enough experience as a dancer, to make a hit with the dance of the seven veils."⁵⁹ In fact, the media went a little wild. *Life Magazine* featured a series of photographs of Curtin dancing provocatively in a diaphanous and flowing costume, her legs mostly bare (Figs. 5.1 and 5.2).⁶⁰ The caption for the final photograph (Fig. 5.2)—"FINAL VEIL FALLS as Salome turns away. Miss Curtin, 30, is wife of Swarthmore history professor"—highlighted the transgressive appeal of Curtin's performance.⁶¹ In 1959, a reporter for a small newspaper based in Beckley, West Virginia, recalled that Curtin's performance, combined with the *Life* photographs, "catapulted" the soprano "to fame overnight."⁶² The reporter also gleefully recalled the language *Life* had used to describe Curtin's performance: "Long-limbed, lush-voiced and intense, Phyllis Curtin electrified her audience as she twisted and wriggled her way through 'The Dance of the Seven Veils.'"⁶³

Five years earlier, however, not everyone in West Virginia had been so proud of or amused by Curtin's performance. When Floyd met Curtin in Aspen in the summer of 1954, she told him how a Clarksburg preacher had censured her from the pulpit, questioning "the appropriateness" of

---

56 See Curtin, "Phyllis Curtin: In Her Own Words."
57 Born in Philadelphia, Pennsylvania, and raised in Webster Springs, West Virginia, Philip D. Curtin (1922–2009) was a noted historian on Africa and the Atlantic slave trade. He earned his PhD at Harvard University in 1953. Over the course of his academic career, he taught at Swarthmore College, the University of Wisconsin, and Johns Hopkins University. He is best known for his 1969 book *The Atlantic Slave Trade: A Census*.
58 Curtin, *On the Fringes of History*, 69.
59 Ibid.
60 See "'Passionate' Salome," 81–84.
61 Ibid., 84. The originals of these photographs may be found in the Phyllis Curtin Collection (Box 2, Folder 13), Howard Gotlieb Archival Research Center, Boston University. I am grateful to Claudia d'Alessandro for her permission to include reproductions of these photographs.
62 "Concert Association Announces Two Selections for New Season."
63 Ibid.

Figures 5.1. and 5.2. Photographs of Phyllis Curtin Performing the "Dance of the Seven Veils," Published in *Life Magazine*, April 12, 1954, © Gene Cook.

her *Salome* performance.⁶⁴ Floyd's biographer reports that "matters compounded" when Curtin and Gene Cook, the photographer who had taken the photographs for *Life*, "fell wildly in love"; Phyllis and Philip Curtin eventually divorced, and Phyllis married Cook.⁶⁵ Thus in the 1950s, Curtin was ideally positioned to approach the story of Blitch and the Valley Elders using their religious authority to put Susannah in her place as something akin to what she had experienced in West Virginia, where she too was at least briefly construed as a dangerous young woman, one who did not properly adhere to the expectations of a wife.⁶⁶

As Floyd noted, when he first met Curtin, she was enticed not only by the story he had written but also by the two arias he had composed for Susannah. In 1960, music critic and composer Herbert Elwell suggested that these arias were not really arias, but rather, "more like extended ballads."⁶⁷ Elwell was one of those early commentators who took *Susannah* to be a folk opera. Indeed, he claimed that Floyd had written the opera "in the language of hillbillies."⁶⁸ Yet as I demonstrate below, "Ain't it a pretty night!" is essentially a da capo aria. Even "The trees on the mountains," which is reminiscent of the ballad, a genre popularly connected to Appalachia, is clearly operatic.⁶⁹ Taken together, "Ain't it a pretty night!" and "The trees on the mountains" are dazzling arias that showcase a singer's vocal prowess and ultimately serve to emphasize Susannah's loss of innocence, hope, and self over the course of her ordeal in New Hope Valley.

Without a doubt, it is sopranos' fondness for "Ain't it a pretty night!" and "The trees on the mountains"—on stage, in concerts, and on recordings—that has contributed to *Susannah*'s enduring popularity overall.⁷⁰ According

---

64   Floyd, interview with the author.
65   Holliday, *Falling Up*, 123. Cook went on to photograph Curtin for the NYCO's *Susannah*. In his memoir, Philip D. Curtin wrote that his wife's meeting with Cook "in connection with *Salome* probably touched off changes that would have happened sooner or later in any case." See *On the Fringes of History*, 69. He also reported that their divorce "was final in April 1956, and that Phyllis married Eugene Cook in Las Vegas the next day" (p. 92).
66   Curtin was not the first artist to identify with Susanna(h). Garrard reads Artemisia Gentileschi's painting *Susanna and the Elders* (1610) in terms of Artemisia's own experience of sexual harassment and rape. See "Artemisia and Susanna," 162–167.
67   See Elwell, "Tennessee 'Susannah' Is Moving Spectacle."
68   Ibid.
69   On the ballad's connection to Appalachia, see Spencer, "Ballad Collecting: Impetus and Impact," 3.
70   A number of high-profile singers have recorded Susannah's arias. See Giddens and Turrisi, *There Is No Other*; Futral, *Great Operatic Arias*; Fleming, *I Want*

to Holliday, Floyd "was once approached by an adoring soprano who told him that the heroine's first aria was 'our national anthem.'"[71] Soprano Phyllis Treigle has revealed her deep—and profoundly personal—attachment to this aria as well. The daughter of Norman Treigle, she was named Phyllis Susannah in honor of both Phyllis Curtin and the title heroine in Floyd's opera. She notes that the front of her birth announcement featured a quote from "Ain't it a pretty night!" Inside, the birth announcement read: "The Norman Treigles present their new soprano." As a result, Treigle "felt destined" to be a singer and, eventually, to tackle the role of Susannah.[72]

"Ain't it a pretty night!" celebrates the mountainous Appalachian landscape and Susannah's potential, as though grafting them together and establishing Susannah as a particularly American heroine. According to Treigle, the aria requires that a singer have "an understanding of Susannah's innocence and her dreams, as well as an ability to take on this persona, so that when those dreams are crushed we can see what exactly was destroyed."[73] The aria opens in G-flat major, with Susannah's entrance preceded by a single sustained tonic in the French horn. Susannah then exclaims "Ain't it a pretty night!" over an expansive, ascending major seventh that falls by step to settle on a major sixth above the opening pitch (Ex. 5.1). As if confirming her pronouncement, the cellos echo Susannah. This sweeping melodic gesture sets the tone for the opening verse, in which Susannah marvels at the sky above her, noting that it "seems so heavy with stars that it might fall right down out of heaven."[74] She then launches into another verse, prefaced by a reprise of the ascending major-seventh motive, and she begins to imagine the world that stretches out beyond her home, citing big cities such as "Nashville and Asheville an' Knoxville," as well as "the folks" she has seen pictured "in the mail-order catalogues."[75] Here, she sounds very much like Laurie Moss, dreaming of the world beyond the picket fence and her family's farm.

Magic!; Upshaw, *The World So Wide*.
71   Anonymous soprano, quoted in Holliday, *Falling Up*, xx.
72   Phyllis Treigle, email correspondence with the author, March 19, 2015. Phyllis Treigle is an accomplished singer and teacher. She sang Susannah in a 1999 production by the Jefferson Performing Arts Society in Metairie, Louisiana. Michael Devlin, a protégé of her father, sang the role of Olin Blitch. Over the course of her career, she has appeared with numerous companies including the NYCO, Houston Grand Opera, Pittsburgh Opera, and the Sarasota Opera Association. She currently serves as classical voice department chair at the New Orleans Center for Creative Arts.
73   Ibid.
74   Floyd, *Susannah, Libretto*, 8.
75   Ibid.

Example 5.1. Floyd, *Susannah*, mm. 308–312.

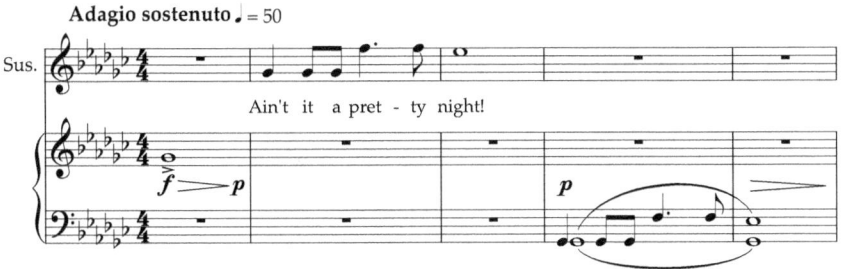

As is typical in a da capo aria, the middle section of "Ain't it a pretty night!" intensifies emotionally as Susannah, much more assertively than Laurie, informs the listener of her desires:

> I aim to leave this valley some day
> An' find out fer myself:
> To see all the tall buildin's
> And all the street lights
> An' to be one o' them folks myself.[76]

Floyd thickens his orchestration, and the singer must have the strength to soar above, finally reaching up to an A♯ above the staff and emphasizing her agency with the word "myself." Wondering if she might "get lonesome fer the valley," Susannah backpedals for a moment, but at Floyd's indication of *con moto*, as the orchestral texture thickens again, she asserts that she "could always come back," and she concludes:

> Someday I'll leave an' then I'll come back
> When I've seen what's beyond them mountains.[77]

The musical and dramatic climax occurs on the word "mountains" as Susannah reaches up to the highest note of the aria for a second and final time (Ex. 5.2). "Ain't it a pretty night!" concludes with a brief recapitulation of the A section. Floyd begins with a variation on the ascending major-seventh motive, decorating it with an ascending major ninth as though alluding to the longstanding da capo practice where a singer embellishes the final A section. Notably, Floyd writes additional embellishments into this final reprise as well.

At the beginning of Act II, Scene 3, Susannah sings "The trees on the mountains," a melancholy number that serves to show how Susannah's

---

76 Ibid.
77 Ibid.

Example 5.2. Floyd, *Susannah*, mm. 346–351.

dreams are gradually being crushed by the weight of her experience in New Hope Valley. Floyd has acknowledged that with this aria, he "wanted something that sounded like a folk song" and thus sought to imitate one of those "old timey ballads," invoking the "familiar theme" of "the false-hearted lover."[78] Yet even as "The trees on the mountains" gestures toward folk tradition, the number requires a decidedly operatic technique. As Phyllis Treigle points out, the aria "is quite lyrical, and the singer has to have both a lush middle and a pretty easily accessible top."[79] The refrain is punctuated

---

78 Floyd, interview with the author.
79 Treigle, email correspondence with the author.

by a repeated octave leap that eventually expands to a tenth, and the number concludes with three exposed octave leaps over a decrescendo from *piano* to *pianissimo* (Exx. 5.3 and 5.4). The exposed conclusion to "The trees on the mountains" recalls the end of "Laurie's Song," which as soprano Alice Hotopp noted was so challenging to sing *pianissimo*.

As an onstage song, "The trees on the mountains" connects to another operatic convention, this one stretching back to the very beginning of the seventeenth century.[80] When Susannah finishes the song, Blitch, who has followed her home and who, according to Floyd's stage directions, "has come onstage and stood listening," compliments her "mighty pretty singin'."[81] Treigle suggests that Blitch "hears" the "resignation" in Susannah's voice as she sings this number.[82] In fact, he comments, "That's a right sad song," noting that it "don't look like it'd do y' much good."[83] He then tries to convince her to confess, and when she refuses, he rapes her, taking advantage of her resignation, her vulnerability, and her song. After this scene, all of the hopes and dreams that Susannah expressed so optimistically in "Ain't it a pretty night!" appear utterly destroyed.

Still, in 1977, Floyd insisted to Harry Haskell of the *Kansas City Star* that Susannah's final moments on stage, two scenes later, symbolize a kind of victory.[84] As the angry crowd disperses from her property, backing away from Susannah and her shotgun, Little Bat remains, watching Susannah "wide-eyed and frightened."[85] Susannah reasserts her agency, composing a new song for the occasion. Purposely harnessing her sexuality for the first time in the entire opera, she begins to seduce Little Bat. In this, she follows a longstanding operatic tradition, her sudden reliance on sexual attraction for her strength recalling heroines such as Carmen, Lulu, and Delilah. Susannah tells Little Bat to take advantage of her, to love her up the way he claimed he had in his earlier testimony before the Valley Elders.[86] As she repeatedly urges him to "come on," she emphasizes the innuendo with vocal glissandi. She issues her final appeal on a dark, moaning glissando in the very low end of her range (Ex. 5.5). Little Bat approaches Susannah tentatively. According to Floyd's stage directions, as he moves to put his arms around

---

80   Claudio Monteverdi's *L'Orfeo* (1607), for example, makes ample use of onstage song.
81   Floyd, *Susannah, Libretto*, 25.
82   Treigle, email correspondence with the author.
83   Floyd, *Susannah, Libretto*, 26.
84   Floyd, quoted in Haskell, "'Susannah' Composer Aims for Believability."
85   Floyd, *Susannah, Libretto*, 35.
86   Her words recall Little Bat's confession in Act I, Scene 5.

Example 5.3. Floyd, *Susannah*, mm. 1045–1052.

Example 5.4. Floyd, *Susannah*, mm. 1085–1087.

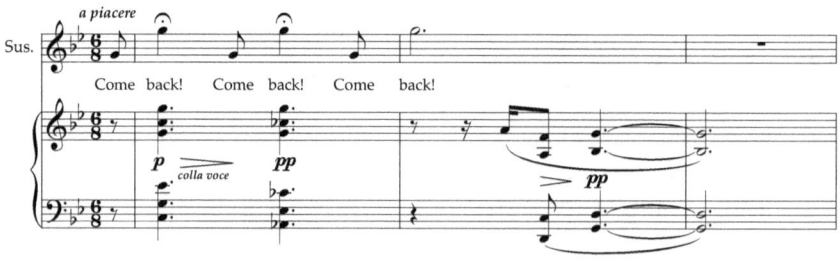

Example 5.5. Floyd, *Susannah*, mm. 1472–1481.

her, she "slaps him viciously across the face," sending him "yelping down the steps and across the yard."[87]

As I noted at the outset of this chapter, in her final moments on stage, Susannah transforms before her audience's eyes and ears. Like many of the tragic heroines who have come before her, Susannah sings until the curtain falls, but her final song—no longer really in the soprano register—sounds strange. At the same time, for all its strangeness, its sudden shift in tone and register, the song is eerily familiar. As Susannah sings, the clarinets trill incessantly in the background, recalling the conclusion to *Salome*, the opera that got Curtin in so much trouble in West Virginia in 1954 (Ex. 5.6). Floyd has insisted that any allusion to *Salome* by way of this extended trill was entirely

---

87 Floyd, *Susannah, Libretto*, 36.

Example 5.6. Strauss and Lachmann, *Salome*, mm. 3202–3210.

coincidental.[88] But perhaps it was subconscious. When Susannah sings for and then slaps Little Bat, her behavior, far from being unnecessarily cruel, reaffirms her right to her own existence, her right to perform for no man.[89] Notably, this is a right Salome is denied. After she dances her provocative "Dance of the Seven Veils," demands the head of John the Baptist, passionately kisses his lips, and then raves about it, Herodes calls for her death. Strauss's trill introduces Salome's final sung number, and the trill is unsettling, as though pointing to her impending punishment; indeed, just before the trill, Herodes announces that something terrible will happen. Floyd's trill is also full of foreboding, but it ultimately serves to signal Little Bat's, rather than Susannah's, punishment. Susannah's final moments on stage do not exactly compel *her* to submit to the gendered violence that Clément believes to be inherent in the operatic form. Moreover, if we really listen to Susannah's song, we might begin to grapple with the ramifications of gendered violence not only in *Susannah* but in so many other operas as well.

Grappling with such violence, however, is no easy work. As soprano Sharon Daniels recalled, when she first began singing the role of Susannah in

---

88   Floyd, interview with the author.
89   This argument becomes tricky, however, if Little Bat is understood and portrayed as having some kind of developmental or cognitive disability. It is potentially disconcerting to watch Susannah punish another marginalized character who may not fully understand the situation in New Hope Valley.

the 1970s, she "couldn't stand the ending."[90] She remembered asking Floyd: "Why doesn't [Susannah] just leave and go to Nashville or Ashville?"[91] According to Daniels, Floyd responded: "She has to stay there; she has to be embittered; she has to protect that property."[92] Floyd maintained that the moral of the story depended on a bitter ending, whereas Daniels noted that "as a young singer with [her own] feminist ideas," she would have preferred a more obviously heroic ending, with Susannah "transcending the tragic circumstances of her situation in some way."[93] When I asked Floyd what he imagined Susannah's future to hold, beyond the bounds of the opera's conclusion, he responded: "You know what Phyllis says? She says [Susannah] becomes a pine tree."[94] I posed the same question to Curtin, who simply called Susannah a "strong girl," arguing that she would remain "up there on that hillside all by herself."[95]

Curtin's commitment to this bleak conclusion can be further understood if we reexamine some of the decisions that Floyd made as he adapted the tale of Susanna and the Elders for his opera. Notably missing from Floyd's adaptation is the rescuer Daniel. Before the opera's FSU premiere, a writer for the *Florida Flambeau* explained that Floyd had turned Daniel into the itinerant evangelist Olin Blitch.[96] Like Daniel, it is Blitch who learns of Susannah's innocence, but unlike Daniel, Blitch discovers her innocence by committing a crime of his own. Blitch also fails to convince the people of New Hope Valley of the error of their ways. Thus in Floyd's opera,

---

90 Sharon Daniels, interview with the author, June 24, 2015, Boston, MA. Daniels is Associate Professor Emeritus of Music at Boston University. She has sung the role of Susannah professionally on numerous occasions. She has also directed the opera. Advised by both Floyd and Curtin, she directed Boston University's 2010 production of *Susannah*, cited earlier in this chapter.
91 Ibid.
92 Ibid.
93 Ibid. In a later email exchange, Daniels elaborated: "I believe that Carlisle would contend that Susannah's transformation from the pure hearted free spirited young woman into the embittered and hard woman behind that gun at the end, chasing the people off her property (even her only friend Little Bat), was absolutely the strongest most honest choice for the character, and therefore leaves the audience with the message of the story." Sharon Daniels, email correspondence with the author, April 29, 2017.
94 Floyd, interview with the author.
95 Phyllis Curtin, telephone interview with the author, March 17, 2015.
96 "Premiere of 'Susannah' Stars Curtin, Harrell February 24th," *The Florida Flambeau*, January 11, 1955, in Scrapbook 6 (January 1954 – July 1956), Historical Scrapbook Collection, Warren D. Allen Music Library, Special Collections, Florida State University, Tallahassee, FL.

there is no one to come to Susannah's defense. There is no heroic tenor role—so familiar in the world of nineteenth-century European opera—in Susannah's world. Blitch, the Biblical hero who has become a sexual predator, is a baritone. Susannah's brother Sam is a tenor, but he is far from heroic. Driven by his thirst for adventure and the bottle, he leaves Susannah alone in New Hope Valley in Act I. At the end of Act II, when he sets out to avenge Susannah's honor, shooting and killing Blitch, he leaves Susannah alone again. Consequently, when the people of New Hope Valley advance on the Polk property, Susannah has two options: run or defend herself. In 1977, Floyd emphasized to Haskell that at the end of *Susannah*, "she chose self-exile."[97] "It's a dreadful choice," he admitted, "but it's a choice."[98] Susannah's victory is her ability to stand up for herself, to claim her agency, but none of this erases her trauma. She takes up a gun, moreover, because if she is going to stay in New Hope Valley, she is going to need it. Unlike Laurie Moss, Susannah Polk is a woman who has been deemed unworthy of protection in a patriarchal world.

Susannah's Rape and Race

But why is Susannah supposedly so unworthy of protection? And why is she actually a victim of rape? This second question has often bothered me because in the Biblical tale, it would appear that Susanna is never physically violated.[99] Why did Floyd feel he had to write rape into *Susannah*? And why the rape of a virgin? In the Biblical tale, Susanna is married to a wealthy and respected man and presumably *not* a virgin. Initially, I assumed that Floyd was simply giving voice to the contemporary obsession with the seeming rising tide of sex crimes. Yet the rape that Blitch commits and that Susannah endures does not quite resemble the way rape was understood in the US in the 1950s. Blitch is not coded as a scary Black man, and Susannah—even though she is a virgin—is not exactly coded as a chaste white woman.

For years, music critics did not even use the word "rape" to describe Blitch's crime, perhaps suggesting that because Floyd was not relying on what scholars call the "myth of the Black rapist," they could not understand

---

97 Floyd, quoted in Haskell, "'Susannah' Composer Aims for Believability."
98 Ibid.
99 Indeed, as Garrard points out, Susanna "as a potential rape victim who emphatically halted the proceedings, is a rare heroine in biblical mythology—her extremism in defense of virtue is topped only by that of Lucretia." See "Artemisia and Susanna," 152.

Blitch's crime as rape.[100] Instead, music critics used the word "seduction," a confusing term to parse because they sometimes employed it as a more polite euphemism for rape and sometimes to indicate that Susannah was a previously chaste woman who had consented to sex outside marriage.[101] Floyd himself initially used the term "seduction," apparently for its euphemistic qualities. His synopsis for the NYCO's 1958 production of *Susannah* for the World's Fair in Brussels described Susannah's rape as follows: "At a revival meeting Susannah is called upon publicly by Blitch to confess and repent, and when she refuses she is pursued to her home by Blitch, who is still convinced of her guilt and reputation for lechery. He fails to force a confession and Susannah, exhausted and broken, succumbs to his advances and is seduced by him."[102] Yet in the Washington Opera's program booklet for *Susannah* in 1999, Floyd claimed that "seduction is the wrong word to put on the scene."[103] In 2015, Floyd spoke with me in similar terms, pausing on the word "seduction" and noting that to him, it "always implies assent."[104] Floyd also remembered that during a press conference prior to the Met's 1999 production of *Susannah* (which starred Renée Fleming), both Curtin and Fleming "took great offense" when someone referred to the scene between Blitch and Susannah as "a seduction scene."[105] Relying on Curtin's and Fleming's interpretations, Floyd explained how "it should never look as if [Susannah] willingly follows through" in this scene.[106] Phyllis Treigle has reflected on this scene as well, asserting that when Susannah declares that she is "so tired I just can't fight no more," she is "verbalizing the

---

100 See Davis, "Rape, Racism and the Myth of the Black Rapist" in *Women, Race & Class*, 172–201. See also Lerner, "A Woman's Lot." The myth of the Black rapist is clearly on display in Harper Lee's novel *To Kill a Mockingbird*, first published in 1960.
101 I have argued previously about the importance of using the term "rape," rather than "seduction," to describe Blitch's crime against Susannah. See "Seduction or Rape?"
102 Floyd, "The Story of 'Susannah,'" synopsis by the composer, reprinted by permission of the Publishers and Copyright owners, Boosey and Hawkes, Inc., in *Playbill* 1, no. 7, June 25, 1958, p. 18, loose in Box 2, Carlisle Floyd Papers.
103 Floyd, quoted in Nancy Tague, "Sweet Music Indeed: An Interview with Carlisle Floyd," Washington Opera program, August 1999, p. 20, loose in Box 2, Carlisle Floyd Papers.
104 Floyd, interview with the author.
105 Ibid.
106 Ibid. Ellie M. Hisama addresses the importance of careful staging of rape scenes in her examination of Juilliard Opera's 2015 production of *The Rape of Lucretia*. See "A Feminist Staging of Britten's *The Rape of Lucretia*."

feelings of all those who have been molested by people in authority."[107] As Treigle concludes, Susannah "feels hopeless and helpless and powerless and numb."[108] Treigle was born in 1960, five years after *Susannah*'s premiere. She was fifteen years old in 1975, the year Susan Brownmiller published *Against Our Will: Men, Women and Rape*, a book that, despite its shortcomings, began to productively challenge the way many Americans understood rape.[109] According to Brownmiller, rape was "nothing more or less than a conscious process of intimidation by which *all men* keep *all women* in a state of fear."[110] Treigle came of age in a culture that no longer relied *quite as exclusively* on the myth of the Black rapist.[111] She did not need that myth to interpret the violence in Floyd's opera because for Treigle, rape was, at its core, about an abuse of power.

Race, however, is still at play in *Susannah*. There are subtle clues embedded throughout Floyd's libretto, suggesting that we might understand Susannah as a woman suspected of having African American ancestry.[112] If we read *Susannah* in this way, the opera does more than challenge the racist formulation of rape as a crime committed by Black men against white women: it potentially serves to highlight the long history of sexual violence against Black women in the US.

To begin this reading, it is important to remember that from the outset of the opera, Susannah and her brother exist somewhat apart from the tight-knit community of New Hope Valley. As a result, Susannah and Sam rely heavily on each other, and even though Sam ultimately fails Susannah, he clearly loves his sister. The two are bound together, both in their care for one another and in the songs they sing together. In Act I, Scene 2, just after

---

107 Treigle, email correspondence with the author.
108 Ibid.
109 Scholars such as Angela Y. Davis and bell hooks critiqued *Against Our Will* shortly after its publication. Davis pointed out that Brownmiller was still heavily influenced by the myth of the Black rapist. See *Women, Race & Class*, 178–183. hooks noted the limitations of Brownmiller's focus on the rape of Black women during slavery (and not any of the repercussions beyond slavery). See *Ain't I a Woman*, 51–53.
110 Brownmiller, *Against Our Will*, 15.
111 The words "quite as exclusively" are crucial here, because the myth of the Black rapist continues to be dangerous well into the twenty-first century. In 2015, for example, before he gunned down a room full of Black worshippers in Charleston, South Carolina, Dylann Roof reportedly proclaimed: "I have to do it. You rape our women and you're taking over our country. And you have to go." See Wade, "How 'Benevolent Sexism' Drove Dylann Roof's Racist Massacre."
112 I have briefly examined this possibility previously. See "Seduction or Rape?"

she completes "Ain't it a pretty night!," Susannah and Sam sing and dance to a humorous, lighthearted number called the "Jaybird" song, its text taken from a rhyme Floyd happened to know. This rhyme was first catalogued by the African American chemist and folk song collector Thomas W. Talley in his 1922 collection *Negro Folk Rhymes*.[113] Talley's "Jaybird" includes four verses and a chorus. The second verse goes as follows:

> Dat Jaybird a-settin' on a swingin' lim.'
> He wink at me an' I wink at him.
> He laugh at me w'en my gun "crack."
> It kick me down on de flat o' my back.[114]

Floyd's version of "Jaybird" is comprised of a single repeated stanza, similar to Talley's second stanza:

> "Oh, jaybird sittin' on a hick'ry limb,
> He winked at me and I winked at him.
> I picked up a brickbat
> An' hit him on the chin.
> 'Looka here, little boy, don't you do that agin!'"[115]

In the opera, Sam sings the stanza first, and then Susannah joins in, repeating it with him (Ex. 5.7). As Floyd recalled to me in 2015, he knew the "Jaybird" rhyme because his grandfather had recited it to him when he was a young boy; it always "tickled me," Floyd noted.[116] He went on to say that he had decided to incorporate the rhyme, composing his own music, as "the theme-song of the guileless, youthful Susannah."[117]

Despite Floyd's rather benign explanation regarding his inclusion of "Jaybird," this number, the composer's only foray into any kind of quotation, might be taken to musically mark Susannah and Sam as racial outsiders. In fact, the syncopations on display, which sound in contrast to the rest of Floyd's score, may be reminiscent of Blackface minstrelsy.[118] Like "The

---

113 Talley, *Thomas W. Talley's Negro Folk Rhymes*, 11–13. Talley was a collector of African American folk songs and a professor of chemistry at Fisk University.
114 Ibid., 12.
115 See Floyd, *Susannah, Libretto*, 10.
116 Floyd, interview with the author.
117 Ibid. Talley's "Jaybird" also includes a melodic transcription. "This," editor Charles K. Wolfe points out, "is one of the few pieces for which Talley provided music in the original edition." See *Thomas W. Talley's Negro Folk Rhymes*, 12. Floyd's melody, however, appears unrelated to the one Talley recorded.
118 See Morrison, "Race, Blacksound, and the (Re)Making of Musicological Discourse." In this article, Morrison defines Blacksound both as an object of study ("the sonic and embodied legacy of blackface performance as the origin

trees on the mountains," the other onstage song in the opera, "Jaybird" is presented as something of a family song.[119] Susannah begs Sam to sing it to her, imploring:

> Don't go to bed right yet, Sam.
> Sing me the "Jaybird" song first.
> Remember how Pa used to always sing me "Jaybird"
> Afore I'd go to bed.
> You ain't sung it fer me in a long time now,
> An' it always makes me feel real happy.[120]

No one else in the opera ever sings this song as if to suggest a tangible reason for Susannah's and Sam's outsider status in New Hope Valley. The song's isolation is all the more intriguing because Susannah's two arias permeate Floyd's score. "Jaybird" does not. The "Jaybird" melody appears just twice, first, at the end of Act I, Scene 2, and second, in the following scene when Susannah hums the melody as she bathes in the creek. Susannah is humming the song that potentially marks her as "other" at the moment she is discovered by the Elders, who respond by plotting to run her out of New Hope Valley. When Little Bat rushes to tell Susannah that she is in trouble, he explains:

> They was lookin' fer a baptism crick
> An' they found it, only you was in it,
> A-bathin', naked as a jay-bird.
> They say it were a shameful sight.[121]

Thus, the word "jaybird" becomes significant in and of itself.

These kinds of musical and textual revelations are not exactly unprecedented on the American musical stage. In Jerome Kern and Oscar Hammerstein II's musical *Show Boat* (1927), Julie La Verne reveals that she is "passing" for white

---

of all popular music, entertainment, and culture in the United States," p. 789) and as a methodology (that "considers the systemic and property conditions under which popular music is produced," p. 790). Morrison also offers a close analysis of two popular minstrel songs, "Jim Crow" and "Zip Coon." His analysis of the "Zip Coon" tune, also known as "Turkey in the Straw," reveals how "Jaybird" may recall the sounds of minstrelsy. As Morrison points out, the "Zip Coon" melody "consists of small, repeated cells featuring arpeggiated leaps and dotted figures, suggesting the fiddling styles of both African and Irish folk traditions" (p. 814).

119 In Act II, Scene 3, Susannah tells Blitch that her mother taught her "The trees on the mountains." See Floyd, *Susannah, Libretto*, 26.
120 Ibid., 9.
121 Ibid., 14.

Example 5.7. Floyd, *Susannah*, mm. 394–397.

when she sings the song "Can't help lovin' dat man."[122] The ship's cook Queenie overhears Julie singing the song and is surprised, noting that she has only ever heard Black folks sing this number. One could interpret Susannah and Sam's "Jaybird" as speaking to their racial heritage as well, albeit in a subtler way than in *Show Boat*. Yet if one combs through Floyd's libretto, one can find additional examples of racially coded language. For example, near the end of Act I, Scene 1, Mrs. McLean, the wife of one of the Valley Elders, asserts that "they's bad blood in that family," referring to Susannah and Sam.[123] Little Bat later repeats this rumor to Susannah:

> My ma says they's bad blood in yo' family
> But I like to look at you.[124]

---

122 See Decker, *Show Boat*, 65–66.
123 Floyd, *Susannah, Libretto*, 6.
124 Ibid., 7.

The reference to "bad blood" calls to mind the "one-drop rule," first an informal rule and later a legal principle asserting that "anyone with any known trace of black blood was considered black," as sociologist Nikki Khanna writes.[125] At the end of the opera, as the mob advances on Susannah, one of the Elders warns her:

> You're mockin' us with yer laughter.
> Y'll regret it, y'll see,
> When yer brother's caught
> An' strung on a tree.[126]

The Elder's words, coupled with Mrs. McLean's comment about "bad blood" and Susannah and Sam's song of African American origin, allude to the history of white mob justice and the practice of lynching Black men in the South. Although Susannah and Sam's racial identity is not *the* story in this opera, it weaves like a subtext throughout Floyd's plot and language.[127]

This subtext is crucial, for when we allow for the possibility that Susannah might be coded as a Black woman, the opera takes on additional national baggage. According to historian Deborah Gray White, there were two primary stereotypes about Black women that arose from slavery, the Mammy and the Jezebel. The Mammy was asexual, maternal, and deeply religious; the Jezebel was a slut.[128] As White explains, "in every way Jezebel was the counterimage of the mid-nineteenth-century ideal of the Victorian lady."[129] Like Susanna(h), Jezebel originates in the Bible. The wife of Ahab, King of Israel, Jezebel appears in the Books of Kings. She dresses in finery and wears makeup; she also convinces her husband to abandon the worship of Yahweh in favor of Baal and Asherah. She is eventually punished for her faithlessness, thrown out of a window by members of her own court and then eaten by stray dogs. In the US, the name Jezebel gradually came to refer to sexually promiscuous women, and sexually promiscuous Black women in particular. bell hooks points out that "black women have always been seen by the white public as sexually permissive, as available and eager for the sexual assaults of any man, black or white."[130] As a result, Black women have historically been more likely to be burdened with the Jezebel label than white women. Gerda Lerner puts the Jezebel label in direct contact with the myth of the Black

---

125 See Khanna, "'If You're Half Black, You're Just Black,'" 98.
126 Floyd, *Susannah, Libretto*, 35.
127 On the topic of Blackness in opera and Black opera, see André, *Black Opera*. See also André, Bryan, and Saylor, eds., *Blackness in Opera*.
128 White, *Ar'n't I a Woman*, 46.
129 Ibid., 29.
130 hooks, *Ain't I a Woman*, 52.

rapist, explaining that "the myth of the black rapist of white women is the twin of the myth of the bad black woman—both designed to apologize for and facilitate the continued exploitation of black men and women."[131]

When we consider the way Susannah is perceived through the eyes of the people of New Hope Valley, combined with the way she is marked in Floyd's libretto, we can see how she is being construed as a Jezebel, that creature who in White's words "did not lead men and children to God," "saw no advantage in prudery," and was solely concerned with "matters of the flesh."[132] All of this may help to explain why the people of New Hope Valley are so quick to regard Susannah as a mere sex object. At the square dance at the very beginning of the opera, the Elders vie for Susannah's attention, trying to get into her square. Mrs. McLean, frustrated by her own husband's obvious attraction to Susannah, describes Susannah as "a shameless girl."[133] She elaborates:

> Showin' herself to all the men.
> Look at her throwin' her head back
> And look at the cut of her dress ...[134]

Later she states sharply:

> Susannah an' Sam is evil, I say.
> They's bad blood in that fam'ly.
> It's too pretty a face an' wicked them eyes,
> She'll come to no good, mark my words.
> She'll come to no good, mark my words.[135]

Mrs. McLean's "words" foreshadow the events to come in the opera, and they seek to hold Susannah responsible for the crime that Blitch ultimately commits. Initially, plenty of music critics were willing to lay the blame at Susannah's feet as well. In 1960, for example, *Chicago Sun-Times* music critic Robert C. Marsh suggested that Susannah was not a rape victim but Blitch's willing sexual partner, and he complained about the overall message that Floyd was sending in his opera: "Floyd's Susannah is not a woman made strong by faith, but one unable to make a strong stand for the right even when she knows she is without moral blame. Indeed, she will do something she knows to be wrong in hope of being restored to the good graces

---

131 Lerner, "Black Women Attack the Lynching System," 193.
132 White, *Ar'n't I a Woman*, 29.
133 Floyd, *Susannah, Libretto*, 4.
134 Ibid.
135 Ibid., 6.

of the community."[136] This clipping appears in Floyd's papers at the South Caroliniana Library, and someone (possibly Floyd) wrote an X and two exclamation points next to this paragraph.

Fortunately, as Americans' understandings of rape and abuse have changed, so too have perspectives on *Susannah*. In 1993, for example, the Lyric Opera of Chicago almost attempted to deal with race and gender in *Susannah*. As music critic John von Rhein reported, Lyric Opera director Robert Falls "read through [Floyd's] score during the 1991 Anita Hill–Clarence Thomas hearings," and he described "the oppression of single women in a patriarchal society" as "more relevant today than when 'Susannah' was new."[137] Indeed, in 1992, Rebecca Walker wrote powerfully in *Ms. Magazine* about the deeply painful spectacle of the Anita Hill–Clarence Thomas hearings: "A black man grilled by a panel of white men about his sexual deviance. A black woman claiming harassment and being discredited by other women."[138] Walker admitted that she could not bring herself "to watch that sensationalized assault of the human spirit."[139] For her, "the hearings were not about determining whether or not Clarence Thomas did in fact harass Anita Hill. They were about checking and redefining the extent of women's credibility and power."[140] I wonder if Falls had Walker's analysis in mind as he contemplated *Susannah* in the early 1990s, for Falls acknowledged that "the idea of woman-as-presumed-seducer, ostracized by the male world, remains very relevant, from a political and human stance."[141]

The Lyric Opera production of *Susannah*, which starred Renée Fleming, used the Anita Hill–Clarence Thomas hearings only as a backdrop, yet in the future, a company might consider a very different kind of production, taking the cues from Floyd's music and libretto to support the casting of a Black soprano in the role of Susannah and thereby using the opera to

---

136 Robert C. Marsh, critic-at-large, "American Tragedies: *Susanna* and *Susannah*," hand-dated March 1960, in "Susannah" Folder, Box 2, Carlisle Floyd Papers.

137 Rhein, "Oh, Susannah!"

138 Walker, "Becoming the Third Wave," 39. Nominated by President George H. W. Bush, Clarence Thomas succeeded Thurgood Marshall, becoming the second African American to serve on the Supreme Court of the US. Anita Hill, an African American lawyer, testified at Thomas's confirmation hearings that Thomas had sexually harassed her when she worked for him at the Department of Education and Equal Employment Opportunity Commission. The US Senate ultimately confirmed Thomas's nomination by a vote of 52–48.

139 Walker, "Becoming the Third Wave," 39.

140 Ibid. See also Walker, "Anita Hill Woke Us Up."

141 Falls, quoted in Rhein, "Oh, Susannah!"

address racism and sexism together. To be clear, however, I offer this reading of Susannah as a Black woman as *an* interpretation, not *the* interpretation. I would be sorry to see *Susannah* flattened by any definitive interpretation, because so much of the opera's strength stems from the fact that despite its origins in the constrained culture of the US of the early 1950s, *Susannah* itself is not at all constrained.

Contemplating *Susannah* in the Twenty-First Century

In 1997, Phyllis Curtin noted that she sang *Susannah* "many times and places until I felt that no matter how well I sang and played it, no matter how deeply I loved to do it, I was getting too old—that awful word—to *look* right for that healthy, lovely, free young girl. And I needed her to *be* herself."[142] Curtin's words demonstrate that if she initially saw a piece of herself in Susannah, she also grew to regard Susannah as someone separate from herself. Like Patricia Neway, who felt that Magda Sorel became more than Gian-Carlo Menotti's creation, Curtin eventually "needed" Susannah to be a fully autonomous character.[143]

Curtin retired from singing in 1984, fully embracing a second career as a teacher and administrator. She had long been associated with the Berkshire Music Center at Tanglewood, as both an artist-in-residence and teacher.[144] In 1974, she joined the faculty at the Yale School of Music, and in 1979, she became the first female Master (now Head of College) of Yale's Branford College.[145] In 1983, she was appointed dean of the College of Fine Arts at Boston University, where she founded the Opera Institute in 1987.[146] Over the course of her teaching career, Curtin helped several young singers discover Susannah. One of those singers was Cheryl Studer, who studied with Curtin at Tanglewood from 1975 to 1977, sang the role of Susannah in a production at the University of Tennessee, where she earned her bachelor's degree in 1979, and then sang the role on the first complete recording of the opera in 1994. According to reporter Mary Campbell, Studer regarded Susannah as "a feminist who faces down an entire community, even though

---

142 Curtin, "Phyllis Curtin: In Her Own Words." Italics in original.
143 I discuss Patricia Neway's perspective on Magda Sorel (from Gian-Carlo Menotti's *The Consul*) in Chapter 1.
144 See Sheridan, "Profile: Phyllis Curtin."
145 See "In Memoriam: Phyllis Curtin, Soprano."
146 See Seligson, "BU Mourns CFA Dean Emerita Phyllis Curtin."

she was created before the women's movement."[147] Like Curtin, Studer latched onto Susannah's agency and autonomy.

Susannah may be a feminist, as Studer asserts, but I think the opera asks us to go a step beyond simply labeling the title heroine. When the final curtain descends and nothing is resolved, we are left to ponder a number of questions. Will Susannah remain traumatized, or will she find a way to recover? Will she tell her story? Will anyone listen to her? Will anyone believe her? The uncertainty of all these questions is frustrating, as Sharon Daniels noted, but it may also be necessary, as Floyd insisted—for perhaps the future is up to us. What will we learn from Susannah's story?

In 2019, Rhiannon Giddens (b. 1977) devoted an episode of her podcast *Aria Code* to "The trees on the mountains."[148] She also released a haunting new arrangement of the aria on *There Is No Other*, her first collaborative album with Francesco Turrisi. Giddens's arrangement is profound—the echoing piano accompaniment captures Susannah's loneliness and isolation after she is ostracized by the people of New Hope Valley. As Giddens recalled on *Aria Code*, the first time she heard "The trees on the mountains" she thought it was "totally devastating but also, just the most beautiful song."[149] She explained that she had chosen to include the aria on *There Is No Other* because she intended the album to be about "breaking down the artificial barriers between cultures, and instruments, and different types of music."[150] Giddens felt that as a folk song written for an opera, "The trees on the mountains" did just that, and she felt the song was totally accessible, to seasoned operagoers and novices alike.

When Giddens featured "The trees on the mountains" on *Aria Code*, she and her guests, Renée Fleming and writer Leora Tanenbaum, focused heavily on the accessibility of both Floyd's music and text. At the beginning of the episode, Fleming recalled falling in love with "The trees on the mountains" at age twelve, before she even knew what the opera was about. The music was just so compelling to her. She noted that she wanted to sing "The trees on the mountains" on a recital when she was in seventh or eighth grade, but her mother said, "Oh no … I don't think so … it's

---

147 Campbell, "Prolific Composer Says Music 'Illuminates Our Emotional Lives.'"
148 As a singer, songwriter, and banjo player, Giddens has made significant contributions to the American folk music scene. In 2005, she became one of the founding members of The Carolina Chocolate Drops, an old-time string band. In 2015, she released her first solo album. Before turning her attention to the banjo, however, Giddens studied opera. She even sang the role of Susannah in a production at the University of North Carolina at Greensboro.
149 Giddens, "Floyd's *Susannah*." Giddens began hosting *Aria Code* in 2018, marking something of a return to opera for the singer.
150 Ibid.

not appropriate."[151] Later in the episode, as Fleming articulated the opera's "timely" themes of "innocence," "shame," "blame," and "lust," she demonstrated why her mother would have objected to her singing "The trees on the mountains" at twelve years old.[152] Why saddle a young girl with so much baggage? Yet Tanenbaum described how the lyrics of "The trees on the mountains" reminded her of her own experience when she was just two years older than Fleming:

> I remember experiencing those feelings when I was fourteen years old, and I did not have the ability to make sense of what was happening to me when my peers called me a slut because that language did not exist yet. The term "sexual harassment" had just been coined in the 1980s at roughly the same time that I was experiencing sexual harassment, and I really did feel alone, the way Susannah expresses in this aria.[153]

Tanenbaum's words remind us of the many girls and young women who will unfortunately understand Susannah's situation all too well. Tanenbaum's words also remind me of Floyd, pausing over the importance of language in 1999. In the 1950s, Floyd used the term "seduction" instead of the word "rape" when he summarized *Susannah*. He certainly knew the word "rape," but perhaps because it tended to be employed in such a limited (and often racist) way, he could not see that it was the language he needed for his synopsis. By the end of the twentieth century, he realized that he was using the wrong language, importantly, by listening to the women who sang *Susannah*. Thus the story of *Susannah*, both on and off stage, demonstrates the power of women's voices and the power of listening.

---

151 Fleming, speaking on "Floyd's *Susannah*."
152 Ibid.
153 Tanenbaum, speaking on "Floyd's *Susannah*."

Epilogue: "The World So Wide"— Beyond the Virgin or the Whore in the Twenty-First Century

In 1999, writer Leora Tanenbaum argued that "despite three decades of feminism," young women in the US were still largely "defined by their sexuality."[1] To be sure, she acknowledged, "some of the rules ha[d] changed" but "the playing field" was "startlingly similar to that of the 1950s."[2] Almost twenty years later, comedian Hannah Gadsby addressed that "playing field" in her searing live comedy performance *Nanette* (2018). Standing before an audience at the Sydney Opera House, Gadsby joked that studying art history in college taught her that "there's only ever been two types of women: a virgin or a whore."[3] "Most people think that Miley Cyrus and Taylor Swift invented that binary," she continued, "but it's been going on thousands of years."[4] Like Tanenbaum, Gadsby argued that the paradigm of the virgin or the whore was alive and well in the twenty-first century. But what about within the world of American opera? As one might expect, over the latter half of the twentieth century, the landscape for American opera continued to change and the repertory to develop in new ways.[5] Yet some of the old ways persisted. Jake Heggie and Terrence McNally's *Dead Man Walking* (2000) serves as a case in point. An oft-performed American opera with clear ties to the canon established in the 1950s, *Dead Man Walking*

---

1 Tanenbaum, *Slut!*, 20.
2 Ibid.
3 Gadsby, *Hannah Gadsby: Nanette*.
4 Ibid.
5 The rise of minimalism, for example, greatly influenced American opera. See Ebright, "*Doctor Atomic*" and "'My answer to what music theater can be.'"

draws on but eventually departs from the paradigm of the virgin or the whore that is so central to *The Tender Land*, *Susannah*, *The Ballad of Baby Doe*, and *Lizzie Borden*.

Heggie (b. 1961) and McNally (1938–2020) began talking about writing an opera together in 1996. According to Heggie, McNally arrived in San Francisco the following year with "a list of ten ideas, only one of which he really wanted to do."[6] McNally started to read the list, beginning with *Dead Man Walking*, a 1993 book by the Roman Catholic nun Sister Helen Prejean (b. 1939) about her work counseling men awaiting the death penalty.[7] As Heggie recalled:

> The hair on the back of my neck stood up and I immediately started to hear music. This was the right story. [Terrence] continued reading, but to this day, I can't remember any other idea because I was already figuring out how Dead Man Walking would sound. What kind of architecture would the music have? What kinds of musical motifs? The range of characters and their transformations was incredible. There would be room for large ensembles and great possibilities to build emotional tension, to find transcendence in musical terms. Fortunately, that was the idea Terrence was most enthusiastic about, too.[8]

The San Francisco Opera gave the premiere of *Dead Man Walking* in 2000, and over the last twenty years, opera companies large and small have mounted subsequent productions.[9]

In a variety of ways, *Dead Man Walking* picks up where *Susannah* left off.[10] Carlisle Floyd's biographer writes that when Heggie began working on the opera, he sent Floyd "a list of pressing questions."[11] Floyd

---

6   Heggie, "The Journey of *Dead Man Walking*."
7   At this point, *Dead Man Walking* was also well known as a movie. In 1995, Tim Robbins's film adaptation, starring Susan Sarandon and Sean Penn, had opened to great acclaim in movie theaters throughout the country. *Dead Man Walking* was nominated for four Academy Awards. Sarandon won Best Actress.
8   Heggie, "The Journey of *Dead Man Walking*."
9   According to Opera America, *Dead Man Walking* is currently the sixth most-produced North American opera. Since 2000, *Dead Man Walking* has been presented by opera companies throughout the US and Canada. These include the Cincinnati Opera, NYCO, Michigan Opera Theatre, Pittsburgh Opera, Houston Grand Opera, Tulsa Opera, Opéra de Montréal, Central City Opera, Washington National Opera, Lyric Opera of Kansas City, Vancouver Opera, Kentucky Opera, and Lyric Opera of Chicago. *Dead Man Walking* has also been produced in Europe. See "North American Works Directory."
10 *Dead Man Walking* may also recall another opera from the 1950s, Francis Poulenc's *Dialogues des Carmélites* (1956).
11 Holliday, *Falling Up*, 357.

responded, becoming a mentor to Heggie. Interestingly, during his teenage years in Orinda, California, Heggie had taken composition lessons with Ernst Bacon (1898–1990), then in his eighties.[12] Some forty years earlier, Floyd had also studied with Bacon, first at Converse College and then at Syracuse University. Bacon encouraged Heggie to study Floyd's operas, but Heggie noted that as a teenager, he was not "a big opera fan."[13] Later, as a student at the University of California Los Angeles, he rediscovered Floyd and opera: "All my singer friends were doing the arias from *Susannah*. So beautiful and immediate and charismatic. There's such a profile to his music, it struck me right away."[14] Floyd's musical influence can be gleaned throughout *Dead Man Walking*, particularly in "He will gather us around," the haunting hymn that Heggie weaves throughout the opera.

Thematically, *Dead Man Walking* also owes a debt to *Susannah*. Set in the backwoods of Louisiana, the opera begins with rape and murder. According to the stage directions, a teenage boy and girl are parked on a rural lover's lane. They are "mak[ing] love" on a blanket on the ground when they are viciously attacked by two brothers, who take turns raping the girl before they kill both the girl and her boyfriend.[15] Because the crimes are staged at the outset of the opera, there is no question about who committed them, no debate about what may or may not have transpired, and no gradual buildup. We do not sit in the audience, wringing our hands, worrying about a young woman who could be "ruined," and we do not wonder about her potential complicity. Instead, we witness a horrific crime, and we are tasked with dealing with the aftermath—with some of the questions that *Susannah* left unanswered.

As soon as the violent prelude comes to its crashing conclusion, Sister Helen appears on stage. She is teaching a hymn to a group of schoolchildren, but she is clearly distracted by her plans to visit Joseph De Rocher, one of the murderers and rapists seen in the prelude, in the Louisiana State Penitentiary (often known as Angola, after the plantation previously located on the territory). Once there, the prison chaplain tells her she is wasting her time. When Sister Helen finally meets De Rocher, their interaction is not particularly pleasant, and even though she believes he is guilty, she agrees to support him as he prepares for his execution. She stands by his mother as she pleads for her son's life before the Pardon Board. She listens to the parents of De Rocher's victims as they rebuke her for seeming to side with a murderer. Finally, just before De Rocher is led to the execution chamber, he

---

12   Ibid., 356–357.
13   Heggie, quoted in ibid., 357.
14   Heggie, quoted in ibid.
15   See Heggie and McNally, *Dead Man Walking*, 6.

admits his guilt. Sister Helen forgives him, assuring him that God forgives him as well. The opera concludes with De Rocher's execution.

In all of its manifestations—book, movie, opera—*Dead Man Walking* reveals how Sister Helen Prejean came to be one of the most vocal advocates for the abolition of the death penalty. Prejean began writing to inmates on death row in the 1980s. She wrote first to Elmo Patrick Sonnier (1950–1984), the inspiration for Heggie and McNally's De Rocher. Along with his younger brother Eddie, Sonnier was convicted of the 1977 rape and murder of eighteen-year-old Loretta Ann Bourque, as well as the murder of her boyfriend, seventeen-year-old David LeBlanc. Sonnier received the death sentence, his younger brother, life without parole. Prejean eventually asked to visit Sonnier at Angola, and when Sonnier asked her to serve as his spiritual advisor, which meant seeing him through to his execution, she agreed. She went on to write to and advise other death-row inmates including Robert Lee Willie (1958–1984).[16] In her book *Dead Man Walking*, she asserted her unfailing belief that "killing by anyone, under any conditions, cannot be tolerated."[17] This "include[d] the government," which as she pointedly noted, could not "be trusted to control its own bureaucrats or collect taxes equitably or fill a pothole, much less decide which of its citizens to kill."[18]

Dead Man Walking is a story that challenges. As mezzo-soprano Joyce DiDonato explains, what Sister Helen seeks to do at the outset of the opera is save a man's soul, an enormous challenge.[19] Indeed, in Act I, Scene 4, the prison chaplain warns Sister Helen that he has already tried to save De Rocher—and he has "a degree in psychology."[20] He assumes that Sister Helen, whom he regards as a mere woman accustomed to taking care of children with "a hug and a lollipop," will be unsuccessful as well.[21] But Sister Helen is uniquely determined. She truly believes she can help De Rocher by convincing him to confess to his crimes and ask for forgiveness. Thus *Dead Man Walking* turns the story of *Susannah* on its head. Whereas Olin Blitch misguidedly set out to save a "ruined woman," Sister Helen sets out to save

---

16   On May 28, 1980, Robert Lee Willie and Joseph Vaccaro kidnapped, raped, and murdered eighteen-year-old Faith Hathaway. Three days later, they kidnapped and raped sixteen-year-old Debbie Cuevas. They also kidnapped and tortured Cuevas's boyfriend, twenty-year-old Mark Brewster. Cuevas eventually managed to escape and lead police to rescue Brewster. In 1998, Cuevas (now Morris) published an account of her survival and efforts at forgiveness. See *Forgiving the Dead Man Walking*.
17   Prejean, *Dead Man Walking*, 31.
18   Ibid., 31, 21.
19   Joyce DiDonato, speaking in *Dead Man Walking*, promotional video.
20   See Heggie and McNally, *Dead Man Walking*, 70–71.
21   Ibid., 77.

a ruined man. She does so on the premise that every human being is worthy of redemption. According to Prejean, when Heggie and McNally began to work on their opera, Prejean told them that her priority was that they capture "the theme of redemption."[22] In the end, Prejean found that Heggie and McNally captured this theme and more:

> [The opera] is a window onto a whole new world for most people, and it shows all sides of the issue. The savage and heinous crime is not ignored, but fully revealed. The emotional pain experienced by the family members of the victims is explored. *Dead Man Walking* is an artistic reflection on what happens behind the scenes, away from the public eye, when we as a society condemn and execute a person.[23]

Thus *Dead Man Walking* challenges its audience to confront and contemplate the realities of crime and capital punishment, alongside the notion of redemption.

Dead Man Walking also challenges popular notions of nuns as sweet, demure virgins or strict, authoritarian spinsters, for Sister Helen does not conform to either of these stereotypes. Both in real life and on the opera stage, Prejean redefined the meaning of "virgin." In *Dead Man Walking* in 1993, she reflected on the path that led her to work as an advocate for social justice, and in her 2019 memoir *River of Fire: My Spiritual Journey*, she applied her understanding of her mission as a nun to her understanding of virginity. Born into privilege in Baton Rouge, Louisiana, Prejean joined the Sisters of Saint Joseph of Medaille in New Orleans in 1957. As she recalled in the beginning of *Dead Man Walking*, in 1980, she and her sisters made a commitment to the poor.[24] Prejean admitted, however, that she made the commitment reluctantly, explaining how she "didn't want to struggle with politics and economics."[25] Yet after hearing Sister Marie Augusta Neal (1921–2004) speak at a convention in Terre Haute, Indiana, Prejean changed her tune.[26] Neal helped Prejean understand that "to claim to be apolitical or neutral" was "a very political position to take, and on the

---

22 Prejean, "Still on the Journey."
23 Ibid.
24 Prejean, *Dead Man Walking*, 5.
25 Ibid.
26 Sister Marie Augusta Neal, SND earned her PhD in sociology from Harvard University in 1963. In 1965, she became the director of the research committee of the Conference of Major Superiors of Women Institute (CMSW), conducting an examination of the resources of nuns in the US for the work of the Church in a post-Vatican II period. She also taught in the sociology department at Emmanuel College for almost forty years.

side of the oppressors."[27] Prejean noted that the way Neal "presented the message of Jesus ... caused the most radical shift" in her perspective.[28] Neal helped Prejean to see her work as that of an activist.

In the tumultuous year 2020, Vintage Books reissued *River of Fire* with a new subtitle, *On Becoming an Activist*, one that left absolutely no question as to the trajectory of Prejean's life and work in the Catholic Church and in American society. Interestingly, for Prejean, becoming an activist required something of a reframing of the Catholic Church's obsession with virginity. As she argued in *River of Fire*, although virginity had "come to be super-identified with biology," she believed the "spiritual meaning" of virginity lay "deeper than biology," ultimately asserting that it was "single-heartedness" or "purity of intent" that lay at the core of virginity.[29] Prejean's single-hearted devotion to social justice work, already reflected in *Dead Man Walking* the book, movie, and opera, shatters the old notion of virginity that has long helped to fuel the paradigm of the virgin or the whore.

❦ ❦ ❦

Like the most enduring American operas of the 1950s, *Dead Man Walking* revolves around women—historical women, women characters, and women performers. *Dead Man Walking* also revolves around the notion of virginity. Yet as I hinted above, this notion of virginity is unusual. More important, the paradigm of the virgin or the whore is not really at play in the opera. By centering a single-hearted (virgin) activist, Heggie and McNally ultimately moved beyond the paradigm, walking through the door that Prejean had opened to new stories and struggles.

Susan Graham (b. 1960), Joyce DiDonato (b. 1969), and Patricia Racette (b. 1965) demonstrated that sopranos in the US were committed to tackling those stories and struggles with abandon. Graham created the role of Sister Helen in San Francisco in 2000. Two years later, DiDonato sang the role with the NYCO. She sang it again in 2011, this time with the Houston Grand Opera, and before the COVID-19 pandemic she was slated to sing it at the Met, as part of the 2020–2021 season.[30] In 2019, Racette, the soprano who claimed *Susannah* brought her to opera, sang Sister Helen at

---

27 Prejean, *Dead Man Walking*, 5–6.
28 Ibid., 6.
29 Prejean, *River of Fire: On Becoming an Activist*, 223. To be clear, Prejean explained that for her, "bodily integrity does [still] matter." She pointed out that she believed "it would be highly hypocritical to engage in casual sex with one person after another while staking the claim" of being a virgin.
30 Because of COVID-19, the Met canceled its 2020–2021 season in its entirety.

the Lyric Opera of Chicago. American sopranos have played such a key role in bringing *Dead Man Walking* to life that writer Fred Cohn attributes much of the opera's success to these women and their affinity for the role of Sister Helen.[31] According to Cohn: "Sister Helen is a diva. I mean in no way to suggest that the nun – either the actual person or her operatic incarnation – is vain or capricious; on the contrary, as presented here, she is a woman of rare compassion. But her quest toward the understanding of the nature of divine forgiveness is like that of a great singer working to achieve musical transcendence."[32] Commending DiDonato's 2011 performance with the Houston Grand Opera, recorded and released by Parlophone Records in 2012, he argued that DiDonato flourished in the role of Sister Helen "not just because she is a wonderful singer but because of the *kind* of singer she is—one driven to create meaning through sound."[33] "The intense focus of DiDonato's art becomes a correlative for Sister Helen's religious calling," he concluded.[34] In other words, DiDonato's single-hearted devotion to her work as an artist serves as a foil for Prejean's devotion. Cohn's perspective on Sister Helen, the real woman, the fictional character, and the singers who embody her, reveals yet again the blurring of history and fiction on the American opera stage.

At the same time, there is a new kind of clarity, for the difference between *Dead Man Walking* and *The Tender Land*, *Susannah*, *The Ballad of Baby Doe*, and *Lizzie Borden* largely comes down to perspective. To be sure, Jake Heggie and Terrence McNally were both men, writing about a woman's experience, but to do so, they sought out that woman's experience. They read *Dead Man Walking*, and they spoke with Sister Helen Prejean. The other operas featured in this book were written by men—and women entered the picture only later. Sometimes composers and librettists welcomed those entrances, and when Beverly Sills and Phyllis Curtin worked to reshape *The Ballad of Baby Doe* and *Susannah*, they clearly imprinted the operas with their perspectives. At other times, the imprints of women's voices remained rather vague. While I found it difficult to resurrect and amplify the voices of singers like MaVynee Betsch, Rosemary Carlos, and Alice Hotopp, it was almost impossible for me to recover Brenda Lewis, the soprano who first depicted Lizzie Borden.

But I did speak with Lewis. Approximately a year and a half before her death, I drove out to her home in Westport, Connecticut. I listened as the ninety-five-year-old singer described the process of looking back on her life

---

31 Cohn, "Heggie: *Dead Man Walking*."
32 Ibid.
33 Ibid.
34 Ibid.

and career in the 1950s and 1960s as something akin to reaching into the "attic" of her memory.[35] She recalled in vague terms, for example, that as she prepared for *Lizzie Borden* in the 1960s, she was going through a particularly painful divorce.[36] Similar to Beverly Sills in the late 1950s, Lewis responded to the difficulties in her personal life by throwing herself into her work. In February 1965, she made her final appearance at the Met, singing the role of Marie in *Wozzeck*. A month later, she made her final appearance with the NYCO in the role of Lizzie. Thus she portrayed two exceedingly demanding roles—both dealing in domestic violence—within two months of each other, and she left the New York stage.[37] What did these performances mean for her? I do not exactly have an answer to this question. When I spoke with Lewis, it was hard for her to recall the kinds of details I sought. Perhaps it was also painful, as metaphors involving the attic often are. Activist Tarana Burke invoked the metaphor in her memoir in 2021, writing that her "internal dusty attic ... held violence, death, disappointment, and all their cousins."[38] Lewis referred to the attic of her memory multiple times during our interview in 2016. Never elaborating, she simply reminded me of the space's existence in her mind, making it clear that this was where she kept her experience with *Lizzie Borden*.

Lewis's reference eventually led me to reflect on Sandra M. Gilbert and Susan Gubar's *The Madwoman in the Attic: The Woman Writer and the Nineteenth-Century Literary Imagination*. First published in the US in 1979, the same year the original French version of Catherine Clément's *Opera, or the Undoing of Women* appeared in France, *The Madwoman in the Attic* remains a key text in feminist interpretation. Gilbert and Gubar focus their attention on nineteenth-century women writers, yet I cannot help but notice how much their analyses speak to the topic of women in American operas of the 1950s. As Gilbert and Gubar explain, the literary women they studied "were literally and figuratively confined."[39] They were "enclosed in the architecture of an overwhelmingly male-dominated society" and "trapped in the specifically literary constructs of what Gertrude Stein was to call 'Patriarchal poetry.'"[40] So too were the women in American operas of

---

35 Brenda Lewis, interview with the author, Westport, CT, March 7, 2016.
36 Ibid. See also Kellow, "Brenda Lewis, 96." Kellow reports that "Lewis looked back on the weeks of the original Lizzie Borden run as a time of great emotional turmoil."
37 After retiring from opera and musical theatre, Lewis joined the faculty at the Hartt School at the University of Hartford. She also produced and directed productions of the New Haven Opera Theater.
38 Burke, *Unbound*, 217.
39 Gilbert and Gubar, *The Madwoman in the Attic*, xi.
40 Ibid.

the 1950s. Thus when we look back on this decade and on this repertory—which continues to form and influence the American-opera canon—we need to remember the attic. This is often where we find women's voices, sometimes soaring, sometimes still tucked away, among the rafters.

Bibliography

Abbate, Carolyn. *In Search of Opera*. Princeton, NJ: Princeton University Press, 2001.

———. "Opera; or, the Envoicing of Women." In *Musicology and Difference: Gender and Sexuality in Music Scholarship*, edited by Ruth A. Solie, 225–258. Berkeley: University of California Press, 1993.

———. *Unsung Voices: Opera and Musical Narrative in the Nineteenth Century*. Princeton: Princeton University Press, 1991.

Abbate, Carolyn and Roger Parker. *A History of Opera*. New York: W. W. Norton & Company, 2012.

Abrams, Nathan and Julie Hughes, eds. *Containing America: Cultural Production and Consumption in 50s America*. Birmingham: University of Birmingham Press, 2000.

Agee, James and Walker Evans. *Let Us Now Praise Famous Men*. Boston: Houghton Mifflin Company, 1939, 1940, 1941, 1960, 1969, 1988, 2001.

Ahlquist, Karen. *Democracy at the Opera: Music, Theater, and Culture in New York City, 1815–60*. Urbana: University of Illinois Press, 1997.

"Alice Hotopp Is Chosen to Sing with Bicentennial Group." *Daily Advocate* (Greenville, OH), July 15, 1976.

Allen, Ray. "An American Folk Opera? Triangulating Folkness, Blackness, and Americaness in Gershwin and Heyward's 'Porgy and Bess.'" *Journal of American Folklore* 117, no. 465 (2004): 243–261.

Allen, Warren D. "American Traditions Set to Music." *Tallahassee Democrat*, February 25, 1955.

Anderson, Marian. *My Lord, What a Morning*. New York: Viking Press, 1956.

André, Naomi. *Black Opera: History, Power, Engagement*. Urbana: University of Illinois Press, 2018.

André, Naomi, Karen M. Bryan, and Eric Saylor, eds. *Blackness in Opera*. Urbana: University of Illinois Press, 2012.

Ansari, Emily Abrams. *The Sound of a Superpower: Musical Americanism and the Cold War*. New York: Oxford University Press, 2018.

Ardoin, John. "The Consul." *Musical America* 82 (May 1962): 25.

———. *The Stages of Menotti*. Garden City, NY: Doubleday & Company, Inc., 1985.

Atkinson, Brooks. "At the Theatre." *New York Times*, January 23, 1953.
Austern, Linda Phyllis and Inna Naroditskaya, eds. *Music of the Sirens*. Bloomington: Indiana University Press, 2006.
"Baby Doe." *Time*, July 16, 1956, 42.
Bailey, Alice A. *The Problem of the Children in the World Today: Essentials of Post War Education*. New York: Lucis Publishing Company, 1946.
Bailey, Beth. *Sex in the Heartland*. Cambridge, MA: Harvard University Press, 1999.
Bancroft, Caroline. "Silver Queen: Baby Doe Tabor's Life Story as Told to Sue Bonnie." *True Story* 37 (January 1938): 30–33, 90–91; 38 (February 1938): 34–37, 86–92; 38 (March 1938): 48–50, 127–133; 38 (April 1938): 40–42, 54–59; 38 (May 1938): 40–42, 67–72.
———. *Silver Queen: The Fabulous Story of Baby Doe Tabor*. 9th ed., reprinted 2016. Cabin John, MD: Wildside Press LLC, 1950.
Barnes, Jennifer. *Television Opera: The Fall of Opera Commissioned for Television*. Woodbridge: Boydell Press, 2003.
Bauch, Jason Norman. "Amahl and the Night Visitors: Menotti's Wondrous Legacy to Music Education." *Music Educators Journal* 47, no. 1 (1960): 112–114.
Beeson, Jack. "The Autobiography of *Lizzie Borden*." *The Opera Quarterly* 4, no. 1 (1986): 15–42.
———. *How Operas Are Created by Composers and Librettists: The Life of Jack Beeson, American Opera Composer*. Lewiston, NY: Edwin Mellen Press, 2008.
Beeson, Jack and Kenward Elmslie. *The Sweet Bye and Bye: An Opera in Two Acts*. The Kansas City Lyric Theater Orchestra. Conducted by Russell Patterson. Citadel Records CT-DOS-2000, 1995. Compact disc.
Beeson, Jack, Kenward Elmslie, and Richard Plant. *Lizzie Borden*. Directed by Kirk Browning. Pleasantville, NY: Video Artists International DVD 4563, 1967, 2013.
Beeson, Jack, Kenward Elmslie, and Richard Plant. *Lizzie Borden: A Family Portrait in Three Acts, Piano-Vocal Score*. New York: Boosey and Hawkes, 1967.
Belmonte, Laura A. *Selling the American Way: U.S. Propaganda and the Cold War*. Philadelphia: University of Pennsylvania Press, 2008.
Benedict, Helen. *Virgin or Vamp: How the Press Covers Sex Crimes*. New York: Oxford University Press, 1992.
Benjamin, Arthur. "The Consul." *Music & Letters* 32, no. 3 (1951): 247–251.
Berend, Zsuzsa. "'The Best or None!': Spinsterhood in Nineteenth-Century New England." *Journal of Social History* 33, no. 4 (2000): 935–957.
Biancolli, Louis. "'Baby Doe' Gets City Premiere." *New York World-Telegram and Sun*, April 4, 1958.

Bick, Sally. "*Of Mice and Men*: Copland, Hollywood, and American Musical Modernism." *American Music* 23, no. 4 (2005): 426–472.

Blackmer, Corinne E. and Patricia Juliana Smith, eds. *En Travesti: Women, Gender Subversion, Opera*. New York: Columbia University Press, 1995.

Bloechl, Olivia, Melanie Lowe, and Jeffrey Kallberg, eds. *Rethinking Difference in Music Scholarship*. Cambridge: Cambridge University Press, 2015.

Bolick, Kate. *Spinster: Making a Life of One's Own*. New York: Crown Publishers, 2015.

Breines, Wini. *Young, White, and Miserable: Growing Up Female in the Fifties*. Chicago: University of Chicago Press, 1992.

Brett, Philip, Elizabeth Wood, and Gary C. Thomas, eds. *Queering the Pitch: The New Gay and Lesbian Musicology*. New York: Routledge, 1994.

Briggs, John. *Requiem for a Yellow Brick Brewery: A History of the Metropolitan Opera*. Boston: Little, Brown and Company, 1969.

Brown, Helen Gurley. *Sex and the Single Girl*. New York: Bernard Geis Associates, 1962.

Brownmiller, Susan. *Against Our Will: Men, Women and Rape*. New York: Simon and Schuster, 1975.

Brown-Montesano, Kristi. *Understanding the Women of Mozart's Operas*. Berkeley: University of California Press, 2007.

Buchwald, Emilie, Pamela R. Fletcher, and Martha Roth, eds., *Transforming a Rape Culture*. Rev. ed. Minneapolis, MN: Milkweed Editions, 2005.

Burke, Tarana. *Unbound: My Story of Liberation and the Birth of the Me Too Movement*. New York: Flatiron Books, 2021.

Cahill, Ann J. *Rethinking Rape*. Ithaca, NY: Cornell University Press, 2001.

Caldwell, Erskine. *God's Little Acre*. New York: Viking Press, 1933.

———. *Tobacco Road*. New York: Grosset & Dunlap, 1932.

———. *Tragic Ground*. New York: Duell, Sloan and Pearce, 1944.

Caldwell, Erskine and Margaret Bourke-White. *You Have Seen Their Faces*. New York: Modern Age Books, Inc., 1937.

Caldwell, Jay E. *Erskine Caldwell, Margaret Bourke-White, and the Popular Front: Photojournalism in Russia*. Athens: University of Georgia Press, 2016.

Calico, Joy H. *Brecht at the Opera*. Berkeley: University of California Press, 2008.

Cameron, Ardis. *Unbuttoning America: A Biography of "Peyton Place."* Ithaca, NY: Cornell University Press, 2015.

Campbell, Mary. "Prolific Composer Says Music 'Illuminates Our Emotional Lives.'" *Associated Press*. Printed in *Standard-Speaker* (Hazleton, PA), April 28, 1999.

Caputi, Mary. *A Kinder, Gentler America: Melancholia and the Mythical 1950s*. Minneapolis: University of Minnesota Press, 2005.

"Carlos." *Catholic Advance* (Wichita, KS), August 3, 1978.
Caute, David. *The Great Fear: The Anti-Communist Purge under Truman and Eisenhower.* New York: Simon and Schuster, 1978.
Ceriani, Davide. "Italianizing the Metropolitan Opera House: Giulio Gatti-Casazza's Era and the Politics of Opera in New York City, 1908–1935." PhD diss., Harvard University, 2011.
Chafee, Zechariah, Jr. "Book Reviews: American Visa Policy and Foreign Scientists." *University of Pennsylvania Law Review* 101, no. 5 (March 1953): 703–713.
Chaney, Karen Elizabeth. *New England Remembers Lizzie Borden.* Beverly, MA: Commonwealth Editions, 2006.
Chapman, John. "'Baby Doe,' a Superb Opera, Gets Swift, Touching Premiere in West." *New York Daily News,* July 9, 1956.
Chase, Gilbert. *America's Music: From the Pilgrims to the Present, Revised Third Edition, with a Foreword by Richard Crawford and a Discographical Essay by William Brooks.* Urbana: University of Illinois Press, 1987.
Childress, Alice. *Like One of the Family: Conversations from a Domestic's Life.* Foreword by Roxane Gay. Introduction by Trudier Harris. Boston: Beacon Press, 1956, 1986, 2017.
Citron, Marcia J. "Feminist Approaches to Musicology." In *Cecilia Reclaimed: Feminist Perspectives on Gender and Music,* edited by Susan C. Cook and Judy S. Tsou, 15–34. Urbana: University of Illinois Press, 1994.
Clément, Catherine. *Opera, or the Undoing of Women.* Translated by Betsy Wing. Foreword by Susan McClary. Minneapolis: University of Minnesota Press, 1988.
———. *L'opéra, ou, la défaite des femmes.* Paris: B. Grasset, 1979.
Cohn, Fred. "Heggie: *Dead Man Walking.*" *Opera News* 77, no. 5 (November 2012). https://www.operanews.com/Opera_News_Magazine/2012/11/Recordings/HEGGIE__Dead_Man_Walking.html. Accessed September 1, 2022.
Cole, Johnetta B. *Conversations: Straight Talk with America's Sister President.* New York: Doubleday, 1993.
Coleman, Robert. "'Consul' a Dramatic Blast at Brutalitarian Rule." *Daily Mirror,* March 16, 1950.
———. "'Consul' in Park Real Spellbinder." *Daily Mirror,* September 8, 1957.
"Composer Is an Admirer of 'Baby Doe': A Wonderful Woman, Dr. Moore Says." *Cleveland Plain Dealer,* September 8, 1958.
"Composer on Broadway." *Time,* May 1, 1950, pp. 64–66, 68–69.
"Concert Association Announces Two Selections for New Season." *Beckley Post-Herald* (Beckley, WV), March 13, 1959.

"A Concert Draws 1,000." *Kansas City Times* (Kansas City, MO), May 14, 1947.

"Conductor of Met Dies: Victor Trucco, Assistant, Stricken in Atlanta." *Baltimore Sun*, May 19, 1964.

Conforti, Joseph A. *Lizzie Borden on Trial: Murder, Ethnicity, and Gender*. Lawrence: University Press of Kansas, 2015.

The Consul. March 15, 1950–November 4, 1950, Ethel Barrymore Theatre, New York, NY. Internet Broadway Database. https://www.ibdb.com/broadway-production/the-consul-2137. Accessed August 23, 2022.

Cook, Susan C. and Judy S. Tsou, eds. *Cecilia Reclaimed: Feminist Perspectives on Gender and Music*. Urbana: University of Illinois Press, 1994.

Cooke, Mervyn, ed. *The Cambridge Companion to Twentieth-Century Opera*. Cambridge: Cambridge University Press, 2005.

Copland, Aaron and Horace Everett. *The Tender Land: Opera in Three Acts, Vocal Score*. New York: Boosey & Hawkes, 1956.

Copland, Aaron and Vivian Perlis. *Copland since 1943*. New York: St. Martin's Press, 1989.

Cortesi, Arnaldo. "La Scala Offers Menotti's 'Consul' with 2 Members of Original Cast." *New York Times*, January 23, 1951.

Cott, Nancy F. *The Grounding of Modern Feminism*. New Haven, CT: Yale University Press, 1987.

Crawford, Richard. *America's Musical Life: A History*. New York: W. W. Norton & Company, Inc., 2001.

Crist, Elizabeth B. "Mutual Responses in the Midst of an Era: Aaron Copland's *The Tender Land* and Leonard Bernstein's *Candide*." *Journal of Musicology* 23, no. 4 (2006): 485–527.

Croan, Robert. "Composer Floyd Staging His Own 'Susannah' to Open Opera Season." *Pittsburgh Post-Gazette*, October 9, 1980.

The Crucible. January 22, 1953–July 11, 1953, Martin Beck Theatre, New York, NY. Internet Broadway Database. https://www.ibdb.com/broadway-production/the-crucible-2211. Accessed August 31, 2022.

Curtin, Philip D. *The Atlantic Slave Trade: A Census*. Madison: University of Wisconsin Press, 1969.

———. *On the Fringes of History: A Memoir*. Athens: Ohio University Press, 2005.

Curtin, Phyllis. "Phyllis Curtin: In Her Own Words." Liner notes. *Opera Arias*. Phyllis Curtin (soprano) © 1997 VAI, VAI 1152. Compact disc.

Dahlburg, John-Thor. "'Beach Lady' Triumphed over Tide of Development." *Los Angeles Times*, September 28, 2005.

Dalrymple, Jean. *From the Last Row*. Clifton, NJ: James T. White & Company, 1975.

Davis, Angela Y. *Women, Race & Class*. New York: Random House, 1981.
Davis, Peter G. *The American Opera Singer: The Lives & Adventures of America's Great Singers in Opera & Concert from 1825 to the Present*. New York: Anchor Books, 1997.
———. "Rocky Mountain High." *New York Magazine*, April 23, 2001.
Dead Man Walking. Promotional video by the Houston Grand Opera, 2011. https://youtu.be/RIMXdaTzxr0. Accessed August 22, 2022.
Decker, Todd. *Show Boat: Performing Race in an American Musical*. New York: Oxford University Press, 2013.
Delton, Jennifer A. *Rethinking the 1950s: How Anticommunism and the Cold War Made America Liberal*. Cambridge: Cambridge University Press, 2013.
De Mille, Agnes. *Lizzie Borden: A Dance of Death*. Boston: Little, Brown and Company, 1968.
Devlin, James E. *Erskine Caldwell*. Boston: Twayne Publishers, 1984.
Dickinson, Peter, ed. *Copland Connotations: Studies and Interviews*. Foreword by H. Wiley Hitchcock. Woodbridge: Boydell Press, 2002.
Dickstein, Morris. *Dancing in the Dark: A Cultural History of the Great Depression*. New York: W. W. Norton & Company, 2009.
Dizikes, John. *Opera in America: A Cultural History*. New Haven, CT: Yale University Press, 1993.
Dobrin, Arnold. *Aaron Copland: His Life and Times*. New York: Thomas Y. Crowell Company, 1967.
Donovan, Brian. "Gender Inequality and Criminal Seduction: Prosecuting Sexual Coercion in the Early-20th Century." *Law & Social Inquiry* 30, no. 1 (2005): 61–88.
Downes, Lawrence. "Of Poor Farmers and 'Famous Men.'" *New York Times*, November 26, 2011.
Downes, Olin. "Menotti 'Consul' Has Its Premiere: Composer Also Directed Stage Presentation of Opera—Tragic Story of Europe." *New York Times*, March 16, 1950.
———. "Music: Premiere of One-Act Opera; Copland's 'Tender Land' Is Put On at Center." *New York Times*, April 2, 1954.
Driscoll, F. Paul. "All American: Patricia Racette." *Opera News*, September 2014. https://www.metguild.org/Opera_News_Magazine/2014/9/Features/All_American.html. Accessed September 1, 2022.
Duffie, Bruce. "Soprano Phyllis Curtin: A Conversation with Bruce Duffie." August 24, 2003. http://www.bruceduffie.com/curtin.html. Accessed September 1, 2022.
Duggan, Lisa. *Sapphic Slashers: Sex, Violence, and American Modernity*. Durham, NC: Duke University Press, 2000.

Dunar, Andrew J. *America in the Fifties.* Foreword by John Robert Green. Syracuse, NY: Syracuse University Press, 2006.
Dunn, Leslie C. and Nancy A. Jones, eds. *Embodied Voices: Representing Female Vocality in Western Culture.* Cambridge: Cambridge University Press, 1994.
Ebright, Ryan. "*Doctor Atomic* or: How John Adams Learned to Stop Worrying and Love Sound Design." *Cambridge Opera Journal* 31, no. 1 (2019): 85–117.
———. "'My answer to what music theater can be': Iconoclasm and Entrepreneurship in Steve Reich and Beryl Korot's *The Cave.*" *American Music* 37, no. 1 (2017): 29–50.
"Edward Bernard Carlos." *Parsons Sun* (Parsons, KS), July 31, 1978.
Edwards, Anne. *Maria Callas: An Intimate Biography.* New York: St. Martin's Griffin, 2001.
Eisler, Benita. *Private Lives: Men and Women of the Fifties.* New York: Franklin Watts, 1986.
Elwell, Herbert. "'Baby Doe' Best in Last Scenes." *Cleveland Plain Dealer*, March 14, 1960.
———. "Tennessee 'Susannah' Is Moving Spectacle." *Cleveland Plain Dealer*, March 12, 1960.
"Eulah Rose Carlos." *Parsons Sun* (Parsons, KS), September 12, 1977.
Evans, Sara M. "Women's Liberation: Seeing the Revolution Clearly." *Feminist Studies* 41, no. 1 (2015): 138–149.
Eyer, Ronald. "Ballad of Baby Doe." *Musical America* 79, no. 5 (May 1959): 7.
———. "Carlisle Floyd's 'Susannah.'" *Tempo* 42 (Winter 1956–1957): 7–11.
Fariello, Griffin. *Red Scare: Memories of the American Inquisition, An Oral History.* New York: W. W. Norton & Company, 1995.
Farris, Julian E. *The Sin Warriors.* Maple Shade, NJ: Lethe Press, 2012.
Fauser, Annegret. *Sounds of War: Music in the United States during World War II.* Oxford: Oxford University Press, 2013.
Fay, Laurel E. "Shostakovich versus Volkov: Whose *Testimony?*" *The Russian Review* 39, no. 4 (1980): 484–493.
Field, Douglas, ed. *American Cold War Culture.* Edinburgh: Edinburgh University Press, 2005.
Fleegler, Robert L. *Ellis Island Nation: Immigration Policy and American Identity in the Twentieth Century.* Philadelphia: University of Pennsylvania Press, 2013.
Fleming, Renée. *I Want Magic!* Decca 460 567, 1998. Compact disc.
Floyd, Carlisle. *Carlisle Floyd's Susannah.* Directed by Michael Unger. Naxos DVD 2.110381, 2017.

———. *Susannah: A Musical Drama in Two Acts, Libretto.* New York: Boosey and Hawkes, 1956.

———. *Susannah, A Musical Drama in Two Acts, Vocal Score.* New York: Boosey and Hawkes, 1956, 1957.

Fox, Margalit. "Patricia Neway, Operatic Soprano Who Won a Tony, Dies at 92." *New York Times*, February 1, 2012.

Frankel, Haskel. "Teaching in Triplicate." *Saturday Review*, April 10, 1965.

Freedman, Estelle B. *Redefining Rape: Sexual Violence in the Era of Suffrage and Segregation.* Cambridge, MA: Harvard University Press, 2013.

Freeman, Jo. "The BITCH Manifesto." © 1969. https://www.jofreeman.com/joreen/bitch.htm. Accessed September 1, 2022.

Freeman, John W. *The Metropolitan Opera: Stories of the Great Operas*, Vol. 2. New York: W. W. Norton & Company, 1997.

Fried, Richard M. *Nightmare in Red: The McCarthy Era in Perspective.* New York: Oxford University Press, 1990.

Friedan, Betty. *The Feminine Mystique.* New York: W. W. Norton & Company, Inc., 1963.

Futral, Elizabeth. *Great Operatic Arias.* Chandos 3096, 2003. Compact disc.

Gadsby, Hannah. *Hannah Gadsby: Nanette.* Directed by Madeleine Parry. Distributed by Netflix, 2018.

Gardner, Kara Anne. *Agnes de Mille: Telling Stories in Broadway Dance.* New York: Oxford University Press, 2016.

Garland, Robert. "Patricia Neway Great in Fine Musical Drama." *Journal American*, March 16, 1950.

Garrard, Mary D. "Artemisia and Susanna." In *Feminism and Art History: Questing the Litany*, edited by Norma Broude and Mary D. Garrard, 147–171. New York: Harper & Row, 1982.

Garrett, Charles Hiroshi. *Struggling to Define a Nation: American Music and the Twentieth Century.* Berkeley: University of California Press, 2008.

Garrett, Charles Hiroshi and Carol J. Oja, eds. *Sounding Together: Collaborative Perspectives on U.S. Music in the 21st Century.* Ann Arbor: University of Michigan Press, 2021.

Gatti-Casazza, Giulio. *Memories of the Opera.* New York: C. Scribner's Sons, 1941.

Gelb, Arthur. "FOLK MUSIC PLAY MAY BE DONE HERE, Myerberg Is Likely Producer of 'The Ballad of Baby Doe' by Moore and Latouche." *New York Times*, June 18, 1956.

Genovese, Eugene. *Roll, Jordan, Roll: The World the Slaves Made.* New York: Vintage Books, 1972.

Gentry, Philip M. *What Will I Be: American Music and Cold War Identity.* New York: Oxford University Press, 2017.

Giddens, Rhiannon. "Floyd's *Susannah*: Hopeless in New Hope, Featuring Renée Fleming." *Aria Code*. June 21, 2019. Podcast. https://www.wnycstudios.org/podcasts/aria-code/episodes/aria-code-floyd-susannah-rhiannon-giddens-renee-fleming. Accessed September 1, 2022.
Giddens, Rhiannon and Francesco Turrisi. *There Is No Other*. Nonesuch 591336, 2019. Compact disc.
Gilbert, Sandra M. and Susan Gubar. *The Madwoman in the Attic: The Woman Writer and the Nineteenth-Century Literary Imagination*. New Haven, CT: Yale University Press, 1979.
Gilmore, Stephanie, ed., *Feminist Coalitions: Historical Perspectives on Second-Wave Feminism in the United States*. Foreword by Sara M. Evans. Urbana: University of Illinois Press, 2008.
Glenn, Susan Anita. *Female Spectacle: The Theatrical Roots of Modern Feminism*. Cambridge, MA: Harvard University Press, 2000.
Goldberg, Vicki. *Margaret Bourke-White: A Biography*. New York: Harper & Row, 1986.
Gornick, Vivian. *Fierce Attachments*. New York: Simon & Schuster, 1987.
Gouin, Raymond. "Floyd's Susannah in Boston." *Opera Today*, April 27, 2010. http://www.operatoday.com/content/2010/04/floyds_susannah.php. Accessed September 1, 2022.
Graber, Naomi. *Kurt Weill's America*. New York: Oxford University Press, 2021.
Graf, Herbert. *The Opera and Its Future in America*. New York: W. W. Norton & Company, 1941.
———. *Opera for the People*. Minneapolis: University of Minnesota Press, 1951.
———. *Producing Opera for America*. Zürich: Atlantis Books, 1961.
Graham-Bertolini, Alison. *Vigilante Women in Contemporary American Fiction*. New York: Palgrave Macmillan, 2011.
Graves, Karen. *And They Were Wonderful Teachers: Florida's Purge of Gay and Lesbian Teachers*. Urbana: University of Illinois Press, 2009.
Graziano, John. "Musical Dialects in *Down in the Valley*." In *A New Orpheus: Essays on Kurt Weill*, edited by Kim H. Kowalk, 297–320. New Haven, CT: Yale University Press, 1986.
Gresmer, Olive. "It's Purely Personal: Have You Heard …" *News-Journal* (Mansfield, OH), September 1, 1948.
Grieb, Lyndal. *The Operas of Gian Carlo Menotti, 1937–1972: A Selective Bibliography*. Metuchen, NJ: Scarecrow Press, Inc., 1974.
Griffith, Robert. *The Politics of Fear: Joseph R. McCarthy and the Senate*. Lexington: University Press of Kentucky, 1970.
Gross, Klaus-Dieter. "McCarthyism and American Opera." *Revue LISA* 2, no. 3 (2004): 164–187.

Gruen, John. *Callas Kissed Me ... Lenny Too! A Critic's Memoir.* Brooklyn, NY: powerHouse Books, 2008.

———. *Menotti: A Biography.* New York: Macmillan Publishing Co., Inc., 1978.

Gunne, Sorcha and Zoë Brigley Thompson, eds. *Feminism, Literature and Rape Narratives: Violence and Violation.* New York: Routledge, 2010.

Gunter, Freeman. "An Exclusive Interview with Elizabeth Futral." *Classical Singer*, December 1, 2001. https://www.csmusic.net/content/articles/an-exclusive-interview-with-elizabeth-futral/. Accessed September 1, 2022.

Guy, Nancy. *The Magic of Beverly Sills.* Urbana: University of Illinois Press, 2015.

Hageman, William. "Lizzie Borden, Animal Lover." *Chicago Tribune*, September 30, 2014.

Halberstam, David. *The Fifties.* New York: Villard Books, 1993.

Halliwell, Martin. *American Culture in the 1950s.* Edinburgh: Edinburgh University Press, 2007.

Hansen, Patrick. "Patrick's Opera Blog: Why Menotti Operas Are Flawed." Tuesday, November 5, 2013. https://patricksoperablog.blogspot.com/2013/11/why-menotti-operas-are-flawed.html. Accessed September 1, 2022.

Hardee, Lewis J., Jr. "The Musical Theatre of Douglas Moore." MA thesis, University of North Carolina at Chapel Hill, 1970.

———. "The Perils of Baby Doe." *Columbia Library Columns* 23, no. 1 (1973): 3–11.

Harding, Kate. *Asking for It: The Alarming Rise of Rape Culture and What We Can Do about It.* Boston: Da Capo Lifelong, 2015.

Harper-Scott, J. P. E. "Britten's Opera about Rape." *Cambridge Opera Journal* 21 (2010): 65–88.

Hart, Beth. "What Becomes a Legend Most? A Tribute to Beverly Sills." *The Opera Quarterly* 20, no. 4 (2004): 624–656.

Hartford, Kassandra. "A Common Man for the Cold War: Aaron Copland's *Old American Songs*." *The Musical Quarterly* 98, no. 4 (2015): 313–349.

Hartman, Louis F. and Alexander A. Di Lella. *The Book of Daniel: A New Translation with Notes and Commentary.* Garden City, NY: Doubleday & Company, Inc., 1978.

Hartmann, Susan M. *The Home Front and Beyond: American Women in the 1940s.* Boston: Twayne Publishers, 1982.

Harrison, Jay S. "American Opera Hailed Here: 'Ballad of Baby Doe'; The Girl of the Silver West." *New York Herald Tribune*, April 4, 1958.

Harvey, Brett. *The Fifties: A Women's Oral History.* San Jose, CA: ASJA Press, 1993, 2002.

Haskell, Harry. "'Susannah' Composer Aims for Believability." *Kansas City Star*, September 18, 1977.
Haskell, Molly. *From Reverence to Rape: The Treatment of Women in the Movies*. 2nd ed. Chicago: University of Chicago Press, 1973, 1974, 1987.
Heggie, Jake. "The Journey of *Dead Man Walking*." *Lyric Notes*, Lyric Opera of Chicago, November 2019. https://www.lyricopera.org/lyric-notes/november-2019-lyric-notes/jake-heggie-dead-man-walking/. Accessed September 1, 2022.
Heggie, Jake and Terrence McNally. *Dead Man Walking: Opera in Two Acts, Piano/Vocal Score*. San Francisco: Bent Pen Music, Inc., 2000.
Heinsheimer, H. W. "The Future of Opera in America." *Opera News*, March 6, 1950, pp. 11, 29–30.
———. "Opera in America Today." *The Musical Quarterly* 37, no. 3 (1951): 315–329.
———. "Right Kind of Opera Has Market in America." *New York Times*, May 29, 1949.
Hellman, Lillian. *Scoundrel Time*. Introduction by Gary Wills. Boston: Little, Brown and Company, 1976.
Hershberger, Monica A. "Feminist Revisions: Virgil Thomson and Gertrude Stein's Mid-Century Homage to Susan B. Anthony." *Journal of Musicology* 37, no. 3 (2020): 383–414.
———. "Fifty Years Later: Reflections on Douglas Moore's Carry Nation (1966), the University of Kansas's Centennial Contribution to the American 'Year of Opera.'" *The Opera Journal* 49, no. 4 (2016): 3–18.
———. "Seduction or Rape? The Sexual Politics of Carlisle Floyd's *Susannah*." *Journal of the American Musicological Society* 71, no. 1 (2018): 226–232.
Heyman, Barbara B. *Samuel Barber: The Composer and His Music*. 2nd ed. New York: Oxford University Press, 2020.
Hinchman, Mark. *The Fairchild Books Dictionary of Interior Design*, 3rd ed. New York: Bloomsbury Publishing, 2014.
Hinton, Stephen. "Down in the Valley." *Grove Music Online*. 2002. https://www.oxfordmusiconline.com/grovemusic/view/10.1093/gmo/9781561592630.001.0001/omo-9781561592630-e-5000008229. Accessed September 1, 2022.
———. *Weill's Musical Theater: Stages of Reform*. Berkeley: University of California Press, 2012.
Hipsher, Edward Ellsworth. *American Opera and Its Composers*. Philadelphia: Theodore Presser Co., 1927.
Hisama, Ellie M. "A Feminist Staging of Britten's *The Rape of Lucretia*." *Journal of the American Musicological Society* 71, no. 1 (2018): 237–243.

Hitchcock, H. Wiley. *Music in the United States: A Historical Introduction.* Englewood Cliffs, NJ: Prentice-Hall, Inc., 1969.

Hixon, Donald L. *Gian Carlo Menotti: A Bio-Bibliography.* Westport, CT: Greenwood Press, 2000.

Holliday, Thomas. *Falling Up: The Days and Nights of Carlisle Floyd; The Authorized Biography, with a Foreword by Plácido Domingo.* Syracuse, NY: Syracuse University Press, 2013.

Honey, Maureen. *Creating Rosie the Riveter: Class, Gender, and Propaganda during World War II.* Amherst: University of Massachusetts Press, 1984.

hooks, bell. *Ain't I a Woman: Black Women and Feminism.* Boston: South End Press, 1981.

Horowitz, Daniel. *Betty Friedan and the Making of The Feminine Mystique: The American Left, the Cold War, and Modern Feminism.* Amherst: University of Massachusetts Press, 1998.

Hubbs, Nadine. *The Queer Composition of America's Sound: Gay Modernists, American Music, and National Identity.* Berkeley: University of California Press, 2004.

Hudson, Elizabeth. "Gilda Seduced: A Tale Untold." *Cambridge Opera Journal* 4, no. 3 (1992): 229–251.

Hughes, Allen. "Florence Kimball, Teacher, Dies at 87." *New York Times*, November 26, 1977.

Hunter, Evan. *Lizzie.* New York: Arbor House, 1984.

Huscher, Phillip. *The Santa Fe Opera: An American Pioneer.* Santa Fe, NM: Sunstone Press, 2006.

Hutchins-Viroux, Rachel. "Witch-Hunts, Theocracies and Hypocrisy: McCarthyism in Arthur Miller/Robert Ward's Opera *The Crucible* and Carlisle Floyd's *Susannah*." *Revue LISA E-Journal* 6, no. 2 (2008): 140–148.

"Immigrant A Suicide: Woman, Denied Entry to U.S., Hangs Herself on Ellis Island." *New York Times*, February 12, 1947.

Inge, William. *Picnic.* New York: Dramatists Play Service, Inc., 1953.

———. "*Picnic.*" In *Four Plays*, 71–148. New York: Grove Press, 1958.

"In Memoriam: Phyllis Curtin, Soprano." *Yale School of Music.* June 11, 2016. https://music.yale.edu/2016/06/11/memoriam-phyllis-curtin-soprano. Accessed September 1, 2022.

Jackson, Paul. *Sign-Off for the Old Met: The Metropolitan Opera Broadcasts, 1950–1966.* New York: Amadeus Press, 2003.

Jensen-Moulton, Stephanie. "Intellectual Disability in Carlisle Floyd's *Of Mice and Men*." *American Music* 30, no. 2 (2012): 129–156.

Johnson, David K. *The Lavender Scare: The Cold War Persecution of Gays and Lesbians in the Federal Government.* Chicago: University of Chicago Press, 2004.

Jones, Ryan Patrick. "*The Tender Land*: Aaron Copland's American Narrative." PhD diss., Brandeis University, 2005.
Kaledin, Eugenia. *Mothers and More: American Women in the 1950s.* Boston: Twayne Publishers, 1984.
Karsner, David. *Silver Dollar: The Story of the Tabors.* New York: Crown Publishers, 1932.
Kastendieck, Miles. "Tip Your Hat, America, to 'Baby Doe.'" *New York Journal-America*, April 4, 1958.
Kellow, Brian. "Brenda Lewis, 96, Ferociously Intelligent American Soprano Who Premiered Title Role in *Lizzie Borden*, Has Died." *Opera News*, September 16, 2017. https://www.operanews.com/Opera_News_Magazine/2017/9/News/Brenda_Lewis_Ferociously_Intelligent_American_Soprano.html. Accessed September 1, 2022.
Kerman, Joseph. *Opera as Drama.* New York: Alfred A. Knopf, 1956.
———. *Opera as Drama, New and Revised Edition.* Berkeley: University of California Press, 1988.
———. "Susannah, A Musical Drama in 2 Acts, Text and Vocal Score by Carlisle Floyd." *Notes* 15, no. 3 (1958): 478.
———. "Verdi and the Undoing of Women." *Cambridge Opera Journal* 18, no.1 (2006): 21–31.
Kernodle, Tammy L. "Arias, Communists, and Conspiracies: The History of Still's 'Troubled Island.'" *The Musical Quarterly* 83, no. 4 (1999): 487–508.
Khanna, Nikki. "'If You're Half Black, You're Just Black': Reflected Appraisals and the Persistence of the One-Drop Rule." *The Sociological Quarterly* 51, no. 1 (2010): 96–121.
Kirk, Elise K. *American Opera.* Urbana: University of Illinois Press, 2001.
Kittredge, George Lyman. "Ballads and Songs." *Journal of American Folklore* 30, no. 117 (1917): 346–347.
Knapp, Raymond. *The American Musical and the Formation of National Identity.* Princeton, NJ: Princeton University Press, 2005.
———. *The American Musical and the Performance of Personal Identity.* Princeton, NJ: Princeton University Press, 2006.
Kolodin, Irving. *The Story of the Metropolitan Opera, 1883–1950: A Candid History.* New York: Alfred A. Knopf, 1953.
Kolt, Robert Paul. *Robert Ward's The Crucible: Creating an American Musical Nationalism.* Lanham, MD: Scarecrow Press, 2008.
Kowalke, Kim H., ed. *A New Orpheus: Essays on Kurt Weill.* New Haven, CT: Yale University Press, 1986.
Krafft-Ebing, Richard Freiherr von. *Psychopathia Sexualis, with Especial Reference to the Antipathic Sexual Instinct.* Translated by F. J. Rebman. Brooklyn, NY: Physicians and Surgeons Book Co., 1908.

Krebs, Betty Dietz. "Alice Hotopp Selected for Ohio Quartet." *Dayton Daily News*, May 5, 1976.
"Laconia Girl Worries about Brother as She Starts Sentence." *Lewiston Evening Journal* (Lewiston, ME), December 3, 1947.
Landis, Mark. *Joseph McCarthy: The Politics of Chaos*. Selinsgrove, PA: Sesquehanna University Press, 1987.
Lange, Dorothea and Paul Schuster Taylor. *An American Exodus: A Record of Human Erosion in the Thirties*. New Haven, CT: Yale University Press, 1939, 1969.
Langer, Lawrence L. *Preempting the Holocaust*. New Haven, CT: Yale University Press, 1998.
Latouche, John. "About the Ballad of Baby Doe." *Theatre Arts Magazine*, July 1956, pp. 80–83.
Lee, Harper. *To Kill a Mockingbird*. Philadelphia: J. B. Lippincott & Co., 1960.
Lee, Hermione. *Biography: A Very Short Introduction*. Oxford: Oxford University Press, 2009.
Lehrman, Leonard. "An Interview with Jack Beeson." *Opera Monthly* 7, no. 1 (1994): 16–28.
Leinsdorf, Erich. *Cadenza: A Musical Career*. Boston: Houghton Mifflin Company, 1976.
Lerner, Gerda. "Black Women Attack the Lynching System." In *Black Women in White America: A Documentary History*, edited by Gerda Lerner, 193–215. New York: Pantheon Books, 1972.
———, ed. *Black Women in White America: A Documentary History*. New York: Pantheon Books, 1972.
———. "A Woman's Lot." In *Black Women in White America: A Documentary History*, 149–215. New York: Pantheon Books, 1972.
Levi, Primo. *The Drowned and the Saved*. New York: Summit Books, 1986.
———. *Survival in Auschwitz: The Nazi Assault on Humanity*. Translated by Stuart Woolf. New York: Collier Books, 1961.
Levin, David. *Unsettling Opera: Staging Mozart, Verdi, Wagner, and Zemlinsky*. Chicago: University of Chicago Press, 2007.
Levine, Robert. *Maria Callas: A Musical Biography*. New York: Amadeus Press, 2003.
Levy, Beth E. *Frontier Figures: American Music and the Mythology of the American West*. Berkeley: University of California Press, 2012.
Leyland, Winston. *Gay Sunshine Interviews*. Vol. 2. San Francisco: Gay Sunshine Press, 1982.
Leys, Ruth. *From Guilt to Shame: Auschwitz and After*. Princeton, NJ: Princeton University Press, 2007.

Lincoln, Victoria. *A Private Disgrace: Lizzie Borden by Daylight.* New York: G. P. Putnam's Sons, 1967.

Lindsay, Tedrin Blair. "The Coming of Age of American Opera: New York City Opera and the Ford Foundation, 1958–1960." PhD diss., University of Kentucky, 2009.

Locke, Ralph. "What Are These Women Doing in Opera?" In *En Travesti: Women, Gender Subversion, Opera,* edited by Corinne E. Blackmer and Patricia Juliana Smith, 59–98. New York: Columbia University Press, 1995.

Lowndes, Marie Belloc. *Lizzie Borden: A Study in Conjecture.* New York: Longman, Green and Co, 1939.

Luening, Otto. *The Odyssey of an American Composer: The Autobiography of Otto Luening.* New York: Charles Scribner's Sons, 1980.

Lynch, Christopher. "Opera and Broadway: The Debate Over the Essence of Opera in New York City, 1900–1960." PhD diss., State University of New York Buffalo, 2013.

MacKellar, Thomas and C. C. Converse. "Toiling Early (Christian Endeavor Hymn)." In *The Standard Hymnal for General Use,* 43. New York: Funk & Wagnalls Co., 1896.

Maharidge, Dale and Michael Williamson. *And Their Children after Them: The Legacy of Let Us Now Praise Famous Men; James Agee, Walker Evans, and the Rise and Fall of Cotton in the South.* New York: Pantheon Books, 1989.

Malitz, Nancy. "'Susannah' Dares to be Different." *Cincinnati Enquirer,* July 8, 1979.

Maria Golovin. November 5, 1958–November 8, 1958, Martin Beck Theatre, New York, NY. Internet Broadway Database. https://www.ibdb.com/broadway-production/maria-golovin-2713. Accessed August 23, 2022.

Mathers, Daniel E. "Expanding Horizons." In *Copland Connotations: Studies and Interviews,* edited by Peter Dickinson. Foreword by H. Wiley Hitchcock, 118–135. Woodbridge: Boydell Press, 2002.

Matthews, Jean V. *The Rise of the New Woman: The Women's Movement in America, 1875–1930.* Chicago: Ivan R. Dee, 2003.

May, Elaine Tyler. *Homeward Bound: American Families in the Cold War Era, Fully Revised and Updated 20th Anniversary Edition, with a New Post 9/11 Epilogue.* New York: Basic Books, 1988, 1999, 2008.

McBride, Jerry L. *Douglas Moore: A Bio-Bibliography.* Middletown, WI: A-R Editions, Inc., 2011.

McClary, Susan. *Feminine Endings: Music, Gender, and Sexuality.* Minneapolis: University of Minnesota Press, 1991.

———. "Foreword: The Undoing of Opera: Toward a Feminist Criticism of Music." In Catherine Clément, *Opera, or the Undoing of Women,* translated by Betsy Wing, ix–xviii. Minneapolis: University of Minnesota Press, 1988.

———. "Lives in Musicology: A Life in Musicology—Stradella and Me." *Acta Musicologica* 91, no. 1 (2019): 5–20.

McConachie, Bruce. *American Theater in the Culture of the Cold War: Producing and Contesting Containment, 1947–1962*. Iowa City: University of Iowa Press, 2003.

McKenna, Harold J., ed. *New York City Opera Sings: Stories and Productions of the New York City Opera, 1944–79*. New York: Richards Rosen Press, Inc., 1981.

Menotti, Gian-Carlo. *The Consul: Musical Drama in Three Acts, Libretto*. New York: G. Schirmer, Inc., 1950.

Menotti, Gian-Carlo and Rudolph Cartier. *Der Konsul*. Halle: Arthaus Musik DVD, 2010.

Menotti, Gian-Carlo and Jean Dalrymple. *The Consul: A Musical Drama in Three Acts*. Pleasantville, NY: Video Artists International DVD 4266, 1960, 2004.

"Menotti Mania ..." *Opera News*, October 29, 1951, pp. 18–19.

Mermelstein, David. "MUSIC; Vocalism in Her Soul, Drama in Her Blood." *New York Times*, April 8, 2001.

Metalious, Grace. *Peyton Place*. New York: Julian Messner, Inc., 1956.

Meyerowitz, Joanne, ed. *Not June Cleaver: Women and Gender in Postwar America, 1945–1960*. Philadelphia: Temple University Press, 1994.

Midgette, Anne. "OPERA REVIEW; He Fell for Her Bait, and Then She Fell for Him." *New York Times*, April 10, 2001.

Miller, Arthur. *The Crucible: A Play in Four Acts*. New York: Viking Press, 1953.

———. "It Could Happen Here—And Did." *New York Times*, April 30, 1967.

Miller, Dan B. *Erskine Caldwell: The Journey from Tobacco Road*. New York: Alfred A. Knopf, 1995.

Mize, Jane Robbins. "From the Outside In: Walker Evans's Allie Mae Burroughs, 1936." *Ransom Center Magazine* (University of Texas), April 7, 2014. https://sites.utexas.edu/ransomcentermagazine/2014/04/07/from-the-outside-in-allie-mae-burroughs/. Accessed September 1, 2022.

Moore, Douglas. "Opera Productions at Columbia University." *Opera News*, April 16, 1945, p. 13.

———. "Our Lyric Theatre." *Modern Music* 18, no. 1 (November–December 1940): 3–7.

———. "Something about Librettos." *Opera News*, September 30, 1961, pp. 8–13.

———. "True Tale of West: Story of Baby Doe Tabor Turned into an Opera." *New York Times*, July 1, 1956.

Moore, Douglas and John Latouche. *The Ballad of Baby Doe: Opera in Two Acts, Piano-Vocal Score*. New York: Chappell & Co., Inc., 1956, 1957, 1958.
Morgan, Brian. *Strange Child of Chaos: Norman Treigle*. New York: iUniverse, 2006.
Morris, Debbie. *Forgiving the Dead Man Walking*. Grand Rapids, MI: Zondervan Publishing House, 1998.
Morrison, Matthew D. "Race, Blacksound, and the (Re)Making of Musicological Discourse." *Journal of the American Musicological Society* 72, no. 3 (2019): 781–823.
Most, Andrea. *Making Americans: Jews and the Broadway Musical*. Cambridge, MA: Harvard University Press, 2004.
"Music and Musicians: School Memories Are Stirred by the Musical Charm of the Saint Mary College Spring Festival." *Kansas City Times* (Kansas City, MO), April 10, 1948.
"North American Works Directory." Opera America. https://apps.operaamerica.org/Applications/NAWD/index.aspx. Accessed August 22, 2022.
Oakley, J. Ronald. *God's Country: American in the Fifties*. New York: Dembner Books, 1986.
Odets, Walt. *In the Shadow of the Epidemic: Being HIV-Negative in the Age of AIDS*. Durham, NC: Duke University Press, 1995.
Oja, Carol J. *Bernstein Meets Broadway: Collaborative Art in a Time of War*. New York: Oxford University Press, 2014.
———. *Making Music Modern: New York in the 1920s*. New York: Oxford University Press, 2000.
"Opera's Heir Presumptive." *Newsweek*, March 27, 1950, p. 82.
"'Passionate' Salome: American Soprano Is Unveiled as a Talented Operatic Wriggler." *Life*, April 12, 1954, pp. 81–84.
"Patricia Neway, 92, the First Magda Sorel in *The Consul*, Has Died." *Opera News*, January 29, 2012.
Patton, Christopher W. "Discovering *The Tender Land*: A New Look at Aaron Copland's Opera." *American Music* 20, no. 3 (2002): 317–340.
Pearson, Edmund. *Trial of Lizzie Borden, Edited, with a History of the Case*. Garden City, NY: Doubleday, Doran & Company, Inc., 1937.
Perkins, Francis D. "City Opera Gives 'Susannah' Its First N.Y. Performance." *New York Herald Tribune*, September 28, 1956.
"Peter B. Greenough, 89, Former Columnist, Dies." *New York Times*, September 6, 2006.
Picnic. February 19, 1953–April 10, 1954, Music Box Theatre, New York. NY. Internet Broadway Database. https://www.ibdb.com/broadway-production/picnic-2220. Accessed August 23, 2022.

Plant, Richard. *The Dragon in the Forest.* Garden City, NY: Doubleday & Company, Inc., 1948.

———. *The Pink Triangle: The Nazi War against Homosexuals.* New York: Henry Holt and Company, 1986.

Plath, Sylvia. *The Bell Jar.* New York: Harper Perennial, 1971.

Pollack, Howard. *Aaron Copland: The Life and Work of an Uncommon Man.* Urbana: University of Illinois Press, 1999.

———. *The Ballad of John Latouche: An American Lyricist's Life and Work.* New York: Oxford University Press, 2017.

Porgy and Bess. October 10, 1935–January 25, 1936, Alvin Theatre, New York, NY. Internet Broadway Database. https://www.ibdb.com/broadway-production/porgy-and-bess-11998. Accessed August 23, 2022.

Prejean, Helen. *Dead Man Walking: The Eyewitness Account of the Death Penalty That Sparked a National Debate.* New York: Vintage Books, 1993, 2013.

———. *River of Fire: My Spiritual Journey.* New York: Random House, 2019.

———. *River of Fire: On Becoming an Activist.* New York: Vintage Books, 2019, 2020.

———. "Still on the Journey." Liner notes. *Dead Man Walking.* Houston Grand Opera, Jack Heggie, and Terrence McNally. © 2012 Parlophone Records Ltd., 5099960246325. Compact disc.

"Premiere of 'Susannah' Stars Curtin, Harrell February 24th." *The Florida Flambeau,* January 11, 1955.

Preston, Katherine K. *Opera on the Road: Travelling Opera Troupes in the United States, 1825–60.* Urbana: University of Illinois Press, 1993.

"Profile of Douglas Moore." *American Musical Theater Workshop.* WCBS-TV. Videotaped February 24, 1962. Telecast March 4, 1962.

Projansky, Sarah. *Watching Rape: Film and Television in Postfeminist Culture.* New York: New York University Press, 2001.

Radin, Edward. *Lizzie Borden: The Untold Story.* New York: Simon and Schuster, 1961.

Ray, Marcie. *Coquettes, Wives, and Widows: Gender Politics in French Baroque Opera and Theater.* Rochester, NY: University of Rochester Press, 2020.

"Refugees Dodge Trains on Border Bridge As Both Austria and Hungary Bar Entry." *New York Times,* May 20, 1947.

Reitz, Christina L. *Jennifer Higdon: Composing in Color.* Jefferson, NC: McFarland & Company, 2018.

Renihan, Colleen. *The Operatic Archive: American Opera as History.* Ashgate Interdisciplinary Studies in Opera. London: Routledge, Taylor & Francis Group, 2020.

RePass, Richard. "Opera Workshops in the United States." *Tempo,* New Series, no. 27 (1953): 10–18.

"RETHBERG IS SUED BY WIFE OF PINZA; Prima Donna Is Accused of Wrecking Basso's Home—$250,000 Damages Asked." *New York Times*, March 8, 1935.

Rhein, John von. "Oh, Susannah! An American Opera of Lust and Moral Superiority Seems Surprisingly Contemporary after 40 Years." *Chicago Tribune*, October 3, 1993.

"Rites Are Set in New York for Met's Trucco." *Atlanta Constitution*, May 19, 1964.

Robinson, Paul. "It's Not Over until the Soprano Dies." *New York Times Book Review*, January 1, 1989.

Rorem, Ned. "In Search of American Opera." *Opera News*, July 1991, pp. 8–10, 12, 14–17, 44.

Rosand, Ellen. *Opera in Seventeenth-Century Venice: The Creation of a Genre*. Berkeley: University of California Press, 1991.

———. "Review: Criticism and the Undoing of Opera." *19th-Century Music* 14, no. 1 (1990): 75–83.

"Rosemary Carlos." *Parsons Sun* (Parsons, KS), August 20, 1954.

"Rosemary Carlos Has Paola Operetta Lead." *Catholic Advance* (Wichita, KS), May 14, 1943.

"Rosemary Carlos Stars in Opera." *Walnut Eagle* (Walnut, KS), May 19, 1950.

Rudel, Julius and Rebecca Paller. *First and Lasting Impressions: Julius Rudel Looks Back on a Life in Music*. Rochester, NY: University of Rochester Press, 2013.

Rutherford, Susan. *Verdi, Opera, Women*. Cambridge: Cambridge University Press, 2013.

Rymer, Russ. *American Beach: A Saga of Race, Wealth, and Memory*. New York: HarperCollins, 1998.

Safo, Nova. "Menotti, Cultural Giant, Dies at 95." *All Things Considered*. National Public Radio. February 1, 2007. https://www.npr.org/templates/story/story.php?storyId=7120281. Accessed September 1, 2022.

The Saint of Bleecker Street. December 27, 1954–April 2, 1955, Broadway Theatre, New York, NY. Internet Broadway Database. https://www.ibdb.com/broadway-production/the-saint-of-bleecker-street-2490. Accessed August 23, 2022.

Salome, Louis J. "The Queen of the Beach." *Palm Beach Post* (Palm Beach County, FL). April 19, 2003.

Sargeant, Winthrop. "Musical Events: Bonanza." *New Yorker*, April 12, 1958, pp. 70–72.

Scanlon, Jennifer. *Bad Girls Go Everywhere: The Life of Helen Gurley Brown*. New York: Oxford University Press, 2009.

Schnur, James A. "Cold Warriors in the Hot Sunshine: The Johns Committee's Assault on Civil Liberties in Florida, 1956–1965." Thesis, University of South Florida, 1995.

Schrecker, Ellen. *The Age of McCarthyism: A Brief History with Documents*. Boston: Bedford Books of St. Martin's Press, 1994.

Seligson, Susan. "BU Mourns CFA Dean Emerita Phyllis Curtin." *BU Today*, June 8, 2016. https://www.bu.edu/articles/2016/phyllis-curtin-obituary. Accessed September 1, 2022.

Sheridan, Molly. "Profile: Phyllis Curtin." *New Music Box*, April 25, 2002. https://nmbx.newmusicusa.org/PROFILE-Phyllis-Curtin/. Accessed September 1, 2022.

Showalter, Elaine. *The Female Malady: Women, Madness, and English Culture, 1830-1980*, 1st ed. New York: Pantheon Books, 1985.

———. "Killing the Angel in the House: The Autonomy of Women Writers." *The Antioch Review* 50, no. 1/2 (1992): 207–220.

Sills, Beverly. *Bubbles: An Encore*. New York: Grosset & Dunlap, 1981.

Sills, Beverly and Lawrence Linderman. *Beverly: An Autobiography*. Toronto: Bantam Books, 1987.

———. *Bubbles: A Self-Portrait*. Indianapolis, IN: Bobbs-Merrill, 1976.

Smart, Mary Ann. "The Lost Voice of Rosine Stoltz." *Cambridge Opera Journal* 6, no. 1 (1994): 31–50.

———. "The Queen and the Flirt." *Representations* 104, no. 1 (2008): 126–136.

———. "The Silencing of Lucia." *Cambridge Opera Journal* 4, no. 2 (1992): 119–141.

———. ed. *Siren Songs: Representations of Gender and Sexuality in Opera*. Princeton, NJ: Princeton University Press, 2000.

Smith, Craig A. *A Vision of Voices: John Crosby and the Santa Fe Opera*. Albuquerque: University of New Mexico Press, 2015.

Smith, Duane A., with John Moriarty. *The Ballad of Baby Doe: "I Shall Walk beside My Love."* Boulder: University Press of Colorado, 2002.

Smith, Helen. "Faith and Love in New Hope Valley: A Consideration of Community in Carlisle Floyd's *Susannah*." *American Music Research Center Journal* 21 (2012): 67–91.

Smith, Julia. *Aaron Copland: His Work and Contribution to American Music*. New York: E. P. Dutton & Company, Inc., 1955.

Smith, Tim. "Aaron Copland, Dean of U.S. Music, Dies at 90." *South Florida Sun Sentinel*, December 3, 1990.

Smith-Rosenberg, Carroll. *Disorderly Conduct: Visions of Gender in Victorian America*. New York: Alfred A. Knopf, 1985.

Sokol, Martin L. *The New York City Opera: An American Adventure*. New York: Macmillan Publishing Co., Inc., 1981.

Solie, Ruth A., ed. *Musicology and Difference: Gender and Sexuality in Music Scholarship*. Berkeley: University of California Press, 1993.
Spencer, Scott B. "Ballad Collecting: Impetus and Impact." In *The Ballad Collectors of North America: How Gathering Folksongs Transformed Academic Thought and American Identity*, edited by Scott B. Spencer, 1–16. Lanham, MD: Scarecrow Press, 2012.
Stark, Bonnie. "McCarthyism in Florida: Charley Johns and the Florida Legislative Investigation Committee, July 1956–1965." Thesis, University of South Florida, 1985.
Stempel, Larry. *Showtime: A History of the Broadway Musical Theater*. New York: W. W. Norton & Company, 2010.
Stott, William. *Documentary Expression and Thirties America*. New York: Oxford University Press, 1973.
Strongin, Theodore. "The Lizzie Borden Case." *New York Times*, March 21, 1965.
Talley, Thomas Washington. *Thomas W. Talley's Negro Folk Rhymes: A New, Expanded Edition, with Music*. Edited with a new introduction and notes by Charles K. Wolfe. Musical transcriptions by Bill Ferreira. Knoxville: University of Tennessee Press, 1991.
Tanenbaum, Leora. *I Am Not a Slut: Slut-Shaming in the Age of the Internet*. New York: Harper Perennial, 2015.
———. *Slut! Growing Up Female with a Bad Reputation*. New York: Seven Stories Press, 1999.
Taruskin, Richard. *The Oxford History of Western Music: Music in the Late Twentieth Century*. Rev. ed. Oxford: Oxford University Press, 2005, 2010.
Taubman, Howard. "Copland's New Opera: 'The Tender Land,' on American Theme, Grew Out of a Picture in a Book." *New York Times*, March 28, 1954.
———. "Labeling 'The Consul.'" *New York Times*, March 12, 1950.
———. "Opera: 'Baby Doe' Here." *New York Times*, April 4, 1958.
———. "Opera: Rooted in West 'Ballad of Baby Doe' Sung in Colorado." *New York Times*, July 9, 1956.
———. "The Opera: 'Susannah.'" *New York Times*, September 28, 1956.
The Telephone/The Medium. May 1, 1947–November 1, 1947, Ethel Barrymore Theatre, New York, NY. Internet Broadway Database. https://www.ibdb.com/broadway-production/the-telephone--the-medium-1549. Accessed November August 23, 2022.
The Telephone/The Medium. July 19, 1950–October 14, 1950, Arena Theatre, New York, NY. Internet Broadway Database. https://www.ibdb.com/broadway-production/the-telephone-the-medium-2151. Accessed August 23, 2022.
Temple, Judy Nolte. *Baby Doe Tabor: The Madwoman in the Cabin*. Norman: University of Oklahoma Press, 2007.

"'The Tender Land,' Aaron Copland Opera, Heard at Tanglewood." *Boston Globe*, August 3, 1954.

Theroux, Paul. *Deep South: Four Seasons of Back Roads*. New York: Houghton Mifflin Harcourt, 2015.

Thomson, Virgil. "The Music: Pathos and the Macabre." *New York Herald Tribune*, March 16, 1950.

Thurman, Kira. *Singing Like Germans: Black Musicians in the Land of Bach, Beethoven, and Brahms*. Ithaca, NY: Cornell University Press, 2021.

Tobacco Road. December 4, 1933–January 13, 1934, Theatre Masque, New York, NY; January 15, 1934–September 15, 1934, 48th Street Theatre, New York, NY; September 17, 1934–May 31, 1941. Forrest Theatre, New York, NY. Internet Broadway Database. https://www.ibdb.com/broadway-production/tobacco-road-1065. Accessed August 23, 2022.

Tommasini, Anthony. "Beverly Sills, All-American Diva, Is Dead at 78." *New York Times*, July 3, 2007.

Toth, Emily. *Inside Peyton Place: The Life of Grace Metalious*. Jackson: University Press of Mississippi, 1981, 2000.

Toth, Susan Allen. *Blooming: A Small-Town Girlhood*. Boston: Little, Brown and Company, 1978, 1981.

"Treasure Hunters Wreck Cabin of 'Baby Doe' Tabor." *New York Times*, August 14, 1935.

Upshaw, Dawn. *The World So Wide*. Nonesuch 79458, 1998. Compact disc.

Urbanska, Wanda. "Book Review: Ike's '50s and Reagan's '80s: Decades Apart and Yet …" *Los Angeles Times*, August 14, 1986.

"Victor Trucco, 51, Conductor at Met." *New York Times*, May 19, 1964.

Voss, Ralph F. *A Life of William Inge: The Strains of Triumph*. Lawrence: University of Kansas Press, 1989.

Wade, Lisa. "How 'Benevolent Sexism' Drove Dylann Roof's Racist Massacre." *Washington Post*, June 21, 2015.

Waleson, Heidi. *Mad Scenes and Exit Arias: The Death of the New York City Opera and the Future of Opera in America*. New York: Metropolitan Books, 2018.

Walker, Nancy A., ed. *Women's Magazines 1940–1960: Gender Roles and the Popular Press*. Boston: Bedford/St. Martin's, 1998.

Walker, Rebecca. "Anita Hill Woke Us Up." *Huffington Post*, October 27, 2011.

———. "Becoming the Third Wave." *Ms. Magazine* 11, no. 2 (1992).

"Walnut Couple Celebrates 63rd Wedding Anniversary." *Catholic Advance* (Wichita, KS). June 5, 1975.

Warren, Carol A. B. *Madwives: Schizophrenic Women in the 1950s*. New Brunswick, NJ: Rutgers University Press, 1987.

Watt, Douglas. "Copland Opera Has Premiere at City Center." *New York Daily News*, April 2, 1954.

———. "'Falstaff' Gets a Fine Revival." *New York Daily News*, February 21, 1952.

Watts, Richard, Jr. "A Police State in Musical Drama." *New York Post Home News*, March 16, 1950.

Westad, Odd Arne, ed. *Reviewing the Cold War: Approaches, Interpretations, Theory*. London: Frank Cass, 2000.

White, Deborah Gray. *Ar'n't I a Woman? Female Slaves in the Plantation South*. Rev. and with a new introduction. New York: W. W. Norton & Company, 1985, 1999.

Wierzbicki, James. *Music in the Age of Anxiety: American Music in the Fifties*. Urbana: University of Illinois Press, 2016.

Wiesel, Elie. *Night*. Foreword by François Mauriac. Translated by Stella Rodway. New York: Hill & Wang, 1960.

Williams, Mike. "The Once and Future American Beach." *Atlanta Journal-Constitution*, January 3, 1999.

Wlaschin, Ken. *Gian Carlo Menotti on Screen: Opera, Dance and Choral Works on Film, Television and Video*. Jefferson, NC: McFarland & Company, Inc., 1999.

Wolf, Stacy. *Changed for Good: A Feminist History of the Broadway Musical*. New York: Oxford University Press, 2011.

Woolf, Virginia. "Professions for Women." In *The Death of the Moth and Other Essays*, 235–242. New York: Harcourt, Brace and Company, 1942.

Wright, Devon A. "The Florida Legislative Investigation Committee and its Conflict with the Miami Chapter of the National Association for the Advancement of Colored People." Thesis, Florida International University, 2002.

Young, Allen. "Central City Triumph: 'Baby Doe' Praised as Forceful, Original." *Denver Post*, July 8, 1956.

———. *Opera in Central City*. Denver, CO: Spectrographics, Inc., 1993.

Zahra, Tara. *The Lost Children: Reconstructing Europe's Families after World War II*. Cambridge, MA: Harvard University Press, 2011.

"Zimbler Sinfonietta Closes Sixth Season." *Boston Globe*, March 17, 1955.

Zolotow, Maurice. "Patricia Neway Talks of Magda Sorel." *New York Times*, May 21, 1950.

Zwartz, Barney. "Review: Lyric Opera Produces Compelling Performance in The Tender Land." *The Sydney Morning Herald*, May 6, 2014.

Index

An italicized page number indicates a figure or musical example.

1950s, US culture in, 4–5, 17–18, 19–20, 114–15, 138, 174–75
1960s counterculture, 147

Abbate, Carolyn, 10–11
abortion, 6, 8
accessibility, 117–18, 184
Adams, John, 3–4
Adler, Peter Herman, 116
Agee, James, 127–28, 130–32, 148–49
agency of performers: Curtin as Susannah, 15, 16, 36, 161–62, 183, 185, 192; Neway as Magda, 25–26, 36, 67, 183; in opera history, 10–12; Sills as Baby Doe, 2–3, 16, 37–38, 40–41, 66–67, 192; Sills in other roles, 66–67, 72–73
"Ain't it a pretty night!" (*Susannah*), 165–67, *167*, 168
Allen, Warren D., 157
American Beach, 145–47
And Their Children after Them (Maharidge/Williamson), 149–50
André, Naomi, 6
"Angel in the House" ideal, 13, 40–41, 60, 64–65
anti-communism, 5, 20–21, 118–19, 158–61. *See also* McCarthyism
anti-Semitism, 3, 41, 67–68
Aria Code (podcast), 184–85
Aspen Music Festival, 157, 162

autonomy, 88, 115, 148, 183–84. *See also* Moss, Laurie (*The Tender Land* character)

Baby Doe (*The Ballad of Baby Doe* character): angelic transformation of, 2, 13, 15–16, 54–55, 60–61, 64–65; as gold digger / homewrecker, 13, 39–41, 60–61, 64–65; Sills's interpretation of, 2–3, 37–38, 40–41, 69–70, 71–73, 74–76
Baby Doe (historical figure), 3, 13, 37–39, 42–48
Bacon, Ernst, 188
Ballad of Baby Doe, The (Moore/Latouche): creative process of, 33, 48–54, 59–61; Futral on, 74–75; inspiration and sources for, 37–40, 41–48, 52; music and lyrics of, 55, 60–61, *62–63*, 70–71, *72*; in the NYCO's repertory, 31; plot and staging of, 54–55; reception of, 56–57, 58, 64, 75; Sills in, 2–3, 40–41, 58, 67, 69–70, 71–73; Sills on, 37–38, 40–41, 66–67, 69–70, 73, 74–76; virgin/whore dichotomy in, 2, 37–38, 39–41, 64
Bancroft, Caroline, 45–48, 50–54
Beeson, Jack: *Lizzie Borden*, 13–14, 77, 79–80, 82–83, 85–88, 92–95, 102; *The Sweet Bye and Bye*, 79. See also *Lizzie Borden* (Beeson/Elmslie/Plant)

Bell Jar, The (Plath), 114
Benzell, Mimi, 57–58
Betsch, MaVynee, 15, 144–47, 192
"Bird Song" (*Lizzie Borden*), 77, 95, 96–97, 98, *99–100*
bitch, figure of, 102–3, 109, 135
"BITCH Manifesto, The," 103
Black rapist, myth of, 115, 174–75, 176, 180–81
Black women, stereotypes of, 180–81
Blitch, Reverend Olin (*Susannah* character), 156, 162, 169, 173–74
Blount, Nathan Samuel, 154–55, 159–60
Borden, Abbie (*Lizzie Borden* character), 77, 90–91, 95, *96–97*, 98, *99–100*, 102
Borden, Abby (historical figure), 77, 87, 88
Borden, Andrew (historical figure), 77–78
Borden, Andrew (*Lizzie Borden* character): abusing Lizzie, 90–91, 101, 102, 103–4; argument with Abbie, 98; credo, 92, 94–95; Lizzie's resemblance to, 104, *105*, 106–7, *107*, *108–9*, 109
Borden, Emma, 87–88
Borden, Lizzie (historical figure): Beeson's interest in, 85–87, 88; life of, 14, 77–78, 87–89, 111; Plant's interest in, 81–83, 84–85, 91–92
Borden, Lizzie (*Lizzie Borden* character): actions and music of, 90–91, 98, 101–2, 103–4, 106–9, *107–9*; as "Mannish Lesbian" figure, 14, 110, 112; punishment of, 14, 80, 112; as spinster, 2, 78–79, 85–86, 90, 111, 112; transformation of, 15–16, 103–4, 106–9, 111–12
Borden, Margret (*Lizzie Borden* character), 90–91, 92–93, 98, 104, 106

Borden, Sarah, 87
Bourke-White, Margaret, 128, 131, 133
Broadway, 12, 17, 28–29, 32–33, 59. See also *Consul, The* (Menotti)
Brown, Helen Gurley, 9
Brown, Robert J., 55
Brownmiller, Susan, 176
Buckley, Emerson, 56, 58
bureaucracy, depiction of. See *Consul, The* (Menotti)
Burke, Tarana, 9–10, 193
Burroughs, Allie Mae (Annie Mae Gudger), 128n77, *129*, 148–49
Burroughs, Lucille (Gudger, Maggie Louise), 128n77, *129*, 148–50

Caldwell, Erskine, 114, 127, 128, 131–33, 135–36
Callas, Maria, 11n57, 12–13
canon, operatic, 1–2, 12, 36n102. See also European opera; Metropolitan Opera
capital punishment, 187, 188–90
careers in opera, 24, 65–67, 115, 140–45, 183, 192–93
Carlos, Rosemary, 14, 139–43, 192
Cartier, Rudolph, 23
Cassel, Walter, 56
Catholicism, 46–48, 190–91. See also *Ballad of Baby Doe, The* (Moore/Latouche); *Dead Man Walking* (Heggie/McNally)
Central City Opera House Association, 37, 48, 50, 52–53, 55–56
Chafee, Zechariah Jr., 21
Chapman, John, 56–57
Childress, Alice, 5n23, 8n38
Clément, Catherine, 1, 4, 10, 15, 172
Clurman, Harold, 116
Cold War, 5, 8, 12, 19–21, 119, 161. See also 1950s, US

culture in; *Consul, The* (Menotti); McCarthyism
Cole, Johnnetta B., 144n168, 145, 147
Coleman, Robert, 20
Columbia University, 28, 33–35, 49, 86–87
communism. *See* anti-communism; McCarthyism
Consul, The (Menotti): characters and story of, 17, 18–19, 21–26; Menotti and, 12–13, 18, 22, 23, 25–26; Neway and, 17, 22, 23–26, *23*; production history and reception of, 12–13, 17, 18, 19–21, 22, 23–24, 31–32; real-life inspiration for, 12, 19
Cook, Gene, *164*, 165
Copland, Aaron: and the gender politics of *The Tender Land*, 14, 113–15, 124, 136–37, 147–48, 149–50; and inspirations for *The Tender Land*, 114, 127–28, 132–36, 147–48; and McCarthyism, 118–19; music for *The Tender Land*, 121–24, *123*, *125*, 126–27, 134; and performers, 139, 144; on *The Tender Land*, 117–18; *Tragic Ground* (unfinished musical), 114, 121, 133–34; writing and revising *The Tender Land*, 115–17, 124, 127, 134, 136–37. See also *Tender Land, The* (Copland/Johns)
Cowles, Chandler, 19, 32–33, 162
Crist, Elizabeth B., 119–20, 121
Crosby, John, 35
Crucible, The (Miller), 152, 160
Curtin, Philip D., 163
Curtin, Phyllis: Floyd on, 157, 161; investment in *Susannah*, 15, 16, 153, 157, 161–62, 165, 175, 183; as Salome, 163, *164*, 165

Daniels, Sharon, 36, 172–73, 184
de Mille, Agnes, 89, 134
Dead Man Walking (Heggie/McNally), 186–92
death penalty, 187, 188–90
Defrère, Désiré, 66
depression, 82–83
DiDonato, Joyce, 189, 191, 192
disability, 65, 156n17, 172n89
Ditson, Alice M., 34
divorce, 13, 38, 47, 67–68
Doe, Harvey, 38, 43–45, 46–47
domestic violence, 90, 102, 193. See also *Lizzie Borden* (Beeson/Elmslie/Plant)
domesticity, 4–5, 16, 77, 89
Down in the Valley (Weill/Sundgaard), 117–18, 158
Downes, Olin, 17, 18, 137, 140
Duncan, Todd, 144–45

Eastman School of Music, 86
eco-feminism, 146–47
Elgar, Anne, 98
Elmslie, Kenward: *Lizzie Borden*, 13–14, 78–81, 82, 85–86, 87, 93–95, 101–2; *The Sweet Bye and Bye*, 79. See also *Lizzie Borden* (Beeson/Elmslie/Plant)
Elwell, Herbert, 64, 165
Europe, 18, 19–21, 145. See also *Consul, The* (Menotti)
European opera, 1, 28, 36n102, 152–53
Evans, Walker, 127–28, *129*, 130, 131, 148
evil stepmother, figure of, 85–86, 95

Fall River Legend (Gould/de Mille), 89
Falls, Robert, 182

Faull, Ellen, 98
Feldy, Sofia, 12, 19
Feminine Mystique, The (Friedan), 8, 110
feminism, 4, 5–6, 8–10, 16, 78–79, 146–48, 150. See also feminist musicology; women's liberation
feminist musicology, 1, 10–11
fictionalization of real events, 3, 6–7. See also *Ballad of Baby Doe, The* (Moore/Latouche); *Lizzie Borden* (Beeson/Elmslie/Plant)
Flanigan, Lauren, 14, 106, 112
Fleming, Renée, 15, 175, 182, 184–85
Florida State University (FSU), 154, 157, 159–61
Floyd, Carlisle: career of, 154n8, 155n14; on Curtin, 15, 36, 157, 161, 165; experience of McCarthyism, 159–61; and Heggie, 187–88; *Of Mice and Men*, 156n17; on *Susannah*, 36, 155, 160–61, 175, 185; writing *Susannah*, 32, 154–57, 158. See also *Susannah* (Floyd)
folk opera, 117–18, 152–53, 157–58
folk songs, 117–18, 177
Ford Foundation, 31
Freeman, Jo, 103
Freudian psychology, 84
Friedan, Betty, 8, 9, 110
FSU. See Florida State University (FSU)
Futral, Elizabeth, 74–75

Gadsby, Hannah, 186
Garland, Robert, 18
Gatti-Casazza, Giulio, 28n62
Giddens, Rhiannon, 184–85
Gilbert, Sandra M., 193
gold digger stereotype, 37, 39–41, 45, 60–61, 64–65
Goldman, James A., 59
Graf, Herbert, 35

Graham, Susan, 191
Green, Paul, 48–52
Greenough, Meredith Holden, 65
Greenough, Peter Bulkeley, 67–69, 75–76
Greenough, Peter Bulkeley Jr., 65
Gubar, Susan, 193
Gudger, Annie Mae (Allie Mae Burroughs), 128n77, *129*, 148–49
Gudger, Maggie Louise (Lucille Burroughs), 128n77, *129*, 148–50

Halasz, Laszlo, 32
Hanson, Howard, 86
Hardee, Lewis J. Jr., 49–50
Harrell, Mack, 162
Hart, Beth, 70–71, 73
Heggie, Jake, 187–88, 190, 191, 192. See also *Dead Man Walking* (Heggie/McNally)
Hill, Anita, 182
Holocaust, 80–81, 82–85
homewrecker stereotype, 37, 39–41, 42, 60–61, 64–65
homosexuality, 80, 83–84, 89n54, 119, 126n67, 150
Hoover, J. Edgar, 4–5
Hotopp, Alice, 15, 143–44, 169, 192
housewife image, 21–22

incest, 6–7
Inge, William, 137–38
intersectionality, 153
Isaacs, Lewis M. Jr., 51

"Jaybird" (*Susannah*), 177–79, *179*
Jezebel, figure of, 2, 153, 156, 180–81
Johns, Charley Eugene, 159
Johns, Erik: Carlos on, 139–40; and the gender politics of *The Tender Land*, 14, 113–15, 124, 136–37, 147–48, 149–50; and inspirations for *The Tender Land*, 114, 127–28, 134,

136, 147–48; writing and revising *The Tender Land*, 115–17, 124, 127, 134, 136. See also *Tender Land, The* (Copland/Johns)
Juilliard School of Music, 141

Karsner, David, 43–45, 49, 53
Kerman, Joseph, 1, 27
Koussevitzky Foundation, 53
Krafft-Ebing, Richard Freiherr von, 14, 110

Lane, Gloria, 23, *24*
Lange, Dorothea, 131
Latouche, John, 13, 37, 39–40, 52–54, 59–60, 79. See also *Ballad of Baby Doe, The* (Moore/Latouche)
Laurie. *See* Moss, Laurie (*The Tender Land* character)
"Laurie's Song" (*The Tender Land*), 124, *125*, 144, 169
League of Composers, 115
Leinsdorf, Erich, 162
Let Us Now Praise Famous Men (Agee/Evans), 14, 114, 127–28, *129*, 130–32, 148–49
Levi, Primo, 81n13, 84–85
Levine, Rhoda, 103
Lewis, Brenda, 79, 80, 98, 101, 192–93
Life Magazine, 163, *164*
Lipton, Martha, 56–57
Little Bat (*Susannah* character), 156–57, 169, 171, 178, 179
Lizzie Borden (Beeson/Elmslie/Plant): Act I, 90, 92–95, 103–4, *105*, 106, *107*, *108*; Act II, 77, 90, 95, *96–97*, 98, *99–100*, 101, 106; Act III, 78, 91, 102, 106–7, *108–9*, 109; as anti-feminist, 103, 109, 110–12; creative process for, 79–83, 84–87, 91–95; gendered stereotypes in, 2, 13–14, 78–79, 85–89, 102–3, 112; historical source material for, 77–78, 81–82, 87–89, 91–92, 93; Lewis on, 192–93
Luening, Otto, 35
Lyric Opera of Chicago, 182

madwomen in opera, 25, 79n5. *See also* Borden, Lizzie (*Lizzie Borden* character)
Magda. *See* Sorel, Magda (*The Consul* character)
Maharidge, Dale, 149
"Mannish Lesbian" stereotype, 14, 110, 112
Manon (Massenet), 65–66, 72–73
Marsh, Robert C., 181–82
masturbation, 91, 102, 106, 133
Mathers, Daniel, 150
May, Elaine Tyler, 5, 138
McCarthyism, 21, 118–19, 120–21n43, 152–53, 158–61. *See also* anti-communism
McClary, Susan, 10, 15, 25, 79n5, 154–55n12
McNally, Terrence, 187, 190, 191, 192. See also *Dead Man Walking* (Heggie/McNally)
McPherson, Aimee Semple, 79
Menotti, Gian-Carlo: *Amahl and the Night Visitors*, 29, 116; *Amelia Goes to the Ball*, 27; *The Bridge* (unproduced script), 19n14; career of, 26–29, 32, 33; *The Consul. See Consul, The* (Menotti)*The Island God*, 28; *La Loca*, 29n66; *Maria Golovin*, 33; *The Medium*, 28–29, 33, 34–35; *The Old Man and the Thief*, 27–28; *The Saint of Bleecker Street*, 33; *The Telephone*, 22n32, 29
Metalious, Grace, 6–7, 7n35, 111–12. See also *Peyton Place* (Metalious)

#MeToo Movement, 9–10
Metropolitan Opera, 1, 27–30, 31–32, 36n102, 59, 86, 142
Midgette, Anne, 75
Milano, Alyssa, 9–10
Miller, Arthur, 160
minstrelsy, 177, 177–78n118
Moore, Douglas: and Beeson, 79–80, 86; *Carry Nation*, 80; at Columbia University, 33–35, 49, 86; comments on *The Ballad of Baby Doe*, 37, 42, 53, 57–58, 64, 70; composing *The Ballad of Baby Doe*, 39–40, 48–54, 59–61; inspiration for *The Ballad of Baby Doe*, 13, 39–40, 41–42; Sills on, 58, 70. See also *Ballad of Baby Doe, The* (Moore/Latouche)
Morel, Jean, 68
Moss, Beth (*The Tender Land* character), 120–22
Moss, Grandpa (*The Tender Land* character), 120–21, 124, 126–27
Moss, Laurie (*The Tender Land* character): and autonomy, 14–15, 115, 119, 139–40, 148, 150; compared to Susannah Polk (*Susannah*), 113, 153, 166–67, 169; depicted by Copland and Johns, 120–21, 124, *125*, 126–27, 136–37, 147–48, 150; future of, 16, 146–47, 149–50; inspiration for, 114–15, 128n77, 136–39, 148–50; "Laurie's Song," 124, *125*, 144, 169; singers who portrayed, 14–15, 139–47, 169; as virgin archetype, 2, 14–15, 113–15
Moss, Ma (*The Tender Land* character), 120–24, *123*, 127
motherhood, 4–5, 65. See also Baby Doe (*The Ballad of Baby Doe* character); Moss, Ma (*The Tender Land* character)

murder, 6–7, 14, 77–78, 86–89, 110–11, 188–89. See also *Lizzie Borden* (Beeson/Elmslie/Plant)
Myerberg, Michael, 59

NBC (National Broadcasting Company), 27–28, 29, 124
NBC Opera Theatre, 116
Neal, Sister Marie Augusta, 190–91
New York City Opera (NYCO). See NYCO (New York City Opera)
Neway, Patricia, 12–13, 17, 22–26, *23*, 36, 67, 183. See also *Consul, The* (Menotti)
nuclear family, as metaphor, 5
NYCO (New York City Opera): history and repertoire of, 29, 30–32, 141–42, 162–63; and *The Ballad of Baby Doe*, 40, 58, 59, 70, 74–75, 79; and *The Consul*, 18, 24, 25–26, 29, 32; and *Lizzie Borden*, 79, 101n90, 103, 112; and *Susannah*, 15, 162–63, 175; and *The Tender Land*, 116, 127, 139, 141–42

Oberlin College, 116, 143, 144–45
Oenslager, Donald, 49, 51, 56
Oklahoma! (Rodgers/Hammerstein), 138–39
one-drop rule, 180
opera: on Broadway, 12, 17, 28–29, 32–33, 59; canon of, 1–2, 12, 36n102; careers in, 24, 65–67, 115, 140–45, 183, 192–93; cultural perceptions of, 18; development in the United States, 26–29; European, 1, 28, 36n102, 152–53; folk opera, 117–18, 152–53, 157–58; for television, 29, 115–16, 117, 118; in universities, 29, 33–34, 117–18, 158
Opera, or the Undoing of Women (Clément). See Clément, Catherine

Opera Workshop, Columbia University, 35

Pancella, Phyllis, 14, 101, 112
patriarchy, 78–79, 102, 109, 113, 153, 182, 193–94
Petrella, Clara, 13
Peyton Place (Metalious), 6–7, 7n35, 8–9, 111–12, 133
Picnic (Inge), 137–38
Pinza, Augusta, 41–42
Plant, Richard, 13–14, 77, 80–85, 91–94. See also *Lizzie Borden* (Beeson/Elmslie/Plant)
Polk, Sam (*Susannah* character), 155–56, 174, 176–79, 180
Polk, Susannah (*Susannah* character): agency of, 171–74, 183, 184; compared to Laurie Moss (*The Tender Land*), 166–67, 169; and Curtin, 15, 153, 157, 161–62, 165, 183; as Jezebel figure, 2, 153, 155–56, 180–81; music sung by, 165–69, *167*, *168*, *170–71*, 171, 177–78, *179*; Racette on, 151–52; racial coding of, 153, 174, 176–81, 182–83; raped by Blitch, 151, 153, 156, 169, 173, 174–76; transformation of, 16, 151, 171
Pons, Lily, 66
Porgy and Bess (Gershwin/Gershwin/Heyward), 12
Prejean, Sister Helen, 187, 188–92. See also *Dead Man Walking* (Heggie/McNally)
Price, Leontyne, 141
propaganda, 8, 20–21, 23, 26
punishment: of Baby Doe, 13, 39, 48, 73, 80; of Lizzie Borden, 14, 80, 112; of Susannah, 153, 181. See also capital punishment

Racette, Patricia, 151–52, 191–92
racial coding, 153, 174, 176–81, 182–83
racism, 145, 174–75, 176, 180–81
rape: anxieties about, 6–7, 113–15, 123–24, 135–36, 174–76; in *Dead Man Walking*, 188–89; in *Peyton Place*, 6–7, 8; and racial stereotypes, 113–15, 153, 174–75, 176, 185; "seduction" as euphemism for, 15, 174–76, 185; in *Susannah*, 15, 113, 151, 153, 156, 169, 173–76, 185; in *The Tender Land*, 113, 123–24. See also sexual violence
real and imaginary, blurring of: as analytical lens, 3, 9, 11–12, 192; in opera as performed, 3, 26, 73–76, 163, 165, 192; in opera as written, 110–12, 148–50, 192
reception: of *The Ballad of Baby Doe* (Moore/Latouche), 56–57, 58; of *The Consul* (Menotti), 17, 18, 20–21, 22, 23–24; of *Susannah*, 152–53, 157–58, 181–82; of *The Tender Land*, 116, 137, 140
Ricketson, Frank Jr., 48, 50–52, 57–58
Rizzo, Frank (director), 26
Roberto Devereux (Donizetti), 66–67
Roberts, Barbara, 6–7, 111
Rorem, Ned, 26, 27, 29
Rosenstock, Joseph, 116, 141–42, 162
Rudel, Julius, 31, 58

Salome (Strauss/Lachmann), 151, 163, *164*, 165, 171–72, *172*
Santa Fe Opera, 35
second-wave feminism. See women's liberation
Secretary, the (*The Consul* character), 18, 21–23, *24*

"seduction" euphemism, 15, 174–76, 185
Serge Koussevitzky Music Foundation, 53
Sex and the Single Girl (Brown), 9
sexual violence, 9–10, 113–15, 120, 123–24, 151, 153, 174–76. *See also* rape
sexuality, shaming of, 5, 15, 113, 153, 163, 165, 180–82, 184–85
Shostakovich, Dmitri, 161n45
Show Boat (Kern/Hammerstein), 178–79
Sills, Beverly: career of, 65–67, 72–74; casting as Baby Doe, 58; life experience of, 2–3, 41, 65, 67–69, 73, 75–76; on *Lizzie Borden*, 112; on Menotti, 29n66; and the NYCO, 31–32; performance as Baby Doe, 2, 13, 40–41, 69–70, 71–73; perspective on Baby Doe, 2–3, 16, 37–38, 40–41, 66–67, 69–70, 73–76
single woman, figure of, 5, 9, 14–15, 88, 182. *See also* spinster, figure of
Smart, Mary Ann, 10–11
Sorel, Magda (*The Consul* character), 12–13, 17, 18–19, 21–26, *23*, 183
spinster, figure of, 2, 78–79, 85–86, 87–88, 90, 111–12
stereotypes: angel, 13, 40–41, 60, 64–65; bitch, 102–3, 109, 135; evil stepmother, 85–86, 95; gold digger, 37, 39–41, 45, 60–61, 64–65; homewrecker, 37, 39–41, 42, 60–61, 64–65; housewife, 21–22; Jezebel, 2, 153, 156, 180–81; "Mannish Lesbian," 14, 110, 112; spinster, 2, 78–79, 85–86, 87–88, 90, 111–12; working girl, 22. *See also* virgin/whore dichotomy
stereotypes, subversion of: in *Dead Man Walking*, 186–87, 190–91; by performers (*see* agency of performers; virgin/whore dichotomy: performers resisting)
Studer, Cheryl, 183–84
suicide, 18–19, 25, 81, 82–83
Sundgaard, Arnold, 117–18, 158
survivor guilt, 80, 82–85
Susanna and the Elders, 154–55, 173–74
Susannah (Floyd): "Ain't it a pretty night!" 165–67, *167*, *168*; compared to *The Tender Land*, 153, 166–67, 169; Curtin's investment in, 15, 16, 153, 157, 161–62, 165, 175, 183; *Dead Man Walking* influenced by, 187–88; *Down in the Valley* as model for, 158; ending of, 151, 153, 156–57, 169, *170–71*, 171–74; Fleming on, 184–85; Floyd on, 36, 155, 160–61, 173, 175; and folk opera, 152–53, 157–58, 165; "Jaybird," 177–79, *179*; Lyric Opera of Chicago production of (1993), 182; and McCarthyism, 152–53, 158–61; Racette on, 151–52; racial coding in, 153, 174, 176–81, 182–83; rape in, 15, 113, 151, 153, 156, 169, 173–76, 185; reception of, 152–53, 157–58, 181–82; synopsis, 155–57; as "too dark for Broadway," 32–33; as traditional opera, 152–53, 165–69; "The trees on the mountains," 165, 167–69, 184–85; virgin/whore dichotomy in, 2, 15, 156, 174–76. *See also* Floyd, Carlisle; Polk, Susannah (*Susannah* character)

Tabor, Augusta Pierce: historical figure, 37, 38, 45, 47; opera character, 64, 71
Tabor, Elizabeth "Baby Doe". *See* Baby Doe (historical figure)

Tabor, Horace: historical figure, 37, 38–39, 43–45, 47–48; opera character, 54–55, 59, 64, 69–71
Tabor, Rose Mary Echo Silver Dollar, 44
Tanenbaum, Leora, 184–85, 186
Tanglewood, 116, 139, 141, 144, 162–63, 183
Taubman, Howard, 20, 56, 64, 69, 157–58
Taylor, Paul Schuster, 131
television, operas for, 29, 115–16, 117, 118
Temple, Judy Nolte, 38–39, 42–43
Tender Land, The (Copland/Johns): anxiety in, 114–15, 120–24, 126–27; Carlos on, 139–40; compared to *Picnic*, 137–38; compared to *Susannah*, 113, 153, 169; Copland on, 117–18; Hotopp on, 144; *Let Us Now Praise Famous Men* as inspiration for, 114, 127–28, *129*, 130–32, 148–49; limits of, 14–15, 147–50; music and lyrics of, 121–24, *123*, *125*, 126–27, 134; reception of, 116, 137, 140; scholarly assessments of, 118–20, 150; synopsis, 113, 120–21; *Tragic Ground* as inspiration for, 114, 127, 133–36; use of folk songs in, 118; and the virgin/whore dichotomy, 2, 14–15, 113–15; writing and revision of, 115–17, 124, 127, 136–37. *See also* Copland, Aaron; Johns, Erik; Moss, Laurie (*The Tender Land* character)
Theroux, Paul, 131–32
Thomas, Clarence, 182
Thomson, Virgil, 17
Tobacco Road (Caldwell), 131, 132–33
Tobacco Road (Kirkland), 132–33
Toth, Emily, 7, 8–9

Tragic Ground (Caldwell), 14, 114, 133, 135–36
Tragic Ground (Copland, unfinished), 114, 121, 133–34
trauma, 80, 82–85, 151, 153, 171–74, 184
"Trees on the mountains, the" (*Susannah*), 165, 167–69, 184–85
Treigle, Norman, 162, 166
Treigle, Phyllis, 166, 175–76
Trucco, Victor, 142–43

universities, opera in, 29, 33–34, 117–18, 158. *See also* Columbia University

verismo, 3–4
victim blaming, 84–85, 135–36, 181–82
victimhood, 1–2, 113. *See also* Clément, Catherine
violence. *See* murder; rape; sexual violence
virginity, 114, 125, 138, 174–75, 190–91. *See also* virgin/whore dichotomy
virgin/whore dichotomy: in art and literature, 2, 6–7, 186; in *The Ballad of Baby Doe*, 2, 13, 37–38, 39–41, 64–65, 72–73; in *The Consul*, 23; *Dead Man Walking* subverting, 186–87, 190–91; in *Lizzie Borden*, 2, 14; performers resisting, 15, 16, 38, 41, 72–73; in *Susannah*, 2, 15, 156, 174–76; in *The Tender Land*, 2, 14–15, 113–15

Watts, Richard Jr., 20–21, 25
weight stigma, 57
Weill, Kurt, 117–18, 158
white supremacy, 145, 174–75, 176n111, 180–81

white womanhood, 8, 14, 110–11, 115, 138, 180–81
whore, figure of. *See* virgin/whore dichotomy
Williamson, Michael, 149
"Willow Song" (*The Ballad of Baby Doe*), 58, 70–71, *72*, 77, 95
Wilson, Dolores, 56–58, 69–70
Woman's Home Companion, 4–5
women's liberation, 8–9, 78–79, 81, 110, 147

Wood, James Madison, 4–5
Woolf, Virginia, 40, 41
working girl, figure of, 22
World War II, 4–5, 80–81, 84–85
Wozzeck (Berg), 193

You Have Seen Their Faces (Caldwell/Bourke-White), 128, 131
Young, Allen, 56

www.ingramcontent.com/pod-product-compliance
Lightning Source LLC
Chambersburg PA
CBHW070801230426
43665CB00017B/2450